D1545570

Lucy is a qualified teacher, an education explorer and an international education consultant. She taught science and psychology at a secondary school in London for three years before turning her sights to research and policy and gaining a distinction in her master's in Politics, Development and Democratic Education at the University of Cambridge.

Since returning from her groundbreaking trip around the world's 'top-performing' education systems, she has published a report on teacher career structures for IIEP UNESCO, advised the UK government as part of a working group on teacher workload, and spoken about her work at conferences in the UK, US and Sweden. She now works as part of a team advising foreign governments on education reform at Education Development Trust. Lucy lives in Bath with her fiancé, Mark.

Praise for *Cleverlands*

'Lucy Crehan's book is a major breakthrough. For the first time we have the human stories and classroom interactions behind the international comparisons of school systems. As an itinerant teacher she has been able to reach deeper than any academic researcher could.'

Sir Michael Barber
Author of *How to Run a Government*,
Chief Education Advisor to Pearson, Managing Partner of Delivery
Associates and co-author of *How the World's Best-performing School Systems
Come Out on Top*

'Lucy Crehan has written a remarkable and original book. Part travel memoir, part research review, she describes her experiences of visiting a number of the highest-performing educational systems in the world. Her conversations with parents and teachers bring these, often very different, cultures to life, and she shows how key features of education systems – more than is often realised – are profoundly influenced by cultural assumptions about the purpose of education and the nature of human potential. This alone would make the book worth reading. But what makes the book a truly important contribution to educational scholarship is the way that these insights are skilfully interleaved with the latest learning and teaching. The result is a book that will be of interest to anyone interested in how to improve education, and should be required reading for anyone studying how we can learn from other education systems.'

Dylan Wiliam
Emeritus Professor of Educational Assessment, University College London

'I first met Lucy at a Head Teachers' conference, where she was presenting. I was instantly impressed by her brilliant talk which was fascinating in so many ways, and now her book, *Cleverlands*, is even more thought-provoking. The book details Lucy's journey across the world to discover the best examples of how education and culture work together effectively. What impressed me most was Lucy's ability to bring to life the sometimes meaningless data, by interactions with real-life characters with whom she immersed herself. This is a must-read, not only for teachers, but anyone involved in the education or coaching of young people today.'

Sir Clive Woodward
OBE Chairman and Founder of Hive Learning,
Rugby World Cup winning Coach 2003,
Director of Sport for Team GB Beijing 2008, Vancouver 2010 and
London 2012 Olympic Games, Director of Sport Apex2100

CLEVERLANDS

LUCY CREHAN

unbound

This edition first published in 2016

Unbound

6th Floor Mutual House, 70 Conduit Street, London W1S 2GF

www.unbound.com

Text Design by PDQ

Art direction by Mark Ecob

A CIP record for this book is available from the British Library

ISBN 978-1-78352-273-6 (trade hbk)
ISBN 978-1-78352-275-0 (ebook)
ISBN 978-1-78352-274-3 (limited edition)

Printed in Great Britain by Clays Ltd, St Ives Plc

7 9 8 6

To all the teachers who welcomed me into their classrooms and all the teachers who would have done if I'd asked.

Dear Reader,

The book you are holding came about in a rather different way to most others. It was funded directly by readers through a new website: Unbound. Unbound is the creation of three writers. We started the company because we believed there had to be a better deal for both writers and readers. On the Unbound website, authors share the ideas for the books they want to write directly with readers. If enough of you support the book by pledging for it in advance, we produce a beautifully bound special subscribers' edition and distribute a regular edition and e-book wherever books are sold, in shops and online.

This new way of publishing is actually a very old idea (Samuel Johnson funded his dictionary this way). We're just using the internet to build each writer a network of patrons. Here, at the back of this book, you'll find the names of all the people who made it happen.

Publishing in this way means readers are no longer just passive consumers of the books they buy, and authors are free to write the books they really want. They get a much fairer return too – half the profits their books generate, rather than a tiny percentage of the cover price.

If you're not yet a subscriber, we hope that you'll want to join our publishing revolution and have your name listed in one of our books in the future. To get you started, here is a £5 discount on your first pledge. Just visit unbound.com, make your pledge and type **clever** in the promo code box when you check out.

Thank you for your support,

Dan, Justin and John
Founders, Unbound

Contents

Foreword

At the point of publication of this profoundly insightful book, international comparisons, particularly those heavily informed by the large periodic surveys, had become dominant in the thinking of those wishing to reform their education and training systems. Worryingly, the survey findings had increasingly been appropriated in order to instil domestic fear of falling behind – 'Look at them and look at us; now listen to me... '

Alongside this kind of misappropriation and misrepresentation, there have been some prominent mistakes, such as the failure to dig deeply enough into the history of educational reform in Finland. International comparisons carry ethical considerations, which too frequently are neglected. They need to be handled with great care. The data are one thing; their interpretation is quite another. Sound transnational analysis is by necessity demanding and complex, requiring an understanding not only of current circumstances but also of complex interactions in society and economy, and of causes and tendencies which arise from things past. Only then can 'the way things are' in specific jurisdictions be understood to any degree.

Lucy Crehan has added a vital qualitative dimension to quantitively focused international comparison. It is an essential read for all those wishing to draw insights from transnational comparisons, and a tonic to 'cherry picking' – the irresponsible myopia of the single extracted fact. But she has done something more than just add 'colour' to the surveys. Like all good social and natural scientists, she understands that observation is theory-dependent. It requires theory as its lens, and the things seen allow us to further refine our theory. Lucy's text gives far more than colour – it penetrates deeply into the way education works in different national settings. This yields extraordinary insights, of value to those looking with curiosity at other cultures and to those wishing to reflect on their own practices. This is a book which should be read cover-to-cover by teachers, parents and policy-makers.

Tim Oates CBE
Group Director for Assessment Research and Development,
Cambridge Assessment

Chapter 1: PISA, Politics and Planning a Trip

As I approached the guard sitting by the entrance barrier to the school, I realised I was biting the inside of my cheek. I became more aware of my walking, the way the sticky Shanghai summer made smart shoes uncomfortable, and I rehearsed my limited Mandarin phrases in my head. 'Wǒ shì lǎoshī' (I am a teacher). 'Wǒ shì yīngguó rén' (I am English person). 'Wǒ kàn xuéxiào ma' (I look school?)

I'd arrived first thing in the morning before the children turned up in their colourful tracksuits, not wanting to cause too much disturbance to the school day, but all the same I had anticipated the guard's initial reaction – confusion, followed by a shrug. He waited, I waited; he expected me to leave, I stayed where I was; I smiled, he picked up the phone. My Mandarin was not good enough to understand what he said on his call, but I imagine it went something like: 'There's a strange British woman standing outside the gates asking if she can look at the school; could you send someone down who speaks English?' He hung up the phone. 'Xièxiè' (thank you). He gave me a nod.

A small, trim lady in a floral dress hurried across the courtyard a few minutes later, her expression displaying a mixture of curiosity and nerves.

'Hello!' I said. 'I am so sorry to disturb you; I'm sure you're very busy.'

She smiled and gave a polite shake of the head, 'How can I help you?'

I told her that I was a teacher from England, and that I was interested in the education in Shanghai because their students do so very well in the international tests. 'I'd love to come and see your school and learn what you are doing, if it's not too much trouble. Can I come back on another day?'

Just turning up at the front gate was a last resort when my opportunity to visit a school in that kind of neighbourhood fell through. I'd already spent a week teaching in a school in a very poor area of Shanghai, and a week teaching, interviewing and observing in an experimental school in a well-to-do area, so I was keen to visit a regular neighbourhood school in Shanghai's dense suburbs, near the house of the teacher I was staying with. My plan was to get an understanding of the school system in China's largest city by living with its teachers, chatting to its students and listening for the cultural subtleties that aren't picked up by 'big data'. I was here because Shanghai's 15-year-olds had outperformed teenagers in every other education system in tests of reading, maths and science, and I wanted to know how.

I'm a teacher by trade. I taught for three years in a secondary comprehensive school in a deprived part of London, a school that catered for young people from some difficult backgrounds and, for not unrelated reasons, a school that didn't 'produce' particularly good exam results. It was hard work; there were days when I didn't have time to eat lunch, or even use the loo, because I was running around finding students to chase up missed homework, or photocopying the worksheet that I'd stayed up until 11.30 the night before making. I moaned to my family, but I didn't really mind about this bit – I assumed at the time that it was an inevitable part of the job.

What got to me was that the hard work I was putting in wasn't making much difference to the children in my care. Much of it – lengthy lesson plans, extensive marking and regular data entry – was required by the school management to help them meet external targets and pass high-stakes school inspections. What time and energy I had left didn't seem enough to overcome the systemic disadvantages that many of my students faced. Students like Dana in my Year 10G4 science class. This means she was 15 at the time, in the fourth science set out of eight, and had been working towards a 'vocational' qualification since she was assigned to this class two years ago. Her course was entirely coursework-based, and because it was not as rigorous as the alternative exam-based qualification, it precluded her from taking science at the next level (and therefore from studying anything science-related at university).

At parents evening, I told Dana and her mother that on this vocational course, she was working at a C-grade equivalent. Mum's eyes lit up. 'That's great!' she said. 'I knew Dana was good at science. She wants to be a science teacher.' Dana smiled and agreed, 'Yeah, I've arranged to spend some time at my auntie's school so I can get more experience.' By this stage in the English system, without the possibility of taking science at the next level, it was too late for Dana to achieve – or even work towards – that goal. But it needn't have been. Had she been in a better school, had better teachers, better resources and better support from the beginning – in other words, had she been educated in a better system – she could have at least had a shot.

I wanted to understand how education systems could be run better – how they could support their students to get better outcomes and have better opportunities without running their staff into the ground – and I looked beyond our borders to find the answers. But how can you tell which countries are doing 'better'? Are there any objective measures that compare educational outcomes in different countries? And are they educational outcomes that we ought to care about?

The Politics of PISA

'Europe is Failing its Students'[1]
'Worldwide Survey Finds US Students Are Not Keeping Up'[2]
'PISA Tests: UK Stagnates as Shanghai Tops League Table'[3]
'PISA Report Finds Australian Teenagers Education Worse Than 10 Years Ago'[4]
'Norway is a Loser'[5]
'OECD Study: Finnish Teenagers are Best Readers'[6]
'Canadians Ace Science Test'[7]

Every three years, the papers are flooded with headlines like these. They refer to the results of an international test called PISA – the Programme for International Student Assessment – which covers reading, maths and science. Each country that chooses to participate enters a representative sample of 15-year-olds to sit the papers, and in 2000 when the programme began, 43 countries took part. In the following 15 years, as the tests became more famous, more and more countries have signed up: 71 participated in PISA 2015, making up approximately nine-tenths of the world's economy. You might think this is an odd way to express the number of children taking an education test, but there's a good reason for it; the organisation that runs these tests is an economic organisation – the Organisation for Economic Co-operation and Development (OECD).

Why do so many countries choose to take part in this testing programme? There are two answers to this question, one quite straightforward, the other more cynical. Firstly, the OECD suggests that the tests measure 'to what extent students at the end of compulsory education can apply their knowledge to real-life situations and be equipped for full participation in society'. This gives governments information that complements the results of another international test – the Trends in International

4

Mathematics and Science Study (TIMSS), which measures how well eighth grade students have learnt the maths and science curriculum in their countries, rather than whether they can apply it.[8]

The results of both studies are broken down by subject, by type of question and by student background, allowing governments who opt in to the testing programmes to see where their education system's strengths and weaknesses are, and to make those areas the target of education reform, capacity building or additional financial support – in an ideal world. Additionally, because PISA is carefully designed to measure students' ability to apply and use knowledge, rather than just memorising it and reproducing it, participation in the programme can be a useful way of tracking the extent to which the education system is doing this successfully. This was one reason that China chose to enter students from Shanghai into PISA in 2009, and from several other Chinese cities in 2012 and 2015.

What is the more cynical reason that countries choose to take part in international tests? Well, it stems right from the inception of the PISA programme. An unusual coalition of US Republicans and French Socialists first set the ball rolling for PISA's design and implementation. Ronald Reagan, reeling from the dispiriting findings of the 1983 'Nation at Risk' report on American education (the clue to its conclusion is in the name), wanted to implement national reform. However, he was met with resistance by state-level governments who considered education to be solely within their own mandate. He was therefore looking for a way to make education policy an international issue, so that he could bring it under presidential control.

Across the Atlantic, the French Minister of Education Jean-Pierre Chevènement sought to demonstrate the failings of what he considered to be an elitist French education system in order to justify his own educational reform. What both men needed was an international education survey that would allow for comparisons of educational outcomes between countries, and they looked to the OECD to provide it. It took a while to develop (as attempting to accurately assess problem-solving ability in three subjects across many different cultures is an enormously ambitious undertaking), but in 2001 the first PISA test results were published, and they were used as an excuse for reform by governments around the world. In Norway, the Secretary of State at the time of these early PISA results described using Norway's poor performance as a 'flying start' to implement their reforms.[9] In America, the PISA results were used as a key justification for a federal school accountability programme known as 'Race to the Top'. And in New Zealand, the use of OECD data in defending controversial reform has been described by some educators as an 'OECD hangover'.[10]

Using PISA results as an impetus for reform is, in itself, no bad thing. The German people went through 'PISA shock' in 2001 when they realised that what they had thought was a world-leading education system was in fact below average in reading, maths and science, and one of the most inequitable in the OECD. It provoked educational discussion, soul searching, and a TV series, and led to various evidence-based reforms across its many states that brought about an improvement in their education system and their PISA standing over the next 10 years.

Of course, one of the major selling points of the PISA tests is that it allows us to identify success in a particular area of education, and learn lessons from other systems that appear to be doing this better. Certainly that is what politicians say they're doing. But this is sadly not always the case. Politicians (along with the rest of us) have been known to cherry-pick evidence; to choose to mention only the data or the features of top-performing systems that back up their pre-existing ideas, and ignore the evidence that throws doubt on their proposed reforms.[11] It is therefore particularly important that the wider public know a little more about what these successful systems are doing, and what the analysis that's been conducted on the data suggests, so that we can hold our politicians to account before they conduct expensive and potentially ineffective reforms.

My Motivation and Approach

There is information about all of these matters out there already, but not enough people are reading it. It's in the form of country reports and cross-country analysis by the OECD (who produce new publications that I want to read at a rate I can't keep up with), and additional reviews, analysis and commentary by consultants, academics and journalists.[12] This book includes some of this analysis, and its conclusions are consistent with the conclusions drawn by the OECD – but they are not driven by it. While the analyses by various consultants and academics are immensely valuable and carried out by people far more talented than myself, they offer only half of the picture. They include the effect sizes, but leave out the people. They can tell you what correlates with what, but not how each thing interacts with a culture. You can learn about the 'what', but not the 'why' or the 'how'.[13]

As I read about 'top-performing' countries and their education systems from rainy England, I craved a more holistic, visceral understanding of them. 'What does that look like in the classroom?' I wondered. 'Do the Singaporean parents think they have a good education system, or is the grass always greener?' 'What does it mean for the children in Finland that they don't start school until aged seven, and would I want my own children to go to school there?' I could read all about the governmental approaches of various nations in these OECD reports, and about the effects of specific policies in the academic literature, but I couldn't find out how education worked as a whole in each particular country context without seeing it for myself; I couldn't join the dots to see the bigger picture.

At the time I was asking myself these questions, I was just finishing my masters and had no permanent job, no mortgage, and no children; nothing to keep me in the country. So I decided to go on what has since been described by a friend as my 'geeky gap year'. I started drafting emails to teachers in top-performing systems abroad whose addresses I'd found on the internet, asking if I could come and help out in their schools for a bit, and asking whether I could stay with them for a few weeks too (no wonder my mum wasn't a fan of this plan at the time). I then realised that no one would say yes in case I was a lunatic, so I set up my iPad and made a little video introducing myself to would-be hosts, attempting to appear as sane as possible.

Of the top 10 PISA performers at the time, I chose Shanghai and Singapore because they got phenomenal scores, Japan because it was a large country rather than a small city-state, Finland because it has until recently been one of the only Western countries to outperform the East Asians and Canada because they performed well despite being culturally and geographically diverse. I sent out emails to teachers in Finland, the first country on my intended itinerary, and waited. I was half thinking that no one would reply and that I'd have to revert to my backup plan of sitting in coffee shops in Helsinki with a big sign saying 'I'd like to hear your views on education, come and talk to me!' when, much to my delight and amazement, a teacher called Kristiina emailed me back – we'll meet her in the next chapter. I found educators all over the world to be remarkably generous and open-minded in welcoming me into their schools, and I owe them a huge debt of gratitude for their essential role in the making of this book.

My approach in each of the countries I visited was to stay with educators to get a deeper understanding of their lifestyle and culture; to visit schools through informal means to avoid being directed towards 'sparkly' schools that were unrepresentative of the rest of the system; and to stay in one of the schools in each place for at least a week until the staff got to know me and felt relaxed in my company.[14] I spent about four weeks in each country and three of those inside schools; sometimes teaching, sometimes helping out, always asking questions. Some of my interviews were formal and recorded, others were informal chats on the subway on the way home, or over a bowl of noodles. I talked to enthusiastic school caretakers, distinguished school leaders, frantic high-school students and despairing parents. I learnt a huge amount about different approaches to (and ideas behind) education this way, and I will share some of this with you in this book as I take you on a tour of education in some of the world's 'top-performing' systems.

What Matters? My Outlook

When I first started giving talks about my work at conferences, a common question at the end of my presentation was the kind of question that is actually a comment: 'Why should we care about PISA? There is more to education than test results.' This is an excellent point; if we don't care about PISA, then we certainly shouldn't care what countries that do well in PISA are doing. It is an excellent and oft-made point, because there is a perception that the furore around PISA results has caused governments to focus on a very narrow measure of education, to the detriment of other important educational goals, such as developing children's knowledge of the arts, their appreciation of citizenship and their personal and social attributes. I don't doubt that this is happening in England and some parts of America, and I don't defend it; it is an example of governments giving PISA rankings too much weight, rather than using the broader data as helpful information to inform the direction of their education systems. Nevertheless, I don't think this makes PISA (or TIMSS) irrelevant.

Just as most people would agree that there is more to education than reading, maths and science, most people would agree that this broader education ought to include reading, maths and science. One of the questions I set off to research was whether top-performing PISA systems only did so well in these subjects at the expense of everything else, or whether there are ways of bringing about improved understanding and ability in maths, reading and science without hugely increasing the time spent on them. It *is* important that young people reach at least a basic level in these subjects to prepare them for their lives after school. And at the moment, in the UK, we are not preparing all of them sufficiently: 17 per cent of British 15–16-year-olds who took the PISA test in 2012 did not attain the baseline proficiency level in reading (Level 2), which means the OECD consider them to 'lack the essential skills needed to participate effectively and productively in society'. In mathematics, the number failing to reach the baseline level was 22 per cent, which is more than one in five.

Box 1: What does Level 2 actually mean?

Failing to reach Level 2 means not being able to answer questions like this:

Level 2 PISA maths question:

On one trip, Helen rode 4 km in the first 10 minutes and then 2 km in the next 5 minutes.
Which one of the following statements is correct?

A. Helen's average speed was greater in the first 10 minutes than in the next 5 minutes.

B. Helen's average speed was the same in the first 10 minutes and in the next 5 minutes.
C. Helen's average speed was less in the first 10 minutes than in the next 5 minutes.
D. It is not possible to tell anything about Helen's average speed from the information given.

In reading, almost one in five 15–16-year-olds are working at the following level, or below:

Level 1a PISA reading question:

BRUSHING YOUR TEETH
Do our teeth become cleaner and cleaner the longer and harder we brush them?

British researchers say no. They have actually tried out many different alternatives, and ended up with the perfect way to brush your teeth. A two-minute brush, without brushing too hard, gives the best result. If you brush hard, you harm your tooth enamel and your gums without loosening food remnants or plaque.

Bente Hansen, an expert on tooth brushing, says that it is a good idea to hold the toothbrush the way you hold a pen. 'Start in one corner and brush your way along the whole row,' she says. 'Don't forget your tongue either! It can actually contain loads of bacteria that may cause bad breath.'

What is this article about?

A. The best way to brush your teeth.
B. The best kind of toothbrush to use.
C. The importance of good teeth.

D. *The way different people brush their teeth.*

As you can see from the questions included here, the baseline proficiency level is pretty basic, especially for someone who has been in school for 11 years and is close to the end of their compulsory education. The OECD hasn't plucked this level out of thin air; it is based on studies of young people in Australia, Canada, Denmark and Switzerland, which followed them over a number of years and found that those who performed below this baseline level (Level 2) often faced severe disadvantages in their transition into higher education and the labour force.[15] This is not only a problem for the economy. Whatever you want to do with your life – becoming a pro skateboarder, opening your own restaurant or starting a family – lacking these basic skills makes your life more difficult and reduces the opportunities available to you.

The proportion of students that achieve at least these basic levels in any system is therefore one outcome measured as part of PISA which I believe to be important – but that isn't all we'll look at. Another key consideration is what proportion of young people achieve the highest PISA levels – it would be no good having a country where everyone knew the basics but no one was brilliant at solving complicated problems. This in measured by another OECD metric: the proportion of young people who attain Levels 5 and 6. The most famous measures are, of course, the average scores that give us the headlines and act as a simple figure to summarise each country's performance.

But we are not quite done. How would you feel if every child that scored above a Level 6 was from a wealthy background, and every child that missed the baseline was living on or below the poverty line? That wouldn't be quite fair, would it? While much of the cause of the worldwide association between background and results is due to students' home lives, education systems can make this worse or they can make this better (though they needn't be held responsible for fixing it completely). This measure – the impact of student background on outcomes – is called 'equity'. Along with the proportion of students who attain at least a L2, the proportion who attain L5 and L6 and the average measures, we have quite enough to be getting on with. Where relevant, though, I will also bring in things which are harder to measure such as children's mental health and reported happiness as we journey through our five countries.

Caring about particular outcomes does not automatically reveal the way in which it's best to pursue them. There's a key distinction between your values or preferred goals, and 'what works' to bring these desired outcomes about. The former should be shouted from the rooftops by anyone with a stake in education – parents, teachers, politicians and business people. Their values and goals are valid and important in any democratic country – but how should those outcomes be brought about? That is a question that has to be answered by looking to the world; looking at the evidence. By looking at the numbers, the associations and the analysis, but also by watching the children, listening to the teachers, looking for the big ideas and connecting all of these to work towards a more complete picture of how it might all fit together.

In this book, I will share with you a part of that bigger picture. I will join up some of the dots to show you what education looks like in five of the world's most celebrated education systems, and to give some clues as to why they are so successful. You'll learn a bit about their history, elements of their culture, how they deal with the challenge of educating children of different abilities, the various ways in which governments make teaching attractive and how parenting styles and attitudes affect their children's results. You'll also learn how psychology can help explain what underlies the success of their approaches. Come with me to Finland.

Chapter 2: Kindergartens, Parables and Professionals in Finland

Tyvestä puuhun noustaan.
A tree is climbed from its base. (Finnish Proverb)

'Oh I'm sorry I'm late, that's not very Finnish of me!' Kristiina hurried over to find me under the clock at the central station in Helsinki, just a couple of minutes after our arranged meeting time. Kristiina is a typical Finn in many other ways; modest, articulate, reliable and quite private, and yet she had taken a punt on me – an unknown English woman who wanted to come and teach at her school – and had given me the confidence that my trip was not such a hare-brained idea after all. We chatted excitedly about plans for my month there, including my teaching schedule and Zumba class, and were then joined for tea by Elsa, a friend of hers who was also a teacher. Both spoke perfect English, of course, and their only English-language queries were about the names of obscure plants that I hadn't even heard of.

Back at the house, I was welcomed with a 'show' by Kristiina's two blonde daughters, Elina, six, and Venla, four, who leapt around the sitting room, twirling and dancing. Later that evening, I had the first of my 'Finnish lessons' with Elina. Yes, she was six, and no, she couldn't quite read yet, but she had a picture book of everyday objects with the Finnish name written under each one, and she traced the letters with her finger as she 'read' each word. 'Sateenvarjo,' (umbrella) she said, and then looked at me expectantly. 'Sateenvarjo,' I dutifully repeated.

Elina hadn't been taught to read yet, because she hadn't yet started school. In Finland, children don't start school until the August of the year they turn seven (so the starting age ranges from six-and-a-half to seven-and-a-half). Before then, nearly all children attend a year of kindergarten, which is where Elina spent her day, and many also attend state-subsidised preschool in the years leading up to that. The next morning we dropped off Venla, Elina's little sister, at one of these preschools, and I went in with Kristiina as she needed to have a chat with one of the teachers. The courtyard we walked through was full of sandy children in bobble hats, bright coats and wellies, running around, pouring water through little plastic windmills and digging holes in the sandpit with great concentration. On the door there was a sign asking a question, surrounded by lots of words that made no sense to me (despite my Finnish lessons with Elina), and I asked Kristiina what it meant when we passed it again. 'It means, "You only played today?" and it gives all the reasons why play is helpful for children. Children don't do formal learning at desks in preschool or kindergarten, they learn through playing.'

'How can that be?' I thought to myself. 'How can 15-year-olds from Finland be coming near the top in international tests of reading, maths and science when all they did was play until they were seven? Surely they ought to be a couple of years behind teenagers in England (who start school at five), not ahead... '

So I hit the books. First of all, the focus on play in the early years isn't solely because they want children to enjoy their childhood – it is a deliberate strategy chosen by the Finns, based on research showing the benefits of play for children's physical, cognitive, social and emotional development.[16] The kindergarten year does aim to prepare children for reading and mathematics, but it does so through 'preparatory activities' rather than outright teaching.[17] What does this mean?

In addition to a curriculum that aims to develop children's social skills, positive self-concept and ability to reflect on right and wrong, Finnish children are introduced to activities and environments in which they can develop the understanding, skills and attitudes required for learning to read and do maths. The National Curriculum for the preschool age group notes that 'the basis for emerging literacy is that children have heard and listened, they have been heard, they have spoken and been spoken to, people have discussed things with them, and that they have asked questions and received answers.' They do this through discussions of fairy tales, stories, poems and rhymes, and through encouraging and supporting children in their own attempts to read and write.

One such fairy tale may be that of the Finnish Mother of Waters, who gave birth into the sea to a fully-grown man: Väinämöinen. She had been pregnant for 700 years, so her baby had reached maturity already, and from the day of his birth he had great wisdom, a well-painted forehead and a long white beard. He had no need of swaddling and no need of teaching. Normal children don't have beards, and they do need formal teaching. But the question remains: when is the best time to start?

Starting School Late (Playing is Working for a Child)

wow

The Finns have one of the highest literacy rates in the world, but this doesn't rule out the possibility that their late school start has a negative influence on children's later reading skills – it could be that their formal education (once they begin it) somehow compensates for their late start, or that there's something about the culture that overcomes the Finns' misguided romantic idea about children's need to play. Historically there is a strong basis for universal literacy; as long ago as the sixteenth century you weren't able to marry unless you could read a section of religious text, and more recently Finns have demonstrated their love of *wow* reading by annually borrowing an average of 18 books per person from libraries, more than any other country in the world. We might therefore expect Finnish children to be good at reading at age 15 anyway, despite the fact that they are not required to learn until they're seven.

However, international evidence suggests that starting formal schooling when the children are a little older makes no lasting difference to children's later reading ability. Two cross-country reviews have been done in this area that make the most of the fact that different countries start formal schooling at different ages, ranging from age five (24 countries, including 15 small island nations[18]), through age six (143 countries) to age seven (38 countries). Back in 1992, the International Association for the Evaluation of Educational Achievement (IEA) commissioned research to examine the differences in reading ability between children in countries who'd started school at five and those who'd started school at seven. They found that by age nine, those who'd been in school for four years (having started at five) did only marginally better in reading tasks than those who'd only started learning to read just two years earlier.

Intrigued by whether these differences completely evened themselves out as the children grew older, Sebastian Suggate, a New Zealander now based in Germany, ran an analysis using the PISA data of 54 countries (including those where children start at six). He found that by the age of 15, there were no differences in reading achievement attributable to school starting age; the two-year head start made no difference by the end of compulsory schooling.[19] Now, by itself this does not imply that starting earlier is of no benefit. It might be that those countries with a later school start are actually engaging children in school-type programmes in pre-school anyway – those with highly-structured lessons, requiring children to sit still and engage with material in a particular way and to be assessed on set outcomes. I have not looked at the pre-school practices of all 54 countries, but I have looked at research comparing these types of pre-school programmes (or an early school starting age) with less formal, more play-based early-years programmes like those practiced by the Finns, and the results are pretty consistent. While academic programmes at an early age often have positive effects on academic outcomes for the first few grades, these effects tend to wash out by the time children reach the end of primary school, with the later-starters catching up, and in a few cases, overtaking their earlier starting peers. This effect has been Germany, America[20]), between nd England[21]), and in maths as

I became a little less sceptical start. If it made no long-term positive differe outcomes, then what was the harm in play-based learning for a little longer? My scepticism left me almost[23] completely when I went on to look at studies investigating the wider effects of starting formal schooling a little later, and found evidence suggesting that it could have some positive effects. For example, researchers in Denmark found that a one-year delay in the start of school (at six-and-a-half compared to five-and-a-half) dramatically reduced inattention and hyperactivity at age seven, and that this difference persisted at age 11.[24] An analysis of Norwegian data found that boys who started school at an older age were less likely to have poor mental health at age 18, and that girls who started school older were less likely to become pregnant in their teenage years.[25] If delaying formal schooling by one year has no long-term academic effect, but a suggestion of positive social effects, then why rush in?

Yet to leave it there would be misleading. To leave it there might give the impression that it doesn't really matter what children are doing before they start school, as long as they're not starting school too early. And this is most definitely not the case. An in-depth study of 3,000 children in early years settings in England found that preschool attendance has positive outcomes on overall development (as long as it is high quality – see Box 2), that an early start (between two and three) was linked with better intellectual and social development; and that preschool is particularly beneficial for disadvantaged children.[26] More specifically, attendance at preschool matters for later reading skills too; the OECD finds that 'The difference between students who attended pre-primary... and those who have not attended pre-primary averaged 54 points in the PISA reading assessment – or more than one year of formal schooling'[27] – which might be explained by the effect of high-quality preschool on early language skills.[28]

Box 2: Not All Preschools are Equal

Finnish preschools and kindergartens meet many of the criteria that have consistently been found to correlate with, or cause, high quality outcomes.

High staff:child ratio[29]

Ratios and group sizes that allow staff to interact appropriately with children are a feature of high-quality preschools. Finland's maximum recommended ratio, at 1:7 for over threes (1:4 below that), is one of the best in the OECD.

High staff qualifications and understanding of the curriculum[30]

Settings that have staff with higher qualifications have higher quality scores and their children make more progress. In Finland, early years teaching staff need at least a diploma equivalent to the International Standard Classification of Education (ISCED) Level 5 (undergraduate degree level), and are required to take part in subsidised professional development.

A developmentally appropriate curriculum with educational content[31]

Being 'developmentally appropriate' does not mean all activities need be child-initiated – the EPPE study found that in 'excellent' settings, the balance of who initiated the activities, staff or child, was equal. Finland's early-years curriculum is based around learning goals including academic content and social skills, but these are developed through playful activities.

What is going on here? Why doesn't giving children an academic head start at school have a long-lasting effect on their reading and maths skills, and how can a preschool that doesn't teach them these more advanced skills make any difference to their later development? As Finnish children don't start formal school until seven, but attend high-quality play-based preschool before then, what we're really asking is, 'How can Finland's early-years approach be working?'

To answer this question, let us turn to the Bible (bear with me):

> A farmer went out to sow his seed. As he was scattering the seed, some fell along the path; it was trampled on, and the birds of the air ate it up. Some fell on rock, and when it came up, the plants withered because they had no moisture. Other seed fell among thorns, which grew up with it and choked

the plants. Still other seed fell on good soil. It came up and yielded a crop, a hundred times more than was sown. (Luke 8: 5–8)

Suggate uses this parable of the farmer to explain the differences in effects when children are taught to read at different times.[32] Like scattering seeds on a path, trying to teach children to read aged one or two will be unproductive, as they don't have the skills, the language abilities or the cognitive capacity to be able to do it yet. Like scattering seeds on a rock, teaching children to read when they're three or four might be seemingly productive, but will take greater effort and input than waiting until they have fully developed the skills required for reading, and helping them to do so. Meanwhile, spending this time trying to teach them detracts from the time they could be using to develop the knowledge and skills that are needed (such as their awareness of letter-sound correspondences, and their vocabulary).

The equivalent to scattering seeds onto good soil is to focus on developing children's pre-reading skills and pre-maths skills until the soil is good (I'm stretching this analogy now, I'll stop), and only teach and assess them on more advanced content when they're ready for it and when they'll pick it up more quickly. Suggate calls this the 'Luke effect' and this is exactly what teachers in Finland use. They encourage and allow all children to develop the necessary skills before expecting them to read. Not all children start at seven – they are assessed during kindergarten for school readiness, and if they aren't yet ready they stay in kindergarten for another year. At the other end of the spectrum, those that are ready sooner are encouraged to read widely and given support to do so by teachers in kindergarten; crucially though, this is seen as an opportunity for those who are ready, rather than a requirement made of all children.

Motivation and Variance

WOW

Once they do start learning to read, children in Finland pick it up very quickly. I had a long chat with a young primary school teacher called Marjo-Rita after class one day, and she told me that they expect all children to be reading by Christmas of Grade 1 (after just four months of teaching). While this might be possible in Finland, they do have a distinct advantage – the Finnish language has great orthographic transparency. This means that in Finnish, sounds and the letters that represent them tend to correspond on a 1:1 basis, which can be picked up by children fairly easily with enough exposure. In English, on the other hand, the letters 'gh' sound different in the words 'trough' and 'though'. Consequently, it will take English-speaking children longer to learn to read,[33] which some have argued means it is necessary to start teaching them at a younger age. However, this doesn't mean that children can successfully learn without the necessary foundation – the Luke effect still applies.

Even though English-speaking children have more to learn, they still won't be able to read and distinguish between 'trough' and 'though' unless they have first fully understood that sounds correspond to groups of letters, and it won't do them much good anyway if they don't know what a trough is. Teachers understand this, but if a system requires (rather than offers) too much of children too soon, they are forced to rush through the foundational stages of early learning. If you don't see the point in waiting until the majority of the children are ready before having higher requirements for the whole year group, consider the alternative of attempting to teach all children to read graphemes such as 'igh' at five. Some advanced children will be ready at this stage and will pick up the idea that letters have different sounds depending on what they're combined with. Their comprehension will still be limited by their vocabulary, and it won't put them at any longer-term advantage, but they'll be able to decipher what a word sounds like even if they don't know what it means. Others who have only recently understood that letters correspond to sounds will really struggle.

This is consistent with research suggesting that children who start learning to read earlier have less positive attitudes towards learning than their peers who started later,[34] and as Cambridge professor David Whitebread points out[35] – children get good at what they practise. If they enjoy reading and are motivated to read outside of school, they are more likely to become expert readers than those who were put off books by being forced to learn to read before they were ready. When I was in a Finnish primary school, I peeked my head into one classroom to see Grade 1 children silently reading to themselves. Some were reading sizable tomes, which shocked me until I went in and saw that they were reading Donald Duck comics (a big deal in Finland), bound to look like adult books.

Kaisa Kiiveri and Kaarina Määttä at the University of Lapland asked Finnish children themselves how they felt about learning to read, right at the beginning of their first year at school, before they'd started formally learning.[36] Most of the children considered themselves illiterate at this age, but said they could read 'a little bit'. In general, children had trust in their own abilities to learn, and 'learning was considered to be joyful'. A few correctly assessed that they could already read; that they'd taught themselves at home or with friends, and this was an enjoyable and surprising experience for them. 'When you read for the first time, it is like... like you would go for the first time to a roller coaster; I got so madly excited then too!'

We know that children starting school in Finland at age seven-ish have varying reading abilities. But some research also suggests that during the kindergarten years, the differences between different children's reading abilities widen – those who started with better pre-reading skills advance more quickly during this time than the ones who start behind. Hardly a high-equity system then, you might think, but there is a bit more to it than this. Suggate's big international review of school starting ages found that there was a tendency for there to be a greater variability amongst children's scores in systems where they started school earlier – the opposite of what we'd expect if the widening gap between scores at preschool had a longer-term impact. The clue to this puzzle might lie in what happens once Finnish seven-year-olds do start school. Have a look at this graph (Figure 1).

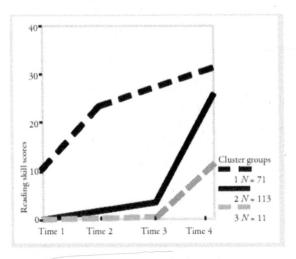

Group 1: 71 children who showed high reading levels early in kindergarten (T1).
Group 2: 113 children who had low levels during kindergarten (T1-T2), then improved rapidly during Grade 1 (T3-T4)
Group 3: 11 children who had low levels during kindergarten (T1-T2), and whose skills developed relatively slowly in Grade 1 (T3-T4).

Figure 1: From Leppanen et al. (2004)[37]

This is taken from a paper by Ulla Leppanen and colleagues, who measured children's reading skills at various key points in their early education: two months into kindergarten (aged six-ish), nine months into kindergarten (six–seven), two months into Grade 1 (seven-ish) and nine months into Grade 1 (seven–eight).[38] In their analysis of the results, they clustered the children into three groups – those who had relatively high skills at the beginning of kindergarten (Group 1), those who had low levels of skill during kindergarten but improved rapidly during Grade 1 (Group 2) and those who had low levels of skill during kindergarten and improved more slowly during Grade 1 (Group 3). Although the differences between initially high performers and low performers widen during preschool, they diminish rapidly during Grade 1 due to the rapid improvement of Group 2, and more modest improvement of Group 3. Leppanen and colleagues explain this by suggesting that learning to read is a similar process for the majority of children, in which there is a rapid qualitative change from being a non-reader to a reader, followed by a slower rate of improvement during which vocabulary and comprehension expand. The difference in the timing of this rapid reading development depends on your initial skills – you need your pre-reading skills to be up to it before the rapid development happens.

But what would happen to those in Group 2 and 3 if someone tried to get them to read before they were ready? The thick black line representing Group 2's progress might be a bit steeper earlier on, but if they found it difficult and unpleasant, I suggest it is unlikely that their skills would accelerate in the way they do in the graph above. Group 3 would likely fare even worse. Suggate hypothesises that the greater variability in scores found in systems that start formal instruction early might well be due to the frustration or low academic self-concept of less able children, brought about when the tasks they are expected to do are overly difficult for the stage that they're at.[39] This same frustration wouldn't affect those children who were developmentally ahead of their peers (often due to them having earlier birthdays), thus exaggerating the gap in ability.

Finland avoids this; by 15 years of age children have one of the smallest variances in scores of all countries, due to the relatively high performance of their 'lower' attainers. But their late start is only part of the story.

Special Needs Support

Some children pick reading up quickly, but some find it hard, even at age seven, due to special needs of various kinds. When this happens, Finnish teachers get straight to it. Before they even start school, children are screened for learning difficulties to allow for early intervention. Marjo-Rita told me, 'Students who are struggling in reading or writing have extra lessons with the class teacher. We give these once a week, before or after school, and we can also ask the special teacher to help support them if they need it.' This is pretty special. These special teachers are trained intervention experts – they are qualified teachers who have completed further training in the kinds of difficulties students face and how to help children to overcome them, and as they don't teach their own classes they are available to offer support where needed. 'All the schools have these resource teachers these days; we are very lucky in that way.'

However, this is not just a case of throwing money (in the form of professionals' salaries) at the problem. Class teachers don't just call on the special teachers to take children out whenever they have an issue – they give them as much support as they personally can first (and must record the support that they give before they can request extra help – a source of some grumbling). There are three different levels of support available to children who are struggling: general, extra and extra extra (not the official terms). General support is provided by the teacher, making use of all the strategies available to her: giving extra lessons after school, sitting the struggling child next to a more able one who can help them, offering extra support to complete tasks during the lesson and more sophisticated strategies that they learn during their teacher training. Another teacher told me, 'Many times I think it's about the methods, you know, you have to know the methods, you have to learn the methods. Of course you can think of ideas yourself, but it's always easier if you've seen examples.'

If after all this the child is still struggling, they get 'frequent' support, which includes having extra support from the special teacher once a week, and a special plan written for the student by the class teacher which they discuss with the parents. Only if all of this has not had its desired impact (of supporting the child to keep up with the rest of the class) is a different curriculum offered for one or more subjects – the assumption is that they will do everything they can to support children to access the usual, national curriculum expectations, before acknowledging that the child's difficulties make this impossible. If the parents agree, and it is passed by the student care team, the child may then be taught in a separate, smaller class, where they can be given more attention.

This is a relatively new system. Students with special needs used to be taught in separate classes as a matter of course, but there is now more of an emphasis on inclusion – hence the various stages before students are given this extra help and different teaching. This has had a mixed reaction from teachers. It obviously makes their job harder, as they are having to cope with a greater range of needs within one class. I also spoke to a special teacher, Mikael, who was concerned that the delay caused by the obligation of teachers to record their initial attempts at addressing the problems themselves meant that children didn't get the intensive specialist support they needed as soon as they needed it: 'It takes such a long time to get to step three that it might take a student who is struggling in seventh grade until the end of eighth grade to get this status. It needs to start from the first grade that it's noticed.'

Multidisciplinary Input

Finnish schools do so much more than teaching children. Finns know that sometimes what causes children to struggle are not learning difficulties but social or emotional difficulties, or health problems. I was privileged to meet the school psychologist, the school social worker and the study counsellor at one of the schools I taught in, but unfortunately didn't have the chance to meet the school dentist, school nurse, speech therapist or family counsellor. All of these specialists are either based in one school or, in areas where schools are smaller (over 30 per cent of Finnish schools have only three or four permanent teachers), they split their time between several.

The multi-disciplinary group known as the child welfare team is a cornerstone of Finnish education, and it is a legal requirement to have one in every school. In big schools, this group meet weekly for a two-hour meeting. During the first hour, the group discuss a particular class with the class teacher – each class being discussed twice a year. They talk through each child individually, spending less time on those who are getting along well socially and academically, and focusing their attention on those who are having problems. The second hour is kept available for any teacher to come along and discuss any student. Mikael explained, 'In the meetings, they analyse the needs for each student as a whole, as a human being, and think, "What are the underlying causes of the problems they're having, and how can we address them?" rather than looking for a specific solution for each problem in isolation.'

This struck a chord for me as a teacher from England. English schools vary hugely in their approaches, but too many will put interventions into place that attempt to deal with a symptom of a problem, rather than its underlying cause. For example, if a student has failed his maths mock exam, he will be often be required to attend extra maths classes after school. Never mind if the reason he failed was that he has depression and can't study, or that he's being bullied, or that he has mild dyscalculia – a specific learning difficulty with arithmetic. Understanding the underlying causes of student difficulties is the best way to address them. This is helped in Finland by the physical presence in school of professionals who have studied these very things. But that's not all of it. There is also a desire for this understanding, because the goals of Finnish schools are so much broader than getting students to pass exams.

The purpose of child welfare work in Finnish schools is to 'create a healthy and safe environment for learning and growing, protect mental health, prevent social exclusion and promote the wellbeing of the school community.' I think it is an advantgage that children's mental health and wellbeing is just as important as (as well as closely related to) their educational achievements. I am sure that other English teachers think so too, and that many English headteachers would give their right arm to have a team full of welfare professionals in school – were right arms accepted as currency in England. But English schools don't have this resource, because it is considered to be too expensive. Arvo Jäppinen, the Director of the Finnish Ministry of Education, had a response to this consideration about cost in his conversation with Dr Jennifer Chung of St Mary's University. 'It is not so costly as if the pupil would be excluded from active life. Later, she or he will cost a lot. We have, by the way, counted if the young boy, for example, will drop out, he will be excluded from active society; he will cost at least 1,000,000 euros.'[40]

The cost of exclusion is pretty pricey in England too. The average cost of a place in youth custody (15–17s) for those that offend is £100,000 a year.[41] The vast majority of these children have been excluded from school at some point, and half of them have only the literacy levels that you would expect of children in primary school. In America, two-thirds of children who can't read by the end of fourth grade end up in prison or on welfare.[42] The strong link between literacy rates and incarceration led to the urban myth that prison planners in Texas used school literacy rates to work out how many prison cells they would need 10 years later. Of course, it would be a mistake to assume, based on these correlations, that a lack of literacy is the sole cause of crime, but some of the factors that are associated with both – e.g. trauma due to abuse or neglect and learning difficulties – are those targeted by Finnish welfare teams throughout children's time in the education system. Yet despite all this input, it is less expensive than the alternative. As Jäppinen says, 'School is cheaper, much cheaper.'

Chapter 3: The Finnish Comprehensive Consensus

Ei oppi ojaan kaada.
Education won't knock you down in the ditch. (Finnish proverb)

November 22nd, 1963, marked the death of President J. F. Kennedy, and the birth of a new education system for Finland. Just before the news of the assassination came in, Finnish politicians had been celebrating the passing of a bill that mandated the creation of a comprehensive education system for all children, to replace the two-tier system that divided children into different types of schools at the age of ten. Looking back to educational changes in the decades leading up to Finland's stellar PISA results in the first round of testing (2000) is very important, as it is these policies that can best give us a clue as to the cause of their success – not what has happened in the decade since.

Maarit, a history and politics teacher I stayed with, who is just recently retired (and makes excellent 'Sister's sausage soup') began her teaching career in this old system as a substitute teacher in an upper elementary school. But this was not the kind of school she went to herself. 'In the old days, when I was at school, I could go to secondary school after the fourth grade, because I got through the exams. Those who didn't pass those exams stayed in elementary and would then go to upper elementary school.'

Ilpo Salonen, Executive Superintendent of Basic Education in a region just outside Helsinki, kindly met with me one rainy morning on the fifth floor of the local government office block to chat to me about his opinions and experiences of Finnish education. He too went to school under the dual-track system. 'The old system was that you had better schools, and then the schools that led to vocational training, and you couldn't change between those tubes. I went through that. From one tube you went to the university, and from the other tube you went into vocational training. And you were 10 when you chose; there were no possibilities to change your mind.'

The education bill that passed in 1963 had been a long time coming; the idea for a comprehensive system had been initially suggested by a cross-party committee (which met 200 times) some 16 years earlier, and it took another 16 years before the system was implemented across the whole of Finland. An idea put forward in 1947 was only fully realised in 1979. This might seem frustratingly slow, and I know I would hate it were I a politician, policymaker or parent involved, but it might also be part of the reason for the system's subsequent stability and success.

The first 16 years between the initial suggestion and its passing in parliament were a time of conflict, debate and, ultimately, consensus-building. There was initially intense criticism from the universities and the grammar school teachers' union, who thought that comprehensivisation would lead to all sorts of ills. A further report in 1959 recommending a move towards comprehensive education was unable to unite different political parties. Eventually, after much debate and discussion, it was realised by a majority (163 in favour with 68 opposed) that Finland could not afford for any of its citizens to leave school without a higher level of education than had been offered to most children at the time. In the words of Ilpo: 'When we are five million, we can't afford to drop anyone. In here everyone counts', and Maarit: 'In Finland, we like to give possibility to everybody.'

Having such a lengthy discussion and building cross-party consensus, rather than having a majority government forcing legislation through regardless, may be why the comprehensive system in Finland has remained relatively uncontested in the years since. Both before and since the surprising PISA results in 2000 when Finland came top in the world, Finnish citizens of all political persuasions have expressed equally high satisfaction in their education system. This is in contrast to their Scandinavian neighbours in Sweden and Norway, where social democratic voters have had a more favourable impression of their education systems than their conservative fellow citizens.

Another factor that may have contributed to its success was the slow lead-in time. The second half of the 1960s was spent developing and piloting a new curriculum for the new schools, to find out what methods worked best for this brand new system in which pupils of different abilities and backgrounds would be taught the same thing. Hundreds of teachers were involved in this process. Even when it was eventually implemented, it didn't happen all at once: it began in the north, in Lapland, where education was most in need of reform, and was rolled out down the country over the next seven years. It was accompanied by special in-service teacher training, to ensure that teachers were able to teach the new curriculum in the way it was intended – quite a task, when teachers had previously been trained to either teach academically-able children academic subjects, or 'less academic' children a watered-down version of this content. This eventual consensus on the importance of educating all children to a higher standard may have had an effect in itself on the Finns' ability to fully implement this reform.

What did this new system look like? All children were to be educated in the same schools, with the same curriculum, for nine years rather than four. The idea was that every child could and would keep up with this curriculum, and would therefore be in a position at age 15 or 16 to choose whether they'd like to go to the gymnasium (an academic school, not a place to work on your abs) or to a vocational school, where they could study to enter the trades.

At the time, this meant merging previously separate 'elementary high schools' and 'secondary schools' into one, which was a bumpy process that could not have happened without a legal mandate. More unusually, the government also made all private schools a part of this system, meaning they became funded by the government and were not allowed to charge fees or select students based on ability. Contrary to popular belief, this means that private schools do still exist in Finland, in that some schools are run by non-state organisations such as the church, but they lack the economic, social or academic selectivity common to private schools in other nations.

Comprehensive Education: Helpful or Not?

Now, just because Finland does something, it doesn't necessarily mean it's a good or useful thing. There are a few measures we can look at when trying to work out if comprehensive schools are useful or not compared to their alternatives: their effect on results, their effect on how much a student's outcomes depend on their parental background (i.e. the equity of a system) and their effect on the dispersion of results (equality). Most would agree that higher results and greater equity are worthy goals, all else being equal (the relative importance of these things is what is more contentious). Not all would agree that equality of results is necessarily a good thing – for many this will depend on whether the narrowing of the gap between the best and worst results is due to the lowest performing doing better, or the highest performing doing worse. There is research out there investigating the effect of comprehensive systems on such things, but as with any system-level research, we should remember to take the findings of this research as clues rather than proofs of 'what works'; the success of an education reform depends only partly on what that reform is, and partly on how (and where) it is implemented.

The kind of research that is relevant here relates to the age at which students are first selected into different schools (often 'vocational' and 'academic') based on their perceived ability. In Finland the comprehensive reform moved the age of first selection from 10 to 15 or 16. Comprehensive education is simply the practice of having all students in the same types of schools, so in other words, a comprehensive school system is one that delays that first selection into different types of schools until children are older.

If overall results, equality and equity are simultaneously improved in a system by having this first selection at one stage over another, then there can be little argument about the direction in which the research clues point. If, on the other hand, equity or equality is at the expense of results, or results at the expense of equity, which option to pursue becomes a question of values about which people will inevitably disagree. Should we sacrifice equity and equality for high performance? Or should we sacrifice the education of the brightest children for the benefit of the masses? Fortunately, the evidence suggests that on this issue, these three goals are not in conflict with one another.

One of the most significant studies in this area was carried out by two economists, Eric Hanushek and Ludger Woessmann, who investigated the effects of early selection on variance in results ('inequality') and average performance.[43] They employed a clever method of comparing countries that allowed them to ensure that the relationship of interest – between age of first selection and inequality – was not caused by any other differences between the education systems, such as the economic inequality in that country, or the quality of teachers. They did this by comparing the inequality within each country at primary school, before selection takes place, and the inequality in the same system at the end of lower secondary school, when selection has happened in some countries but not others. This graph demonstrates the changes in inequality – notice that in all but one of the countries that select (track) early, inequality increases in secondary school, whereas in all but two of the countries that don't select students into different schools until later (not tracked) inequality is reduced by secondary school.

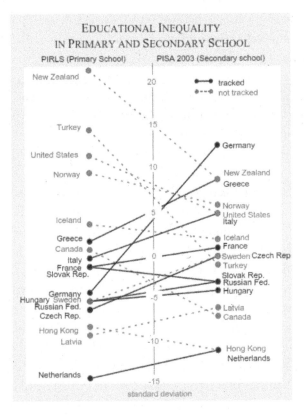

Figure 2: From Woessmann (2009)[44]

Not all will agree that inequality in results is necessarily a problem, especially as this variance could potentially just reflect the brightest from all backgrounds doing particularly well in early-selecting systems, and could therefore be an argument in favour of early selection. A more interesting question then is how this practice effects children from poorer backgrounds, or in other words, 'what effect does early selection have on equity?' Does early selection into different schools support equity by giving academic chances to the brightest from all backgrounds? Or does it reduce equity by denying chances to those who haven't had intensive support at home?

Woessmann and some other colleagues analysed the PISA 2003 data, and used the OECD's measure of student background to investigate its effects on students' scores in countries with different selection arrangements.[45] In line with previous studies, they found that the later the age at which students were selected into different schools, the lower the impact of student background.[46] No matter what common sense may tell you, the empirical evidence suggests that leaving the division of students into different types of school until they are a little older means students' scores at age 15 are more likely to reflect their potential and effort, and less likely to reflect the size of their parents' pay cheques.

This is consistent with the situation in Finland, which has one of the most equal education systems in the world, both in terms of spread of results (equality) and the impact of background (equity). Before you assume that this is just because Finland has fewer social divisions anyway, it is important to note that Finland has not always been a relatively classless society. Shortly after Finland became independent from Russia in 1917, a civil war erupted, leaving deep divisions between different classes in society. Having a more open education system was one of the factors – along with unprecedented prosperity – that contributed towards the gradual dissolution of differences between social classes in terms of taste and conduct (and accent, I was told) over the period since.[47] Of course, having a comprehensive system alone is not enough to bring about relative educational equity – there are other ostensibly comprehensive systems, such as England and the US, with an equity record that is nothing to be proud of, and we will come to why this might be a little later on. Nevertheless, it does seem to help move a system in an equitable direction.

So far then, the comprehensive option is looking sensible. But what about overall performance? Comprehensive education might make the system fairer, but is that at the expense of student outcomes? Hanushek and Woessmann looked at this too. The results aren't quite as clear-cut as those on the age of selection and inequality; they did find a statistically significant difference in scores between students in different types of systems, but this difference – in favour of systems with later selection – was only marginal. Other studies confirm that there is, at the very least, no negative effect on overall performance as a result of delaying selection,[48] and in several individual country cases, including Poland and Lithuania, pushing back the age of selection has had a positive effect on performance.[49]

Another concern raised by critics of Finland's comprehensive reform back in the 1970s was that even if it didn't have a negative effect on performance overall, it might disadvantage the brightest. This is a concern felt keenly by some parents of academically-able children; those who support educational equity, but understandably worry that the pursuit of it may prevent their own children from fulfilling their potential. Thankfully, research in this area suggests that you can have it both ways. Hanushek and Woessmann went on to compare students in selective systems with students in the same part of the ability range in less selective systems, and found that there was no negative effect of later school selection on any group, not even on the brightest five per cent. Similarly, Woessmann and colleagues found that while later selection seems to raise the performance of those from less advantaged backgrounds, students from more privileged backgrounds performed at a similar level in both types of system. More on this later.

System Structure Isn't Everything

The big picture seems to suggest that delaying the selection of students into different schools may be helpful for equity purposes while having minimal effects on average outcomes, but this big picture hides all sorts of nuance and detail that can only be understood by looking in more detail at the individual pieces of the puzzle. As we're in Finland, let's start with that part of the jigsaw.

There was an evaluation carried out on the effects of Finland's comprehensive reform many years after it was implemented. PISA didn't exist back then, nor did any national test of educational achievement that could allow the comparison of scores at the end of schooling in different parts of the country. However, Finland did and still does have an expectation that all its young men will do national service in the army for a year when they are 20 – an understandable policy in a country that has spent most of its history under foreign rule. On signing-up, the new recruits have to take some cognitive tests – one verbal reasoning one numerical reasoning and one logical reasoning.

Of these tests, you might expect the verbal reasoning and numerical reasoning scores to reflect in some way the quality of education the recruits had received, as they'd loosely correspond to what was taught in Finnish and mathematics lessons. Tuomas Pekkarinen, Roope Uusitalo and Sari Kerr, who carried out this analysis, found that recruits who'd been educated under the comprehensive system did, on average, marginally better on the verbal tests than those educated under the old two-tier system, and no differently in the other two.[50] However, entirely consistently with the international evidence, the averages masked significant differences in scores between those students under the different systems whose parents had low levels of education; in all three tests, soldiers from these more disadvantaged backgrounds did better under the new system than the old.

So it seems that the comprehensive reform contributed to Finland's impressively equitable system, but does it add much in explaining their high results? Not by itself, no. But as mentioned earlier, a structural reform itself is only part of the story; Pekkarinen and colleagues evaluated the effects of the first four years of the reform, but there were a number of enabling factors that came into play later on. Here I'll mention three: cultural attitudes, teacher expertise and universal expectations. The first idea was introduced to me by Ilpo.

'The school system – the formal change and the cultural change – are two different things. The structural change happened in the 70s, from 1972–79, coming from up north then coming down south. But the culture of this old system and the comprehensive education that we have now, well, that took a while to change, and I see the old system still sometimes.'

I asked what he meant by the culture of the old system, and he gave me an example of a school that was recently closed down that had held on to the old way of thinking, despite the country moving on around it. 'In this school, they fostered that idea "you are all going to university" and "I hope you understand that you can't go to vocational training; no one from this school goes to vocational school". They had a false pride kind of problem.'

So the old idea was that only certain children are cut out for academic study, and that it is inherently superior to vocational training. This stands at odds with the more modern idea on which the reforms were based – that all children can reach a certain academic level (as set out by the National Curriculum), which will allow them to choose at 16 which of several equally valuable paths they want to go down. The change to the comprehensive system introduced a new structure and with it, this new philosophy – but the latter took a little while to take hold. Teachers' beliefs and expectations have a powerful effect on student outcomes in themselves – a surprising research finding that we'll come back to when we get to Japan. The effects of moving to a comprehensive system will be diminished if the teachers don't embrace the new philosophy, and instead hold on to the idea that only some students can achieve. Thankfully, it is Ilpo's impression that this old way of thinking has largely made way for the new, more inclusive one.

A second enabling factor that is needed to make comprehensive education work is also related to teachers; they need not only the belief that all children can achieve, but the know-how to make this happen. In the first few years of Finland's reform teachers struggled, as they'd been trained for a different education system. I asked Maarit how she initially found teaching in the new type of schools.

'It was more difficult, because I was trained teaching history and politics, so I was trained to teach qualified pupils – is that how you say it? They were chosen. These in the new school were not. It was really difficult; you have to really think of a new way to teach, because it was so heterogeneous. It was difficult I think, in the beginning.'

The government did organise in-school training for the teachers on how to teach this new curriculum, but it took the teachers a little while to get used to it. Nowadays of course, most teachers have been trained for these circumstances right from the beginning, as part of a master's degree in teaching.

There was, though, a third enabling factor that was lacking in the 1970s. Its absence might explain why there was no significant impact of the new system on soldiers' average results for the numerical reasoning task, and is a good example of why we need to take the high-level statistics with a pinch of salt. When the comprehensive reform was first implemented in Finland, students did not actually all follow the same curriculum; there were still different courses for different students in maths and languages. Maarit explained: 'Under the new system I didn't only teach history and politics, I taught an English class of students who were in that class because they were not very good at it. In the beginning we had two or three language groups, those who are better and those who are not so good.'

The practice of putting children into different classes for different subjects based on their ability is called 'setting', and muddies the research waters slightly. In the Finnish case it was done for only two subjects, but in other countries students can be set, or streamed (put in a single ability-based group for all their subjects) in a way that makes it little different from selecting them into different schools in the first place. Yet schools that do this can still officially be called comprehensives. Take, for example, a certain secondary school in England that is not selective, but divides new pupils at age 11 into three ability groups on entry to the school. This school not only teaches them different courses, but teaches them in different buildings and has them wear different uniforms. Is this educationally any different to selecting them into different schools? We need to be aware that selection into different schools, selection into different tracks within a school (streaming) and selection into different classes for individual subjects (setting) fall along a spectrum with little meaningful distinction between them. It isn't surprising then that the research findings on setting into different classes for different subjects are similar to those for early selection into different schools; it has almost no effect on performance, but significantly disadvantages students from lower socio-economic backgrounds.[51]

42

Catering for Difference

In Finland, this setting in maths and languages was much debated, and then finally discontinued in 1983, following internal research showing that the practice of setting was maintaining and deepening regional, social and gender inequality.[52] It became illegal to group children into different classes based on test scores. Most of their classes now include children of different abilities within them, and nearly all are aiming for the same national curriculum goals. Rather than lowering the goals for the less able, they increase the support given. Ilpo thinks this might be one reason for Finland's success in PISA.

'Somehow what I think about PISA results and Finland is that traditionally we have always had heterogeneous classrooms, so that might be one explanation also. So that we don't choose people, and group them in an academic sense but instead we have a "put them together and they get along" kind of thinking. That might be one factor.'

There are sensible exceptions to the mixed-ability trend though – they don't throw all children in together no matter what. As we saw earlier, children with special needs that can't be met by the teacher or by occasional support from the special teacher are taught in a separate, smaller class in which they may pursue a modified curriculum. Children who come to the country as immigrants and don't speak the language are taught in regular schools but in a separate class for a year, where they concentrate on getting to grips with the language before being integrated into mainstream classrooms. Those teenagers that have come from war-torn regions and have never been to school in their home countries remain in separate classes even after this first year, as they have so much catching up to do in addition to learning Finnish which is hard enough by itself, so classes are differentiated to some extent.

One group that is noticeable by its absence, however, is a class for children who are academically gifted. I'm being deliberately specific, because Finland does have provision for students with other gifts: there are schools that specialise in music, in PE and in languages, and these schools will have one class of students within each year group who have a slightly extended curriculum – to include extra music, for example. One such student is Emma. Emma is a budding musician and is now in high school planning her applications to music college next year, but when I met her she was in the Grade 9 music class – the last year of compulsory education. Emma is also a smart cookie (she didn't tell me this herself, she is Finnish after all – it was her teachers that told me how quickly she picks things up), so I asked her how she found it being in a class where not everyone understood the material as quickly.

'It can be rather annoying if you're one of the nerdy kids, for sure. In English, I was always the first one ready, and it would just mean more work for me, just like, "OK oh you're done? Now just do all the other ones." Yeah and they would often ask me to help the other kids too, like, walk around and help others. I mean, it's alright, I didn't mind it, but now that I think about it, it's like, I could have got so much more done just going forward with my own work.'

I'm told that this is an area of great discussion within Finland, with some criticising the system for its failure to stretch the brightest. Yet several of the educators I met seemed quite relaxed about it. One teacher told me:

'The brightest kids, they'll learn anyway, whatever you do with them. They're not the ones that need the help.' She should know, as this particular teacher had five degrees. Ilpo gave a similar argument. 'I think when you are very talented – I mean this is realism, there are more talented and less talented people, that's just the way of life, we are different, luckily – the thing is that when you are more talented you learn, whatever you do. If you stand on your head you learn, that's not a problem. But in the same time, you learn different things when you have to support someone who hasn't got that kind of talent. And if you are in the same group, sooner or later you are in that situation where you say, "well, don't you see, it works like this and this." And then you have a different level of learning inside your head. In that sense you learn more, and differently, and the less talented student also learns; the basic things at least.'

Perhaps for this reason, a lack of advanced classes before the age of 15 doesn't seem to have a great effect at a national level on the scores of top students – in 2009 Finland were fourth in the world for the percentage of students scoring at the PISA top levels (5 and 6) in science, seventh in reading and a less impressive but still substantially above average, fifteenth in maths. From the age of 15 onwards, these students can attend academically selective schools if they choose to, and then on to selective universities from there. Oxford and Cambridge universities have societies of students from 'comprehensive' Nordic countries. Still, if there were one thing to improve on (which of course there is, like any other country), Finland's schools might offer more stretch to the brightest students to keep them on their toes.

Chapter 4: Purpose, Mastery and Trust in Finnish Teachers

Esteet katoavat etevän tieltä.
Barriers will disappear on the path of the skilled (Finnish Proverb)

If I were able to stand the long, cold, dark winters, I should like to be a teacher in Finland (though when I told Emma I might be coming back to Finland in the winter she told me in a very serious voice, 'You might die'). Coming straight from English schools, where I'd been told what colour pen I should use for my marking, teachers in Finland seemed to have a huge amount of freedom over how they did their jobs. In England I had to write out all my lesson plans in a predetermined format and send them in for review, whereas teachers in Finland don't ever have to do this once they're qualified, not even for lesson observations, because they're not observed. Their professional opinion is respected in everything, to the extent that I went to one staff meeting in which the last item on the agenda was which new furniture they should order for the school canteen (lest anyone think my trip was glamorous).

There are no school inspections. There is no teacher evaluation. There aren't even national exams to hold teachers to account – right up to the age of 15 students' grades are decided by the teachers. So how can Finland possibly get such good results in PISA? Not only that – how can these results be similar across schools all over the country? There is more to this story than meets the eye. The first half of the story is about motivation, and the second is about an alternative approach to quality control.

Imagine if your education system had no external exams, no teacher observations and no school inspection. Do you think the teachers would put as much effort into their lessons? Would the schools that needed improving bother to make the necessary changes? Speaking to teachers in Finnish schools, I was reminded of the research on motivation that I studied as an undergraduate, and of a book on the subject that I read more recently: *Drive*, by Daniel Pink.[53] Pink explains how many businesses base their policies and working practices on an outdated model of motivation, which he calls 'Motivation 2.0' (Motivation 1.0 is simply that we have a drive for survival).

Motivation 2.0 is based on the assumption that humans seek reward and avoid punishment, so the best way to motivate people is through extrinsic motivation – with a carrot and a stick (I mean this metaphorically). Without these external incentives, says Motivation 2.0, humans are inert and won't do much. However, research carried out as early as the 1940s suggests that humans have a third drive – intrinsic motivation – which explains why people will continue with some activities without any external reward, simply for the inherent satisfaction they get from the activity itself. Pink calls this 'Motivation 3.0'.

According to research by two eminent psychologists, Richard Ryan and Edward Deci, the three elements that contribute to individuals being intrinsically motivated are:

- mastery – our desire to get better and better at what we do;
- relatedness – our desire to have positive relationships with others; and
- autonomy – our desire to be self-directed.[54]

Based on more recent research,[55] Pink adds a fourth element that contributes to Motivation 3.0:

47

- purpose – our yearning to be part of something larger than ourselves.[56]

Quite unintentionally, the Finns have created a system that plays precisely into the psychological prerequisites for intrinsically motivated teachers.

Purpose

This is the easy one. From a purpose perspective, teaching as a profession sells itself. It isn't only Finnish teachers that go into the profession because they think educating the next generation is important; a study conducted by education think-tank LKMco in England found that the vast majority go into teaching because they want to help children succeed.[57] In Finland, though, the calling to be a teacher has historically been even louder than this: it was literally a call to create a nation.

Ilpo told me, 'The role of education in our culture is huge. In the 1860s we were part of the Russian Empire, but as a separate Grand Duchy, and some of the Russians started to press the Tsar that it's not right that Finland isn't part of Russia. In response, Finnish legislation was ordered to build up the public school, and everyone is obliged to go there, so that they could teach the children that "we are not Swedes, and Russians we don't want to be, let us be Finns".'

In this way, the education system was the foundation of Finland as a nation. The argument at the time was that if they could build up the mass culture and identity as Finnish people, then eventually they could ask for independence. Teachers were therefore seen as bastions of Finnishness with a huge responsibility, and held in very high regard. When many soldiers then went on to become teachers after the end of the Second World War, this reputation was upheld.

Seventy years later, teaching is still popular, but it's no longer looked up to in quite the same way. According to Emma, who is of the age at which young people choose their future careers, 'I do know a lot of people who want to be teachers actually, but I don't know, yeah, it's respected for sure, but it's not a big deal.' She didn't put it on the same level as being a doctor, for example. An international survey by the Varkey GEMS Foundation supports Emma's perspective. They asked a representative sample of 1,000 people of 21 countries to rank various professions based on how much status they had, and the Finnish respondents ranked teachers lower than respondents from Britain or America.[58]

Nevertheless, it is still a hugely popular profession overall, with applications for places on teacher training courses far outweighing places available (by a ratio of 10:1 in the capital, Helsinki), allowing those who run the course to be very picky about those they let in. Primary teaching is particularly popular (though not all secondary teaching subjects are equally oversubscribed – there is a still a national shortage in maths and natural sciences teachers in Finland). To get a place on a teacher training course, applicants have to go through two sets of tests, both written and practical. They first have to read a series of articles related to education, and then write an essay based on them. They then have a practical demonstration of their potential teaching ability, and an interview that checks, among other things, their moral commitment to teaching – selecting for those who already have that sense of purpose.

Why does teaching remain such a popular profession, when its status is not as high as it once was? Emma gives us a clue: 'You do have crazy training to become a teacher. So in that way, yeah, it is respected. It's like, "Oh you're doing all that school? Just so you can teach? That's pretty cool." You really have to work for it – they don't let just everyone be a teacher.' Finns also rank teachers highly when asked for the kind of job they'd like a potential marriage partner to have. So while it's not high status (or particularly high pay – about average for the OECD) it is respected as a job that requires both moral commitment and professional expertise. It is the latter, not the former, which marks it out from the teaching profession in England and America.

Mastery

The 'crazy training' of which she speaks is a five-year masters degree in education, which is funded by the Finnish government. Primary-school teachers spend this time studying education at one of the eight universities in Finland that offer teacher training, in addition to a school placement, and they cover all the subjects that they will have to teach the children in school (including ice-skating, I was delighted to discover, as they have to teach this in PE). Secondary-school teachers, on the other hand, do just a one-year education masters after their subject-based undergraduate degree; they are still studying for five years, but only one of those years is focused on education specifically.

What makes them masters level degrees is that the courses include research training, and all teachers produce a masters level thesis in an educational topic of their choice – Reeta did hers on the gendered language used in English language textbooks. They are taught the latest educational science based on up-to-date research on teaching practice, and complete a placement in a special teacher training school (like a teaching hospital) – an essential part of their training. Emma had a trainee teaching her religion class for almost the whole of her last semester, with the regular class teacher sitting at the back making notes.

Much has been made of this masters level training in various explanations of Finland's PISA success, but as with almost everything else, there is no evidence available on whether this feature itself made a difference.[59] Whether or not adding the masters level qualification itself helped raise Finland's scores, teachers in Finland have been better educated than the rest of the population since the beginning of compulsory education – contributing to the impression of mastery – and even before the introduction of the masters degree, teacher trainees received two–three years of education in how to teach, recognising it as a job that required expertise.

When I asked Marjo-Rita about continuing professional development, she explained that there are a certain number of 'learnings' that teachers have to go to each year, which they choose themselves based on their needs, but that they also have to do a lot of independent studying in their spare time. As someone who worked in the public sector in England, when I hear 'have to' I interpret that as meaning 'forced to and monitored to make sure you've complied'; but that is not what she meant. She meant that you have to read books, study documents, and discuss research with colleagues in order to be a good teacher: 'I don't feel like I can do my job properly if I don't study every now and then.' This, for me, is a pretty good indication that the Finns got the first two prerequisites for intrinsic motivation right in this case – they selected someone who has a sense of purpose, and they trained her to be able to understand and apply her understanding of pedagogical research.

Relatedness

Now, I've no evidence that Finnish teachers have more 'relatedness' – positive relationships with others – than anyone else. In primary schools they do meet at least weekly to plan together. They do have mentors when they first start teaching, and they do have 15-minute breaks between each lesson during which they're able to sit and chat in the staff room over extremely strong coffee. But none of this is particularly unusual. They don't have positions of authority within school other than the principal – all teachers within a subject department, for example, are on an equal professional footing. They don't have performance-related pay, or anything else that might put them in competition with one another. Perhaps these features contribute.

Something that is likely to add to Finnish teachers' (and students') sense of relatedness is the prevalence of small schools. In the early 1990s, there were over two thousand schools with a student population of fewer than 50. These schools were embedded in the community, meaning that your maths teacher was likely to bump into your mum in the queue at the post office at the weekend, and get you in trouble if you hadn't done your homework. However, since the recession of the early 1990s, many of these schools have been shut down and their pupils bussed to bigger schools, with the numbers of rural schools gradually declining over the past two decades to just 660 in 2012. While this does not appear to have affected student outcomes,[60] it may affect the quality of students' and teachers' relationships, and there are fears that closing these schools is a threat to the identity and vitality of surrounding villages, which rely on schools as a centre for the community.[61]

For the sake of the bigger picture, whether or not Finnish teachers have more 'relatedness' than teachers elsewhere, I will share with you some interesting research on why 'relatedness' matters, in addition to its effects on intrinsic motivation. 'Relatedness' is similar to the concept of 'social capital', which describes the strengths of the relationships a person has with others, and the value arising from those relationships. For teachers in a school context, this would include sharing ideas and learning from one another, and having strong social capital would mean these relationships are characterised by high trust and frequent interaction.

The effect of social capital on student achievement was explored in a study of more than 1,000 teachers in elementary schools in New York by Professor Carrie Leana from the University of Pittsburgh. Teachers completed questionnaires about who they talked to when they needed advice, and how much they trusted the source of the advice they received. The researchers also tracked student progress in maths over a year. They found that students showed higher gains in maths achievement when their teachers reported frequent conversations with their peers that centred on maths, and when there was a feeling of trust or closeness among teachers.[62] The relationships between teachers are therefore doubly important – they improve individuals' motivation, and they also appear to be associated with their effectiveness.

Autonomy

Mastery, relatedness and a sense of purpose still might not be enough if Marjo-Rita were to have her efforts to be a good teacher frustrated by bureaucracy or micro-management. Don't get me wrong: there is still bureaucracy involved in being a teacher in Finland – such as the requirement to document the interventions you've made with struggling students before requesting input from a special teacher – but they do have autonomy over *how* they teach, and to some extent, *what* they teach. Teachers really are trusted in Finland. Once they are qualified there is no teacher evaluation process; there is no one looking over their shoulder at what they are doing.

Ilpo explained, 'It goes through our culture that if you're paid for something, you're obliged to do it, and you don't want someone looking over your shoulder; if you get that it makes you perform less in fact. There's also a historical reason for that.' He paused and raised an eyebrow.

'What's that?' I asked.

'Good question! I knew you'd take the bait.' he said. 'Finnish history in short is that in the 1100s came the Swedes, as the crusaders, and well, they kind of got Finland under control over the next two or three hundred years. We were then under Swedes until 1812, and then came Russians. Both Swedes and Russians thought that Finns were second-level citizens, and they looked over our shoulders. And from those hundreds and hundreds of years in our Finnish culture, there's always been a feeling of "Hey, I do my job, go away, you don't have to look over my shoulder".'

This feeling meant that teachers felt it particularly keenly when they were told how to teach during the comprehensive reform in the 1970s. As described earlier, teachers found themselves in a completely new kind of teaching situation where they were faced with children of different abilities, and were expected to get them all to reach a reasonably high academic standard. This required not only new pedagogical techniques, but a new philosophy of education, which not all teachers at the time shared. In addition to on-the-job training, teachers therefore underwent regular inspection, managed by a strictly centralised steering system to check that they were teaching the new curriculum as they were supposed to, and not keeping up the old ways.

It was only once the comprehensive system was firmly established and teachers were doing what they were supposed to do that the inspections were dropped, as was the requirement for schools to use centrally-approved textbooks. In 1985, a new curriculum framework was introduced, allowing municipalities (regional districts) and schools more autonomy over how they interpreted the core national curriculum, although even now there are national requirements over how many hours should be spent on each subject. These days, teacher autonomy is highly valued among Finnish teachers to the extent that many say they would consider leaving the profession were they to lose it.[63]

So while purpose and mastery (by which I mean expertise rather than a master's qualification per se) have been features of the Finnish teaching profession since the beginning of compulsory schooling in Finland, the feature of autonomy has not always been as constant. Surely, autonomy is not always an unqualified good – it depends on the qualities, beliefs and expertise of those who exercise that autonomy. While Finnish teachers have always been highly educated, there was a time when their training and previous experience was no longer sufficient to take on the new, enormous task expected of them – and it is important to remember that this period of reduced autonomy may have been necessary for Finland's later success. Since the 1980s though, when it was decided that inspections were no longer needed due to the consistent quality of teaching being observed, Finnish teachers have had autonomy over how to teach and what resources to use in teaching, thus completing the triumvirate of relatedness, mastery and autonomy that supports intrinsic motivation.

Is it really autonomy?

A group of researchers from the University of East Anglia in England were called in by the Finnish National Board of Education in 1996 to visit 50 Finnish schools and watch lessons across the country, in order to understand how teachers were using the curricular freedoms granted to them. The findings of their report were a surprise:

'Whole classes following line by line what is written in the textbook, at a pace determined by the teacher. Rows and rows of children all doing the same thing in the same way whether it be art, mathematics or geography. We have moved from school to school and seen almost identical lessons, you could have swapped the teachers over and the children would never have noticed the difference.'[64]

Although just a small sample, this was a report of the situation in Finnish schools just four years before the PISA 2000 tests announced Finland's students to have the highest scores of all the countries that took part, and suggests a high degree of consistency between teachers and schools. Emma didn't notice a big variation between teachers at her schools in terms of how their lessons were structured either. She described a typical lesson to me thus:

'We'd come into class and be seated, and go through the homework. If you hadn't done it there'd be such anxiety because they'd call out random people for the answers and if they picked you, you wouldn't know! Then they'd see if anyone had anything to say about it or anything to ask. Then we'd go through the next subject we were going to talk about, like, "This is how it works, and that's how it goes", and we'd make notes and ask questions and discuss, and then they'd give us some exercises to do from our workbooks, and that would be the rest of the lesson. The teacher would go to individual people if they had questions. But it depends on the subject. It was like that in maths, but in languages we'd have sets of work, like oral pair work and games.'

Comparative video-based research on maths teaching in Iceland and Finland also shows Finnish teachers taking a consistently traditional approach with the lessons led by the teacher, but with substantial whole-class interaction, such as class discussion and student presentations.[65] All 20 of the lessons filmed in Finland took a Review-Lesson-Practice structure, similar to the one described by Emma. This is in contrast to the approach taken by Icelandic teachers – a country similar to Finland in many respects but with significantly lower PISA results – in which half of the teachers in the sample took a more individualised approach, with students spending more time working independently on different things, and receiving one-on-one teaching where time allowed. My point here is not that this traditional approach led to Finland's high results, but that there appears to be some evidence of surprising consistency in teaching styles amongst Finnish teachers, compared to elsewhere.

This relative uniformity of approach in Finnish classrooms makes sense of the fact that there is so little variation in scores between different schools and regions in Finland. But does it call into question the idea that Finnish teachers really do have autonomy over how they teach? Is there some hidden pressure on them that means they all take a similar approach? You'd be very sensible to ask these questions, but be assured that the answer to them is actually 'no'. Finnish teachers really can teach how they like – these days. The similar approaches to teaching styles and lesson structures you see across the country are not due to these styles or structures being enforced, but rather come about as a result of quality control in two other areas: teacher training and resources.

A Different Approach to Quality Control

Some people look to Finland's education system, and to their teachers' professional freedoms, and argue that if teachers elsewhere were left to get on with teaching how they saw fit, then their students would score highly in maths, reading and science too. I don't believe that this would uniformly be the case. Students in some schools would do better, but students in other schools would do worse, depending on the quality of the teachers and the school management. There is only value in someone doing what they think is best with no oversight if they have both the right intentions and the required expertise to bring about their intended goals – purpose and mastery. Without the former, teachers may not be bothered to put in the work required (an unfortunately common sight in some developing countries is a teacher asleep at her desk). Without the latter, teachers may charge ahead enthusiastically with some new teaching strategy, without knowing whether it works, or having the practical expertise to make it work.

Finland only gets away with trusting their teachers to the extent that it does because it is able to control both the intentions and the expertise. They have enough people applying for the teaching profession that they can choose to only admit those who are motivated and passionate about educating young people. They then run teacher training programmes in only a handful of highly prestigious universities, allowing for quality control of these courses and the skills of those who graduate from them.

That the Finns have enough people applying to teaching to be this selective is partly historical, but also partly because it's an appealing job for all of the reasons laid out above. Enough good people want to work in a meaningful profession, they like to be experts, and it is appealing to be trusted to do such an important job (without all the extra workload brought on by the monitoring and observations present in some other countries). It seems like a chicken and egg dilemma to replicate the Finnish model, until you remember that teachers in Finland haven't always been trusted as they are now; inspections existed until teacher training – in universities and on the job – made teachers good enough to no longer be inspected (in the eyes of the authorities).

The fact that teacher training courses are nationally coordinated (but not mandated, allowing for some local variation and initiative[66]) might help explain teachers' similar teaching styles. If research suggests that there is a particular way of teaching a certain concept that helps students understand it best, why would you do it any other way? Lessons are still adapted to suit different children's interests and needs by using different examples or different activities, but the fundamentals of how children's brains work do not change across different parts of Finland. In the same way, you would not expect to see huge variation in the way doctors treat appendicitis across the country, or even the world, but that is not because doctors lack autonomy; it is because their practice is guided by research.

A second feature of the Finnish system that is likely to contribute to the consistency of outcomes is the common usage of high-quality textbooks; the vast majority of Finnish teachers use textbooks as the basis for maths and science lessons, for example.[67] Textbooks no longer have to be approved by the National Board of Education, although they did until the mid-1980s. Like the teacher training courses, the contents of the textbooks and suggested activities are based on research of what works best for helping children understand the concepts or learn the skills being taught. This isn't just academic research; the textbooks are also fed into by highly experienced teachers, who have tried out various strategies in classrooms. Teachers are not forced to use these textbooks, but as they are so well designed, it would be waste of time to reinvent the wheel completely.

Maarit's son is a maths and science teacher (I get the impression that teaching is something that runs in families). He told me:

'All the student books have specific teacher guides for them, which are commonly available in all schools. They usually contain suggested plans for lessons, extra resources, such as examples, extra assignments, group work topics, print-outs, amount-of-lessons-per-topic schedules etc. Usually these book providers also have internet materials which the school has access to. There are books available from several publishers for each subject, and the teacher is often allowed to choose which ones to get when it's time to get some new books. This competition between the publishers usually results in pretty high-quality materials being available for both teachers and students.'

A key difference here, compared with many other countries, is that there are no standardised exams until age 18, so most of the textbook companies in Finland compete on their ability to bring about engagement and deep understanding, as opposed to the situation in England where, until recently, the competition seems to have been based on who could design a textbook that would get the students the highest marks in a particular exam specification.

I asked Reeta about textbooks too, and she explained to me why they use them so much:

'In Finnish schools, the textbook is the main tool. Experienced and skilful teachers have come together with the publisher to create an interesting, enjoyable and motivating textbook that is based on the current curriculum. Nowadays teachers have so much other things to do than planning the lessons that I would say all the teachers depend on the materials A LOT. I think this system is really typical for Finland and concerns the whole country. Of course there are some exceptions, teachers who insist doing things on their own and maybe not even using textbooks, but that's really rare. Who has time?'

So do teachers have autonomy then over how they teach? Yes. Is there still some quality control over what is being taught and in what way? Yes. And is this a contradiction? No, strangely enough, it's not. And I still want to teach there, despite the perilous weather.

Looking Forward

In PISA 2006, Finland peaked. By 2009, their results in mathematics, reading and science declined relative to their 2006 scores, and in 2012 they fell further. What could be behind this fall? In truth, no one knows – but there have been some suggestions.

Finland is facing bigger challenges that take us beyond the field of education, which may well relate to their declining scores. Professor Pasi Sahlberg – Finnish educator, author, and de facto spokesperson for Finnish education – points out that income inequality has grown faster in Finland over the past two decades than it has in other OECD countries, and that this is often related to growing social problems, increased poverty and worsening educational attainment.[68] He also points out that according to the Teaching and Learning International Survey (TALIS), teachers' participation in professional development is now low, and teachers rarely receive feedback on their teaching. I wonder if the lack of observations for the sake of autonomy has been a baby and bathwater scenario; teachers can be supported by fellow teachers or principals offering feedback on their lessons without it threatening their professional autonomy.

The 21st century has also brought demographic changes. Like in other countries, the number of foreign-born citizens in Finland has been increasing dramatically; there were almost ten times the number in Finland in 2010 compared to the number in 1990, and most of this increase has been since the turn of the century.[69] While immigrant students in Finland performed better than immigrants in many other countries in 2009, this was no longer the case in 2012, and the mathematics scores in PISA of those not born in Finland is two full years behind their Finnish peers, contributing to Finland's overall decline in results.[70] This is not an inevitable effect of immigration, but like the move to comprehensivisation in the 1970s, it might take a shift in teaching methods and philosophy to meet the challenge of educating this diversifying population.

Despite these challenges, though, Finland is still amongst the top-scoring countries in the world, and on average in 2012, still the highest scoring non-Asian country. Their approach in the early years of starting formal schooling at seven after providing high-quality preschool means that nearly all children can meet the demands of the school curriculum from its outset, and progress through it together. Their decision to delay selection into different schools or classes until the age of 16 is consistent with their remarkably equitable outcomes. And the existence in Finnish schools of all of the conditions for intrinsic motivation for teachers – autonomy, mastery, relatedness and purpose – puts them in the enviable position of being able to choose from the best, which in turn, allows them to grant teachers as much autonomy as they do. Curiously, there are some similarities here between Finland's approaches and that of one of its Asian competitors, despite the enormous cultural differences. Come with me to Japan.

JAPAN

Chapter 5: Authority, Resilience and Not Bothering Others in Japan

出る釘は打たれる
The nail that sticks out will be hammered down.
(Japanese proverb)

I almost didn't get into Japan. The landing form required that I fill in the address at which I was staying, but this was on my phone, which had sadly died after I'd failed to turn it off properly on the plane. I'll be honest – this is not the first time I've arrived in a country without a definitive address, but it'd never before been a problem. Elsewhere they'd tell me to just put down the town, or the address of a hotel: not so in Japan.

A very polite airport assistant was dispatched to help the hapless foreigner. I explained that I was staying with an English teacher called Juliet, who was waiting for me just outside in Arrivals, so they announced over the PA to the whole airport that Lucy Crehan had arrived without the proper information, and could her host please go to the information desk in Arrivals to provide her address. Five minutes later, the assistant had brought through the address to the other side of immigration control, I filled in my form and was free to enter the country, tail between my legs. In Japan, they do things by the book, and to the letter.

Follow the Rules and Don't Complain

Juliet has been living in a small town in southern Japan for 25 years, teaching English at high schools and universities, and bringing up three beautiful, insightful children with her Japanese husband, Yutaka. Hannah, Lily and Maya, now 20, 18 and 15, went to local Japanese schools from elementary school, through junior high to high school, and they weren't shy about discussing their own experiences of having to follow the rules.

'I think junior high is when the teachers get to enforce useless rules,' said Lily. 'They just come up with them for seemingly no reason, and whatever the teachers say, you have to obey – if you don't you get into trouble. They don't even explain why you're not allowed to do certain things, they're just like – "you're not".'

'In assemblies we weren't allowed to sit like this,' Lily shifted from the sofa where we were chatting and sat on the floor with her legs crossed, you had to sit like this,' she put her knees up in front of her and her arms around her knees, 'and your bum would go numb because they talk forever, and your back would start to hurt. But you couldn't move.'

The other girls concurred. Junior high was agreed to be a time when behaviour in schools was strictly enforced, and Hannah's university friends who came from all over the country had similar experiences of the huge difference between elementary school and junior high, at age 13. At elementary school, the children in most regions don't wear school uniform, but at junior high their outfits have to be just so, with particular brands of socks and only certain permitted hairstyles. They described moving to junior high school as 'like joining the army', with the students taught how to march in time during gym lessons, and getting shouted at if they stepped out of line. Lily went as far as to say that those three years of her life 'were like hell; we had no freedom, loads of work and really strict teachers.' Hannah, who is now several years out of school herself and at university, offered a reason for this shift in teachers' attitudes.

'My impression is that junior high schools are really strict because they're trying to get you ready for high school,' she said. 'They're trying to straighten you up really. Also after junior high, some people don't go to high school and go out into the world, so school is trying to get us ready for that too.'

Hannah's comments chime with some academic accounts of Japanese educational history. Edwin Oldfather Reischauer of Harvard University – born in Japan and a prolific writer on its culture and people – suggested that in pre-war Japan, 'education was regarded primarily as a tool of government, to train obedient and reliable citizens in the various skills required by a modern state'.[71] From my conversations with the girls, with Japanese teachers, and with the parents from a Parent Teacher Association two days later, I gather that this is still the case to some degree.

I was sitting at a polished oak table in a cold meeting room, sipping green tea and listening to five Japanese mums from the PTA discussing the education system, when one of them echoed what Hannah had said almost exactly: 'Japan is a country where if you go into society you have to go by the rules, so you have to first learn in school to go by the rules.' This topic had come up when I'd asked them what they thought the best and worst features of the Japanese education system were, and they had identified the lack of freedom in schools as being both simultaneously.

It was good, they said, because in going through this environment, the young people learn to internalise the rules and the behaviour expected of them, so that they no longer need to be told what to do. On the flip side, 'there are students who aren't good at handling this.' Interestingly, they did not give the misery induced in students as a disadvantage of this strict culture, they seemed to accept that this was a rite of passage that everyone had to go through, as they themselves had. This is due to the cultural importance given to *gaman* in Japan, which is a term of Zen Buddhist origin, meaning 'enduring the seemingly unbearable with patience and dignity'. Japanese students are supposed to develop this trait during their schooling, especially in the lead up to their entrance exams for high school and university when they are expected to work extremely hard. One of the mums told me, 'This level of exam pressure is normal, you have to take it, you can't really say it's too much. Everyone's done it, that's how it should be.' Another chipped in, 'The children are too busy sometimes and I do feel sorry for them, but we went through that too, it's just the way it is.'

Another instance where *gaman* is supposed to be practised is in response to the extreme temperature fluctuations in Japanese schools. Apart from in the far north, Japanese schools don't have heating or air conditioning (this is not obviously from a lack of funds, as most schools have swimming pools). In the winter, the temperature in the town I visited varies from two degrees Celsius at night to a peak of 10 degrees during the day, and in the summer it is humid, with temperatures in the 30s. The girls have to wear socks and skirts throughout the winter, with just a thin jumper and blazer, while their teachers (much to Maya's chagrin) can come in wearing coats and gloves if it's chilly. In a great example of teenage ingenuity and subtle rebellion, the girls and boys buy self-heating pads, which they put in their socks and stick to their backs on the really cold days. Maya gave me a couple, and I made great use of these during my school visits in March, under my three jumpers.

A Broader Education

Juliet's second daughter Lily had just finished her university entrance exams when I went to visit, so very kindly agreed to come into schools with me to act as my interpreter. She did a brilliant job, and was not only my interpreter in the traditional sense – she also guided me through the many formalities involved in visiting a school, and interpreted the children and teachers' behaviours when I didn't understand what I was seeing. She warned me, when I was first introduced to the principal of the local junior high school, to accept his business card with both hands, and to keep it on the table for the duration of our meeting, and so saved me from certain rudeness. As it was, he was the kind of man who wouldn't have been offended, or if he had, would certainly not have shown it. With silver hair and eyes that crinkled when he smiled, he was alarmingly gracious, and Lily and I both found him rather charming.

Mr Hashimoto made sense of the conversations I'd had so far, and shone light on the lessons I watched subsequently when he described the purpose of education in Japan as 'to bring up the children'. This encompasses far more than teaching them reading, maths and science. 'A Japanese classroom is not just a place to study, it is a place where you live too. So Japanese class teachers don't only teach them things like academics. They teach moral education, and a whole range of things. It is written in the law that education is to develop students' personalities, and I really agree with that.'

When I first heard Lily's translation of this point, while sitting in the principal's office, I assumed that 'developing students' personalities' meant bringing out the individual personalities of the students and encouraging the differences between them, as it does in the West. In fact, in Japan this couldn't be further from the truth. On reflecting on Mr Hashimoto's words in the context of my other conversations and reading, I believe that what he meant by developing personalities could be better understood in English as developing character, as opposed to developing their individual characters. He went on to describe a teacher meeting they'd had at the beginning of term, when they'd spent two hours discussing the kind of people they wanted their students to be.

Mr Hashimoto wants them to be polite. Parents want them to learn to follow the rules, and to work hard. When I asked the girls what kind of people the school was trying to get them to be, their initial response was 'robots' (accompanied by much giggling) and then, 'they want us to be serious when doing something important' and, 'to be strict on yourself but kind to others'.

The effects of values education are not easily measurable. In data-driven education systems, this can mean that these effects are not valued, so less time is spent thinking about and developing students' traits and behaviours. Some say that this is how it should be – school is about making children cleverer, and nothing else. I think this is an oversight, for two reasons. The first is instrumental; that by deliberately developing student traits of studiousness and resilience, and visibly valuing effort and perseverance, you can increase those more measurable things like grades. Of course there are better and worse ways of doing this, and research should inform the introduction of any such programmes where they don't already exist.

The second reason I think that school should be about more than 'making children clever' is fundamental. While I was in Japan, I visited the Peace Memorial Museum in Hiroshima. As you can imagine, this was an immensely moving and troubling experience, and it made me reflect on the goals of education. Nuclear technology is sophisticated, and was invented by learned individuals who would have scored highly on maths and science exams. But what good is knowledge if it is used for destructive purposes – and what good is it if a child knows all their times tables, if their house is destroyed in a nuclear blast? We need to talk about these things with our children so that we avoid the mistakes of the past. Moral education is important, even if the effects of that education are not seen until many years later, when someone decides not to push the big red button.

*

The definition of moral education in Japan is broader than you might think. In addition to a goal being 'to develop a citizen who is able to make a voluntary contribution to the peaceful international society', it includes goals around individuals' attitudes to work and learning ('always maintain a studious attitude') and to personal grooming ('to keep oneself neat'). However, the main theme that came out of all my research in Japan was the importance placed on teaching the children to live as part of a group. This is fundamental to the Japanese education system, and is a form of socialisation that affects how the students think of themselves as they get older. In fact, this process begins at birth, long before their formal education starts.

Japanese mothers are inseparable from their babies, to encourage a sense of *amae* or dependence. Japanese children commonly sleep in the same bed as their parents until they are four or five years old, and some continue to do so until teenagehood (which might explain the phenomenon of 'love hotels' for couples who get little privacy otherwise). Juliet told me that when Maya first started school, at age six, she went to a parents meeting where the principal impressed upon them the importance of 'skinship', and continuing to sleep and bathe with your child. In this way, the theory goes, children are drawn in to the importance of human relationships, and they are therefore more willing to accept the inevitable constraints on their individuality that come from living as part of a group[72].

On Maya's first day at school, she was put in a *han*; a group of four or five children that she would do everything with for the first month, until the *han* groupings changed. Japanese children sit with their *han*, do classwork with their *han*, eat lunch with their *han* and clean the school with their *han* (this is very cute to watch, though it did make me feel as if I was walking through the orphanage in *Annie*). They are praised as their *han* and scolded as their *han*. But for the purposes of this group socialisation, behaviour management in elementary school looks very different to behaviour management in junior high. It took me a while to understand the reasons for this difference, until it was explained to me by two other foreigners.

I met Sophia and her partner in the local Starbucks – the natural place to meet expats. The two met while working as Assistant Language Teachers (ALTs) in Japan, and have since adopted a little Japanese boy who goes to public school. I asked them what surprised them the most about education in Japan when they first arrived. 'I was shocked by the behaviour in primary schools, it seems really bad,' said Sophia. 'The children are allowed to get up and walk around during lessons, and generally do what they like unless it's considered dangerous.' Another ALT, Adam from Minnesota, had made the same point when I'd asked him about his experiences in primary schools.

'In elementary schools this year I had some pretty bad kids. They were running outside the class during the middle of my lessons, and playing games in the hallway, and I finally started getting after them. I told them to sit down, sternly in Japanese. And they were like, "Stop yelling at us!" The teacher just stood there, and I was like, "this is your classroom!" So the ALTs, we've all noticed that there isn't the same discipline structure. You can't send the kid out into the hall for a detention. In America, if you're interrupting our class we just throw you out of class. Whereas here you're supposed to deal with it.'

I'd been equally surprised when Lily and I had just reached the top floor of an elementary school, and had first heard (and then saw) a group of eight-year-olds careering around the corner, followed by their teacher. Why is it that behaviour seems so bad in Japanese primary schools, from a Western perspective? I think there are two contributing factors. The first is that class sizes are often quite big. Once the number of children reaches 40, you are allowed to split the group into two classes, but that means some classes are as big as 39 students. Hannah had a relatively relaxed time at elementary school in a class of 20, but Lily and Maya were both in big classes, 'which meant the teachers were always stressed' said Maya, 'as they couldn't control the class'. This wouldn't explain the apparent chaos alone though; class size is just a compounding factor that exaggerates the effects of a deliberate teacher strategy.

Sophia came to recognise this strategy after she'd been in Japan for a few months. 'They are expected to learn for themselves how they should behave. Teachers don't tell them off much, as they think the children will naturally want to be part of a group, and their peer group will encourage them to take part in the task.' In other words, teachers are prioritising the need for the children to understand the importance of the group, and to choose to behave well, over the need for peace and quiet in the here and now. For example, if a particular child is out of her chair and not taking part, the teacher might say something like 'yellow *han* group isn't ready yet'. This, of course, has the effect of making the rest of the yellow *han* berate the wayward individual and implore her to come and take part so that they can finish their task. This way children learn that they are needed by the group, and learn to take pride in achievements accomplished as a group. These feelings and beliefs are very important in Japanese society, and stay with individuals through secondary school and adulthood.

Class Identity and Uniformity

The importance of the group continues to be emphasised at junior high although, as we've seen, the behavioural expectations become a lot higher. They still have *han*, but the identity of the whole class becomes more important, so the group that they are expected to feel a part of expands. This class identity is encouraged by having the children stay in the same group, in the same classroom, for all their lessons. It is the teachers who move from room to room. Students take ownership of the classroom decoration, and stick up posters with class slogans they've decided on as a group, and pieces of the students' artwork. Recall Mr Hashimoto's account of this: 'A Japanese classroom is not just a place to study, it is a place where you live too.'

Class identity is also enhanced through setting the classes up in competition with one another. This is fair competition at an academic level, as all classes are mixed ability – there is no setting into classes or selecting into schools in Japan until students go to high school at 15. The classes compete in sports and artistic performance too, and so the overall class performance at sports day and during the annual cultural festival is taken seriously. During the primary years there are sports day rehearsals all day, every day, in the week leading up to the event, in addition to a few hours every day in the weeks prior to that. Similar time is put into the cultural performances, and often in the students' own time. Maya explained, 'My class spent hours preparing our piece for the cultural festival, so you don't want to muck it up because then you'd be letting everyone down.'

All of this fosters a sense of belonging, and shared responsibility for the outcomes of the class. This sentiment is encouraged by the Japanese approach to behaviour management too. Whereas in primary school they were praised or berated as a *han*, in junior high, their behaviour as a class is what matters. This is known as *rentai sekinin* – collective responsibility. Teachers don't often pick out individual children that are being naughty; if one child is misbehaving, it is the whole class's responsibility to make sure they fall into line, otherwise they all get in trouble.

This collective responsibility is formalised by having one boy and one girl as 'class leaders', whose job it is to ensure the class is orderly and on time. Because this role rotates around the class during the course of the year, the students are more inclined to do what these class leaders say, as they'll want that obedience reciprocated when their turn comes around. Poor Maya was class leader several times, and had a miserable time on one school trip to the local national park, where she was called in front of the teachers and told off because some of her classmates had been standing on the back of their shoes.

Hearing Maya telling that story raised my hackles. As a parent, I'm not sure I'd cope with a system in which my child would be punished for the misbehaviour of others, even though I like the idea of children having a sense of collective responsibility. Juliet found it very difficult to stomach this element of the Japanese education system, as she is from England, so doesn't take this Japanese approach for granted as most Japanese parents quite naturally do. And the difficulty with collective identity and responsibility is not purely one of unfair punishment, but of its pernicious effect on individuality of any kind.

Adam and I had been chatting about Japanese socialisation in an empty classroom during his free period, when he summed it up neatly, 'I like the social aspect of it, but getting students here to think outside the box, to think critically about something... I'd have better luck going to the dentist. Because they don't want to be wrong. They don't want to be outside the box. Because they shouldn't be outside of the box. They shouldn't be outside of the group.'

Lily weighed up these pros and cons too, 'There are good things and bad things about this group feeling in a class. You feel close to the others because you all go through hardship together – teachers shouting at you to march in time, etc. But on the flip side, it means you feel controlled, like you can't give your opinion, and you can't think any differently from the rest of the group.'

I wasn't quite clear about the connection between being a functioning member of a group, and not thinking 'outside of the box', so I asked Juliet and Hannah, and they gave me two Japanese concepts that help explain this link. The first is a common saying, 'The nail that sticks out will be hammered down'. This means that if someone is being different or causing trouble, they will be dealt with, because otherwise their actions will affect the whole group and cause disharmony. The other concept is *meiwaku*, which translates as 'bothering others'. Hannah explained a common feeling in Japan that you don't want to cause anyone any bother, so you try and make yourself as small and quiet as possible. 'It's a small island,' Juliet said. 'People are living in close proximity, which is why they emphasise the importance of group harmony.'

My initial reaction, as a Westerner (and one who gives her opinion freely) was that those nails should never be hammered down; in fact, they should be coaxed out of the woodwork. But on examining that initial reaction, I now wonder whether the Japanese and the Anglo-Saxon 'West' are at two extremes of a spectrum. The Japanese try and mould children's personalities so that they can get on well in society. Perhaps, through the cult of individuality, we too often leave our children's antisocial behaviour unchecked, fearing that by telling them on occasion that their opinion is not warranted or their behaviour is inappropriate, we will squash their developing personalities. It would be blissful if the Year 10s I used to teach had the desire to avoid *meiwaku* – bothering others. Instead, their seeking it out caused bother for me, bother for each other and bother when it came round to exam time. And I don't just say this because it would make it easier for me as a teacher. When our young people leave school, don't we want them to be polite and considerate of other people? To know that there is a time for speaking out and a time to listen; a time to criticise and a time to accept the state of affairs?

However, I do wonder whether Japan takes this too far, and leaves children with the impression that there is never a time for speaking out. Hidenori Akiba, a professor of educational psychology at Osaka Kyoiku University, explains that conformity and assimilation in Japan have 'bred the disposition to reject even a slightly different behaviour'[73]. And unfortunately, combined with the schools' approach of 'collective responsibility', the way these nails are hammered down is often through peer pressure and bullying. Of course bullying happens all over the world, and it is notoriously difficult to measure given students' and schools' reluctance to report it. But bullying in Japan seems to have some particular features that grow out of its unique classroom culture. Research shows that 80 per cent of the cases of reported bullying in Japan are collective, with the whole class bullying one student, rather than one or two being 'bad apples'.[74] It is more likely to take place in the classroom itself, rather than in the schoolyard as it does in other countries.[75] And the percentage of students who say that they'd intervene if they saw bullying taking place decreases between the ages of 10 and 14.[76] They are less likely to stand up for outcasts as they get older.

Chapter 6: Samurai, Meritocracy and 'Education Mamas'

大同小異
Big similarity, small difference.
(Japanese proverb)

A Trip to the Museum

Much to Maya's misfortune, we stumbled upon a 'Museum of Education' while walking around Kyoto on a weekend trip. I say misfortune because I imagine there are things 15-year-olds would rather do with their free time than going into an old school and translating signs about the history of education. I gave her a sideways glance as we passed it, and to her credit I didn't even need to ask. 'Do you want to go in here? That's fine!' And in we went.

The building had previously been a school, but was one of 5,000 or so in the last decade to shut due to Japan's declining birth rate. The classrooms were filled with old-fashioned desks, textbooks and other artefacts, and around the walls were old grainy photographs of children lined up outside schools, wearing traditional robes and frowning at the camera. Some of these dated back to the Meiji Era, which was a time of huge change in Japanese history, and which heralded the beginning of the modern education system.

Prior to the Meiji Restoration in 1868, education in feudal Japan was an ad hoc affair, with different types of institutions providing schooling to children from different classes. Samurai, who were members of the military nobility, attended the public schools set up by their feudal domains (also called *han*). Here they learnt Confucian classics, arithmetic and calligraphy. Children of the commoners who worked on the land, if they were educated at all, were given basic training in reading, writing and maths in temple schools. Apart from these, a number of private academies taught specialist subjects such as medicine and Chinese to samurai, and even some commoners.

In 1868, the ruling Tokugawa regime was overthrown by a group of young samurai, who were motivated by growing domestic problems and the threat of Western imperialism (the Japanese had recently been forced to sign a rather unequal treaty with the newly-arrived Americans). They wanted a Japan that could stand up to the Western powers, and believed that the feudal, class-based system was to blame for Japan's current weaknesses. They consequently got rid of the samurais' class privileges and the separate systems of education, and instead, the Government Order of Education in 1872 ruled that there would be elementary and middle schools for all, and higher-level universities for future leaders. They envisaged a future where 'there shall be no community with an unschooled family, and no family with an unschooled person.'[77]

At this stage, attendance at elementary and middle school was not compulsory – that would have been a huge leap given that at the time, only 40–45 per cent of boys and 15 per cent of girls had any kind of education at all, and not enough schools existed. When four years of elementary education was made compulsory some 14 years later, it was very difficult to enforce, as the common people saw almost no need for school-based education.[78]

During the course of the Meiji Era from 1868 to 1912, the numbers of children attending elementary school gradually increased. Though initially elementary schools unofficially retained some class character with upper-class children attending certain schools and commoners attending others, these distinctions faded as the general standard of elementary education improved. Middle school was still not compulsory however, and a number of different types of schools were authorised alongside the national middle schools to cater for children going into work (who could attend part-time) or into vocational training. During the 1900s, there was also an increase in the number of military schools for boys and girls as Japan began to flex its military muscles.

Fully comprehensive education until the age of 15, as Japan has now, was not introduced until another tumultuous time in Japan's history – after their defeat in the Second World War. Calls for a longer period of compulsory education to extend it from six to eight years had been made by factions within the government many years earlier, but not passed a process of political wrangling. What it took to extend compulsory education beyond elementary school was a fundamental restructuring of the education system during the post-war occupation by America.

The aim then was to establish a new, democratic, peaceful Japan, and changing the education system was seen as fundamental to this. The Education Renewal Committee under the authority of General Douglas MacArthur decided to get rid of the selecting of students into different types of middle school at age 12, and instead introduced a single, compulsory, nine-year educational trajectory for everyone – six years at elementary and three years at junior high school. Hence the Japanese calling their middle schools 'junior high schools' (in Japanese), which is what they were called in America. A further three years at high school and then four years at university were available to anyone who passed the exams required to get into them.

This is the system that remains to this day. Children of different classes attend elementary and junior high school together up to the age of 15, and everyone is eligible to take the tests required for further study. High schools have varying levels of prestige, and the best ones are fiercely competitive to get into, as these are more likely to ensure entry into a prestigious university, and subsequently a well-paid job. The final year of junior high school is therefore dedicated to getting students ready for these high-school entrance exams, and the exam papers appear in the newspaper the day after the students sit them so that the whole citizenry can pore over them.

All Can Succeed

Because anyone can take these exams, and everyone is expected to, there is a widely-held belief that the Japanese education system is meritocratic. The Japanese public school system ensures as far as possible that everyone has the same education up to this point, so that no one has any unfair advantages, and so that the test results and subsequent high school access are based on how hard the young person has studied. One way they do this is by transferring teachers between schools based on their evaluations, so that no one school gets all the best teachers (I got quite excited when a principal told me this, and Lily widened her eyes in surprise at my enthusiasm).

Teachers are employed by the local board of education, rather than directly by schools, and are moved every two years initially, and then every four to six years once they are established. While they are given feedback on their evaluations, they aren't told their results (which range from A to E), so no one knows why they are being moved to a particular school. Adam, the American ALT, thinks there are additional advantages to this approach, in addition to the 'balancing out' of schools.

'Rotating teachers around schools forces teachers to care about their jobs and be active in their professional learning. In the American system, after so many years in one school, some of the teachers become kind of stuck in their ways. We just teach on autopilot, and don't really think about our jobs any more. When you move schools, there's a whole new set of kids and a whole new staff, and because those kids have already worked with one teacher they may have certain expectations you have to live up to, or behaviour problems you have to learn to deal with.' Of course the downside of this is that teachers can be moved to locations that are not convenient for them or their families, and some choose to stay in a flat nearby during the week rather than move their families or face a long commute.

Another way in which children have similar educational environments up to the age of 15 is that within their schools, they are not separated into different classes or groups according to their ability – just like in Finland. The same class will contain the student who has their sights set on Japan's most prestigious university, and the student who struggles with maths and squeezes in their homework around baseball practice. I asked the head teacher of a junior high I visited why this was, given my own experience of the setting of students by ability in England, and he said, 'In Japan, we have very strong ideas about providing equal education to everyone. It is the tradition.' But it is not just the case that they believe children should have equal access to educational opportunities despite inherent differences between them; Japanese educators are less likely to believe that there are inherent differences in the first place.[79] And I think this belief makes a difference, over and above the policies that are put in place.

Japan's education system is based on the assumption that everyone is intellectually equal, at least at first, and it is the environment and individuals' work ethic that lead to eventual distinctions in academic ability. This doesn't mean that the Japanese don't have the conception of some children being smarter than others. Juliet used to give lifts to her daughters' friends, and would hear them talking about their classmates as being *atama ii* or *atama warui* – literally 'good head' and 'bad head'. But there is a perception that these differences come about as a result of studying hard or not. Lily explained to me that if you fail a test, it's not because you're stupid – the tests are such that if you've studied, you can definitely pass, even if you don't get top marks.

This belief is conveyed to the students in the way that Japanese teachers relate to the class. As we saw, at the primary level, students do much of their work in groups (*han*), and this work is therefore evaluated as a group effort, playing down any early differences in ability between students. Praise is also reserved for the group, rather than individual students. Adam recounted, 'What I was surprised by, coming from an American or Western mind set, was the way the other teachers responded to me praising individual kids who had done well. A lot of teachers were like, "no, don't do that. Because now all of the other students will be mad. That they sucked, they didn't do good." So I've slowly stopped doing that.' When teachers take pains not to emphasise the differences between students, they perpetuate this idea that all students have equal potential.

I said earlier that I think this belief alone makes a difference to student outcomes, over and above the particular policies of comprehensive education or mixed-ability classes, and here is why: teacher expectations make a difference. Research suggests that if teachers believe that students have great potential, this becomes a self-fulfilling prophecy, and the students are more likely to succeed as expected. This is called the Pygmalion effect, after the mythical King of Cyprus who fell in love with a woman he had carved out of stone, and whose dreams came true when the goddess Aphrodite took pity on him and turned the statue into a real woman. The psychologist Robert Rosenthal was the first to use this term in an educational context in 1968, to describe the results of an experiment he carried out with school principal Lenore Jacobson.[80]

Rosenthal and Jacobson gave the children at Jacobson's school an IQ test at the beginning of the school year. They told teachers that this was a measure of student potential and 'blooming', suggesting that it could tell which students would perform well that year – in fact it could do no such thing. Teachers were told that certain students in their classes had come in the top 20 per cent of this test, whereas actually they were randomly selected from the class list. At the end of the year, the children took IQ tests again to estimate any change, and the students the teachers had expected to do well based on the invented test results had actually improved their IQ scores, relative to the other children. The only explanatory factor was the teachers' expectations of them.[81] On a less positive note, the same thing happens in reverse (the Gollum effect), and when teachers have low expectations of children, it effects their scores in the expected direction too.[82]

So when Japanese teachers believe that all children have equal potential, and are equally capable of succeeding at school (as opposed to some children lacking the innate ability), this actually makes it more likely that they will succeed at school. Sociologist Gail Benjamin writes: 'Japanese educators do not feel that they can be effective only with certain kinds of children or with children from only certain kinds of home backgrounds. All children can learn, all should learn, the same basic lessons, and the same sets of teaching techniques can be effective with all children.'[83] Japan is one of only 10 countries of all those that take part in PISA in which the impact of socio-economic status on maths scores is below the international average, while at the same time keeping those scores above the international average. Perhaps these attitudes have something to do with it.

Even in Japan though, a student's family background significantly relates to the grades she is likely to get. While in many ways, Japan's social and economic environment has been conducive to educationally supportive home backgrounds for many years, with low unemployment, low income inequality and a large middle class (over 90 per cent of Japanese considered themselves to be middle class in 1995), there are still disparities in parental approaches based on social strata.

Yoko Yamamoto at Brown University carried out a series of in-depth interviews with 16 Japanese mothers of different classes about their children's education, and found that though both middle-class and working-class mothers wanted their children to do well at school, it was only the middle-class mothers who considered it their responsibility to engage their young children in learning outside of school. Where working-class mums were sometimes worried about the academic achievement of their children, they didn't have the confidence or the know-how to address these issues.[84] Perhaps for related reasons, children from poorer backgrounds are also likely to spend less time studying outside of school.[85] And more so than in many other countries, mothers in Japan are expected to play a significant role in their children's education.

Mum Says I Have to Study

Students work hard in Japan, but not only because they believe that they can succeed through hard work; nationally education is believed to be of supreme importance. As we have seen, this was not always the case, and when compulsory education was first introduced, many people did not see the point of school. At the time, the government took it upon itself to educate the population about the importance of education, alongside establishing the education system. More recently, the education minister raised teachers' pay above that of other civil servants, so that it would continue to reflect the importance of the job. And now, this education focus can be seen in the manner of the ceremonies that are held for all children on their entering and graduating from school at each stage of their education.

I was privileged to be invited to attend Maya's graduation from junior high school. The school hall was full of parents, dressed mainly in dark, smart suits, but with a few who had made an even greater effort and donned colourful kimono. At the front, by the stage, were 20 or so important-looking people separate from the rest of the audience. I whispered my query to Juliet on my left, and she explained that they were local dignitaries, and that they attended all entry and graduation ceremonies, even those of the six-year-olds starting school for the first time. The hall went from hushed to silent and the graduating students filed in from the back in pairs, some with tears already sliding silently down their cheeks.

The ceremony was a long one, and I got pins and needles in one bum cheek. The principal made a speech, the students came across the stage one by one to receive their graduation certificates, and each of the dignitaries stood up in turn and gave their congratulations to the graduating class. Then all the students came on stage in neat lines, boys on one side and girls on the other, and sang the school song in harmony. Those children were singing their hearts out, the melodies soared to the rafters of the hall, and several children were singing despite the occasional sobs and sniffles that conveyed the depth of their sadness at leaving their classmates and teachers after three intense years together. I looked around, and saw a couple of mums dabbing at their eyes with white handkerchiefs too.

Parents, particularly mothers, are expected to be heavily involved in the education of children in Japan, and they take this role seriously. In England, if a child were staying up all night to study for their exams, their mum might pop their head in the door and remind them to get a good night's sleep. In Japan, their mum is more likely to stay up late with them, and bring them snacks. Some mums have been known to give up something dear to them during the lead-up to the child's exams – their favourite food for example – in solidarity with their child and the sacrifices they are having to make. Consequently, the children feel the weight of their parents' expectations, which motivates them further to succeed at school. Failure does not only have a personal cost; it reflects badly on the family.

This intense involvement in the child's education is expected by society and by the schools. It is bound to have a positive effect on exam results, but significantly impacts on women's career opportunities. For example, a survey of 3,500 25–44-year-old women by Japan's Labour Ministry found that 47 per cent reported being told at work that they were 'causing trouble' or that they 'should retire' when they fell pregnant.[86] It's culturally expected that as a mother you wouldn't do anything which would interfere with your ability to supervise your children's homework, or make their packed lunches for the school trip. Schools send home a list of responsibilities that parents are supposed to take on, such as marking their child's homework. They are told what time students should go to bed, and how much time they should have for playing with friends during the holidays.

Gail Benjamin sent her children to Japanese public school for a year, so received all of the communications that parents get from schools. She writes, 'The constant reinforcement of these values in school communications and the somewhat admonitory tone of the writing probably is in the long term an effective way of enlisting pressure from home on children to enhance the school's attempts to teach proper behaviours and attitudes. Another way of looking at it is that these communications are ways of reminding mothers that their role as *kyōiku mama*, 'education moms,' is one the school system counts on, not one that is optional for them.'[87]

Chapter 7: 'Relaxed Education', Lesson Study and the Japanese Approach to Problem-Solving

泥棒も10年
Even a thief takes ten years to learn his trade.
(Japanese proverb)

Let me take you inside a Japanese junior high school classroom as it is now, and has been for decades. The desks are organised in rows, with space between each one allowing you to walk along the aisles, and see the students' work. Try not to trip over the bulky backpacks as you go. The students wear navy uniforms, which look like sailors' outfits with a white trim; skirts for girls and trousers for boys. All the students wear white plimsolls, and some wear surgical type masks over their noses and mouths to stop their germs from spreading.

It's quiet when we enter. The boy at the back nudges his friend, who looks over at us with raised eyebrows, but both turn back and get on with taking notes. The teacher is at the front, lecturing on the properties of parallelograms. He writes on the blackboard, which is dark green, and stretches across the entire wall at the front of the classroom. He adds each step of his working next to the last on the board, so that were you to come in at the end of the lesson, you'd be able to follow the whole lesson's teaching based on the board work alone. The students are scribbling away, making notes in their exercise books. One girl flicks the hair of the girl in front with a pencil, and borrows a rubber.

When he's finished explaining, the teacher asks the students to repeat the three properties of parallelograms, first to themselves, then as a class. This goes on for 15 minutes. He then instructs the students to move the desks so that each group of four students sit in a huddle, each with two boys and two girls. They do so without a fuss. Each group is given a different, challenging problem to solve, and the classroom is filled with a murmuring as the students chat about how to solve it. The teacher patrols, checking their progress, and shares a joke with one student (sadly, due to my lack of Japanese, I don't get it). As each group finishes, one of their member comes to the front of the classroom, and writes up their solution on the board. I see some groups play 'rock-paper-scissors' to decide whose task that is.

The teacher gets a student from each group to talk through their solutions, which, of course, require an understanding of the properties of parallelograms, and addresses some questions to the class, such as 'is there another method to solve this?' Sometimes we see a hand-up. More often than not, no one volunteers, and the teacher chooses someone to stand up and answer. With the end of the lesson approaching, the teacher assigns the students some practice questions from their work-books for homework, then invites the students to stand. They bow, he bows, he leaves.

You'll have noticed that this looks quite different from the more raucous primary school atmosphere I described above. The behaviour and volume levels aren't the only changes that take place between elementary and junior high schools either. At a primary level, the lessons are more obviously active. I went in and danced to an English song with a class of eight-year-olds, and we learnt how to ask for someone's telephone number in English using a cardboard cut-out phone. There is more group work at primary, and the teachers use a variety of props in the classrooms to demonstrate concepts – building blocks, colanders, balloons.

At junior high and high school, the lessons look far more traditional, with more teacher explanation at the front of the class and less movement. In one class, I even saw a couple of boys sleeping at the back of the room. According to Sophia, who has worked in both elementary schools and junior high schools, the frequency of group work declines partly because students get less outgoing as they get older. 'In elementary school they're better at it, and all keen to get involved, but in junior high school everyone gets shy, and girls won't talk to boys, so they'll sometimes just allocate a leader and let them do all the work.' The teachers' awareness of the hugely important high school entrance exams at the end of junior high is bound to play a part too.

Despite these obvious differences, the psychologists James Stigler and James Hiebert were able to identify some similarities in approach at both levels of Japanese schooling, based on some video-based comparative research they carried out in the 1990s in Japan, America and Germany.[88] They noted that Japanese teachers took great pains to begin teaching mathematical concepts by introducing a real-world problem. They contrasted this with the American approach, which more typically saw teachers introducing the mathematical concepts straight-up, and teaching students the correct procedure to solve the problems. In Japan, the students were reportedly encouraged to solve the problem presented to them through a very carefully planned lesson sequence, during which the students were asked guiding questions at each stage to ensure they came to understand the topic at hand.

In an earlier book, Stigler and his esteemed colleague Harold Stevenson[89] give an example of one Japanese elementary maths lesson, which began with the teacher bringing in a variety of containers – teapots, vases, a beer bottle – and asking the students which they thought held the most water. The students had different ideas about the answer, so they were asked how they might investigate the question. The teacher guided them towards the suggestion that they could fill each one using a cup, and count how many cups of water it holds. They went off and did this, and as students reported their findings to the teacher, she put the information into a bar chart, representing the number of cups per container. At the end of the lesson she asked the students again – how can we tell which has the most water? The students explained what they'd done to discover this, and how the graph represented the answer. They had developed an understanding of what bar charts were and how they are used and useful.

When Stigler and Heibert analysed lessons at Grade 8 level, they found the same structured problem-solving approach used. Recall the lesson on parallelograms, described above. Here the teacher has given the students mathematical problems that he has not told them how to solve. However, he has not left them completely in the dark during this attempt – he has started the lesson by teaching them the relevant content knowledge they will need to solve the problems, even though he hasn't given them an exact 'how to'. The problem-solving is both structured and, as educators say, scaffolded. Just as scaffolding on a building helps you to reach the top through a series of platforms, but doesn't lift you straight to the top with no effort like an elevator, so the teacher gives them a series of prompts and information to help them solve difficult problems, but doesn't give them all the answers.

There seems to be a careful balance that is struck here between giving the students enough information and guidance to allow them to solve the problem, and giving them the space to attempt the problem-solving on their own. If students don't have the prior knowledge necessary to solve the problem, they will become dispirited, and the whole exercise will be a waste of time – hence the teacher lecturing to them first (or in the elementary example, the teacher introducing the structure of a bar chart on the board, rather than getting them to design their own graph). In fact, what Japanese elementary and secondary schools have in common is that students are required to commit a lot to memory, whether that's number facts up to 100 in Grade 1, the times tables in Grade 2 or the three properties of parallelograms in Grade 8 (unrelated but fun fact: one Japanese man has memorised the numerical value of pi up to 111,700 digits). This memorisation is not restricted to mathematics either: Japanese children are expected to know 1,006 kanji (the adopted Chinese characters used in the Japanese writing system) by the time they leave primary school, and a further 1,130 by the time they leave junior high school. Having this knowledge in their long-term memory helps them enormously with other academic tasks, such as comprehension and mathematical problem-solving, for reasons based on the architecture of the brain, and explained in Box 3.

Box 3: Why Memorisation is Helpful for More Than Tests

Humans have a working memory, which is the cognitive structure in which processing occurs – in other words, this is where you process things that you are consciously thinking about. You also know an awful lot of things that you are not thinking about at any one time: your address, the name of your first pet, the lyrics to 'Rocket Man', etc. – these are stored in your long-term memory. When you have to recall the name of your first pet because you set it as the answer to your security question and you've forgotten your password, you retrieve it from your long-term memory, and process it in your working memory, like taking something out of your kitchen cupboard where you've stored it, to use it at your kitchen counter.

Things also enter your working memory through your environment. You see an advert for a new toothbrush that impresses you, or you look up the different types of rock on Google to help you with a geography assignment. You can pop next door to the corner shop for an ingredient you didn't have and add it to your kitchen counter. It does have a limited capacity though – you can only hold so many things in your working memory at any one time, just like you can only fit so many ingredients on your counter. If you've just looked up a phone number on your phone, and you're trying to hold it in your mind between hearing it and dialling it, it's pretty annoying if someone asks you a question – you're likely to forget the number (the memory decays) and have to look it up again. It also doesn't have great sticking power – if you don't repeat the phone number over and over in your head, you're likely to have forgotten it in about 30 seconds. For the sake of my kitchen analogy, I'd like you to imagine that if you leave your new ingredients unattended for more than 30 seconds, your dog comes along and eats them (this doesn't happen for the stuff from your cupboards though, because there's space to store them back on the shelf whenever you're not using them).

Let's return to our Japanese children, who've learnt their times tables and their number facts. These are now in their long-term memory, and they can retrieve them with ease and bring them into their working memory whenever they need to. Their teacher has asked them to solve a maths problem:

If a cake is cut into 12 pieces, how many pieces would you need to eat to have $\frac{1}{3}$ of the cake left?

They are thinking hard about how to solve this, and they have been taught about equivalent fractions, so see that they need to work out how many twelfths would be equivalent to $\frac{1}{3}$ and then take 12 away from this value. They know they need to work out the lowest common multiple of 12 and 3, and because they easily recall from their long-term memory that 3x4=12, they know that the lowest common multiple is 12 and that they therefore need to multiply the numerator by 4. So $^4/_{12}$ is the same as $^1/_3$, which means that the next step is 12-4=8, leaving them with the conclusion that you need to eat 8 pieces. Someone who did not immediately know that 3x4=12 would struggle to find the lowest common multiple. They'd get side-tracked with trying out which multiples both numbers went into using their calculator, and in the meantime, they would have forgotten the other steps they'd decided to take, as it would have decayed from their working memory.[90] It wouldn't only take them longer, it would be a more difficult and demotivating process.

If you're trying to follow a recipe to make a cake, but at every stage of the recipe you need to pop next door to get more ingredients, it takes you longer. It is also additionally difficult if you pop out for butter, only to find the dog has eaten the eggs you so carefully whisked. Now imagine you don't have a recipe at all – you've just been asked to make a cake, and discover the method for yourself. It's going to take you a little while, but if you've got all the ingredients there, your trials and errors aren't going to be as disastrous as if you have to go out at every step and potentially buy the wrong ones. That is why it is helpful to stock up your shelves with the kinds of ingredients that are used in the kind of baking that you do.

On the other hand, if the teacher only got the students to memorise the facts, and didn't ever give them the opportunity to apply their knowledge to novel situations, they would struggle to deal with any problems that didn't follow exactly the same pattern as ones they'd learnt the solutions for. And if Japanese teachers do err on one side or the other, it is this side on which they err. Even now, more than 15 years after problem-solving approaches in Japanese schools were supposedly typical, one Japanese primary school teacher I spoke to at a BBQ said: 'The education system we've taught in for a long time is where the teachers just teach; a one-way education. Nowadays we have to bring in active learning, but there aren't many people who can do it. We've started learning how to do it but we're slow, especially in Osaka.' This is clearly something she and teachers in her school aspire to, rather than something which has been established across Japan for more than a decade.[91]

Nevertheless, Japanese students do particularly well in PISA's international tests of problem-solving (defined as the 'capacity to engage in cognitive processing to understand and resolve problem situations where a method of solution is not immediately obvious'), better even than their high scores in maths, science and reading would lead one to expect, and more than any other country apart from Singapore and Korea. Perhaps the problem-solving tasks that are embedded in some (even if not all) Japanese lessons help contribute to this ability.

While it is impossible to say for sure what teaching approach leads to what outcomes, there is some evidence to show that these approaches are beneficial. The original TIMSS study in 1995 on which Stigler and Hiebert's observations were based included a questionnaire for students on how often reasoning tasks happened in their lessons (defined as: 'explaining the reasoning behind an idea; using tables, charts or graphs to represent and analyse relationships; working on problems for which there is no immediately obvious solution and/or writing equations to represent relationships'). Japanese students reported that they did this in their lessons more than American students did, and the frequency with which they did this made a difference of 14 TIMSS test points within Japan, and 19 points within America.[92]

This suggests that these reasoning tasks could contribute to some of the difference between the two countries' scores, if only a small proportion of it (the gap was about 100 points, and a quarter of American teachers already used these types of tasks frequently). It is important to remember that these reasoning approaches in Japanese lessons are discrete, highly-structured to ensure students have the required prior knowledge, and are introduced with a particular goal in mind. Used in this structured way, problem-solving approaches seem to be beneficial to mathematics scores, and perhaps even more general problem-solving skills too.

Lessons for the Rest of the World

Rather than assuming that one particular approach to teaching is the best in all situations, Japanese teachers have a number of teaching strategies in their repertoire, and every activity within each lesson is carefully chosen with the goal of the lesson in mind. When I asked Mr Hashimoto about the use of group work in Japanese schools, and why they did it (despite the challenges it presents for awkward teenagers) he said, 'There are lots of different aims for it. The teacher decides which student characteristics or abilities they want to improve through the group learning, before they begin. They never just introduce group work for the sake of it, there is always an aim.' The methods chosen for each lesson are based on the question, 'What is the best method to teach this idea?'

Whichever methods they choose, Japanese teachers have an edge on developing students' conceptual understanding for a number of underlying reasons. The first is the practice of 'lesson study', which is common in Japanese elementary schools across the country. I first came across this concept when I was invited to watch a lesson in which 10 teachers and a video camera were squeezed in to the back of an otherwise normal-looking classroom. My palms would be sweating if I were being observed by so many teachers, because observations in England are usually an assessment of your ability as a teacher, and end with a grading on a scale of 1–4. This teacher looked calm though, and I later learned that they have a different type of observation for lesson study in Japan where the focus is on watching how the students are responding to the lesson, so that the teachers can communally feed back on the effectiveness of the lesson plan. But it's even less scary than that – four or five of the teachers sat at the back of the room were involved in planning the lesson with the teacher in the first place, so the teacher isn't even being judged on their planning.

This lesson study approach has a number of advantages beyond the prevention of sweaty palms. Expert teachers feed into all lesson plans, allowing younger teachers to learn from them and avoid the lesson disasters that I unintentionally created in my first year of teaching. The carefully designed, evaluated and tweaked lesson plans are stored centrally so that teachers rarely have to plan from scratch, just edit to suit their particular class. And the regular conversations about the best way to teach a lesson ensure that teachers at all levels are thinking about their practice, rather than growing stale after many years of teaching the same thing.

In their research, Stevenson and Stigler were curious about this lesson study process, and asked a teacher, 'What do you talk about?' The teacher stopped marking and thought for a moment. 'A great deal of time,' she reported, 'is spent talking about questions we can pose to the class – which wordings work best to get students involved in thinking and discussing the material. One good question can keep a whole class going for a long time; a bad one produces little more than a simple answer.'[93] A teacher I spoke with amazed me with the level of detail in which she had planned; for the introduction of a particular maths topic she explained that the number 23 should be used in the example she first shared with the students, as it wouldn't introduce misconceptions or require new maths the students hadn't learnt yet, whereas using the number 24 would. This detailed approach to lesson planning is why I believe that the level of planning evident in the lessons analysed by Stigler and Hiebert was not simply due to the presence of the video camera.

Another advantage that Japanese teachers have, in common with teachers in Shanghai and Singapore, is time. Ask American teachers to plan to that level of detail with their colleagues and they would laugh in your face – they have the longest teaching hours of all the countries that entered the TALIS survey, at 26.8 per week.[94] In Japan however, it's 17.7 – equivalent to about three-and-a-half hours a day, which is made possible by their larger class sizes. According to Andreas Schleicher – the man in charge of PISA – most countries have this trade-off between class size and teaching time, with either larger classes but fewer lessons, or smaller classes but more lessons. Primary school teachers in the UK unfortunately have neither fewer lessons nor smaller classes, due to student-teacher ratios being substantially higher than average (21 children per teacher, compared to an OECD average of 15).[95]

Japanese teachers also have more time on each topic to ensure the children have a thorough understanding of it before they move on, because of the way the curriculum is set out. The Japanese have a national curriculum – content that all students should be taught laid out by subject and by year group. This curriculum is demanding, in that at least in some subjects it covers more difficult content by age 15 than either the English or American curriculum do.[96] And yet it actually covers fewer concepts per year; the textbooks are skinnier, containing about 10 topics a year for maths and science rather than the 30 or 40 covered in America.

How can this possibly lead to a more demanding curriculum? Surely this means it is easier? No. Japanese teachers have the time to cover concepts in depth, and don't move on to the next topic until students have mastered the first. The expectations placed on parents to supervise their children's homework and help them when they are stuck make this more achievable than it might be elsewhere. And because each topic is covered in depth, they don't then need to reteach the same concepts in later years as they would if they'd rushed through them, meaning they can subsequently move on to more difficult topics.

The government is actually concerned with defining a maximum content for the textbooks that should be mastered as well as a minimum that should be covered, so for example, one textbook publisher was asked to remove the label 'cow dung' from a picture of a cow eating grass in the sunshine, lest it gave the impression that the students had to cover the whole of the nitrogen cycle at that stage.[97] I was impressed by this – one of my frustrations as a teacher in England was having to cover lots of content in time for the exam, sometimes ignoring students' important but curriculum-irrelevant questions in doing so. Japanese primary school teachers don't have to do this, because their curriculum in each subject is narrow but deep.

This approach gives the teachers time to bring most of the students with them as they move through the curriculum. The idea is that everyone will understand and move forward together, rather than accepting or expecting that some will race ahead or fall behind. This was evident in one of my conversations with Mr Hashimoto, when I asked him what teachers did if students were falling behind.

'To be honest – say in maths – if a student is behind in maths when they are in second grade of junior high, it is quite difficult to get them to catch up again.' The implication being that this is unusual rather than the norm. 'But what the teachers would do is to try to make the lessons really dense, if that makes sense. Trying to make the best lessons they can make.' So rather than splitting the class into different groups within the lesson, and accepting that some students will just have to do easier work, the teachers make the lessons as efficient as possible to cover whatever the students were behind on, in addition to what they were learning for the first time. Differentiation with different activities for different students is not a focus. It is not a focus to the extent that Juliet's girls, who spoke fluent English, still had to sit through English classes and do the same activities as the rest of the class. What Mr Hashimoto didn't say, but I saw happen, was that teachers also support students who are struggling outside of class. Japanese students have a 10 to 15-minute break in between all of their lessons, and at the end of each class the teacher would often stay at the front desk and talk through things with individual students.

An account of the Japanese education system wouldn't be complete, though, without giving a mention to *juku* (private 'cram school') and the role they play in catering to students of different abilities. When a student is struggling with a particular subject and their parents can't help them, many go to classes after school to continue their lessons. Students who want to get ahead and extend their learning go too, as does almost everyone that is studying to take the university entrance test. Students don't only go because their parents make them – *juku* is seen by many children as a social activity, and a place to make new friends.[98] Kunio Kijima, head of a private association of *jukus* and director of his own *juku* chain, believes that public schools often bore the smartest students and leave the weakest students behind.[99] 'Our goal is to help all kids get ahead,' he said. In countries without such private tuition options (or the parents willing to pay for them), these students would need to be supported by a public alternative or by school teachers, as they are in Finland.

Relaxed Education

At the beginning of the 1990s, students all attended school on Saturday too, and more children attended *juku*. However, as Japan became more self-aware, the Japanese became concerned that students were working too hard, and that they lacked the ability to learn and think for themselves. The government therefore decided that the students needed 'room to grow' – *yutori kyōiku* – and so over the course of the late 1990s and early 2000s, they cut the curriculum down by a third, reduced the number of Saturdays that children had to be at school (eventually eliminating this practice completely) and introduced a period of 'integrated studies' in which students would be given time to pursue studies of their own interest.

Hannah started school just before this *yutori kyōiku* was introduced, and Lily and Maya followed her straight into this 'relaxed education'. They tell tales of going into the nearby forest with the class to search for wild boar tracks, and learning about the plants and different types of bark. They described how they'd visit the local shrine and learn about its history. (They also told me that one teacher used to stick his knuckles into the heads of naughty boys – a reminder that what is officially decreed by the government doesn't always make its way down into schools, even in law-abiding Japan.)

In a move that was quite unusual for the normally prescriptive Department for Education, how the integrated studies were delivered was left largely up to schools. The aim of the programme was to allow students to work independently, and follow their own interests to encourage their individuality – but how much school time was allocated to the programme and what topics were to be covered was not decreed. This went a step further than teachers introducing structured problem-solving into lessons – this time the problems to solve and the questions to investigate were (in most cases) up to the children. The elementary school students loved it. They liked the choice, the open-endedness of the tasks (which are otherwise rarely seen in Japanese schools) and the fact that the content wasn't examined.[100]

Teachers and older students were less sure. While many teachers approved of the philosophical underpinnings of *yutori kyōiku*, they worried about the effects it would have on students' entrance exams. Some embraced it enthusiastically, while others did the bare minimum to meet the official requirements (I must admit I was guilty of the same with certain policies when I was teaching.) A Japanese friend of mine said of her school days in the early 2000s, 'Even though you don't officially have to go, schools make you go on Saturdays by giving lessons and stuff. They say it's optional, but you know "optional".' And while Lily was officially a student of *yutori kyōiku* for her entire education, she still described high-school teachers as 'trying to stuff a textbook down your throat'. The point being that while this was a 'relaxed' period compared to the previous state of Japanese education, if you were to transfer the same requirements onto children to England, they would not find it in the least bit relaxing.

So what were the effects of this *yutori kyōiku*? Professor Kariya found that the average amount of time children spent working outside of school dropped between 1974 and 1997.[101] This was a motivational issue rather than anything else – the proportion of children responding 'yes' to the statement 'I'm fine if my grades are good enough not to fail' rose too. Kariya doesn't think that this motivational drop was solely due to the new 'relaxed education' – he suggests that a lack of employment opportunities due to the economic situation in the 1990s damaged students' belief in the previously solid 'fact of life' that doing well at school led to good jobs. This hit young people from working-class backgrounds the hardest – explaining his second finding that the reduction in motivation was greatest amongst young people from poorer backgrounds. However, he found that in response to the 'relaxed education' reforms, this situation got even worse.

According to Kariya, the relaxed education approach may have given working-class students a false sense of security, believing that academics didn't matter, further disadvantaging them in the job market. Middle-class students were likely to be under no such illusion, thanks to their parents (though I'm sure no one was thanking their parents at the time). In addition, the Integrated Study Time (IST) was of more use to those who already had the academic skills to make the most of it. Professor Christopher Bjork, who visited schools at the time to evaluate the programme, said: 'In all of the junior high schools I visited, intellectually-able, self-directed individuals usually developed thorough IST project plans, used their time wisely and produced impressive reports. As a result, they earned praise for their efforts. Students who were struggling academically, in contrast, tended to flounder. Lacking the organisational skills and/or the ability to synthesise information in insightful ways, they often used time allocated for IST to socialise, doodle or sleep.'[102]

In 2004, when the 2003 PISA results were released and showed that Japan's scores in reading had declined, there was an uproar. Fingers were pointed at the *yutori kyōiku* reforms, and the students of this era were labelled *baka* – stupid. Lily is one of this 'stupid' generation, but recalls this fact with amusement. In response to the criticism the government gradually began to increase the hours spent on maths and Japanese, and in 2011, many of the *yutori kyōiku* reforms were reversed. Textbooks were fattened, and the hours spent on 'Integrated Studies' were reduced to make way for other subjects.[103]

In the frenzy that followed these PISA results, what is rarely considered is that Japanese international test results had been declining for some time, even before the introduction of the *yutori kyōiku*, and that the 2003 results were not a huge drop in comparison. More fundamentally, however, they seem to have forgotten what the reforms set out to do. *Yutori kyōiku* was not supposed to raise PISA results; it was supposed to relieve pressure on students and improve their creativity and problem-solving abilities. According to surveys which Japanese students filled out in 2000 and 2012, their satisfaction with school increased during this period more than in any other country in the world. And in the tests of problem-solving, Japanese students did better than almost all other countries, including PISA chart-topper, Shanghai. Looks to me like they achieved what they set out to achieve.

Japan's education system has always put them above most other countries in the PISA tests, perhaps due to the importance placed on education, the carefully-planned lessons and the cultural belief that all children can and ought to keep up with their mastery-based curriculum. Yet slipping just a few places made the government panic and reverse reforms that seemed to be effective – both in reducing the 'examination hell' lamented by the public and enabling students to be world-beaters at solving unseen problems. This highlights a values-based dilemma which is relevant to other countries too: to what extent are we willing to compromise on maths and reading results to secure other social and educational goods for our children? This question is not only asked by the government in Singapore – our next stop – but by Singaporean parents too.

Chapter 8: Dynamic Intelligence, Eugenics and Streaming in Singapore

You marry a non-graduate, you're going to have problems, some children bright, some not bright.
Lee Kuan Yew, founding Prime Minister of Singapore

My first educational encounter in Singapore was with a small Muslim lady at passport control in the expansive and expensive Changi airport.

'Why have you come to Singapore?'

'I'm researching the world's best education systems.'

She raised one eyebrow and pursed her lips. 'You think Singapore has the world's best education system? No lah, we put too much pressure on kids too young.'

Stereotypes: 1
Surprises: 0

I didn't have the time to ask her what she meant as there was a queue forming behind me, but it pretty quickly became clear. Students begin school the year they turn seven, in Primary 1 (P1). Within each school the classes are mixed-ability at this age, but different primary schools have different levels of prestige (Raffles Girls' Primary School is *de rigueur*), and gaining admission to the top schools is the holy grail of parenting for mothers of tiny children, and a subject discussed with great urgency outside the preschool gates.

First priority for admission to any primary school goes to those with a sibling currently at the school, followed by those whose parents or siblings are alumni. This helps community cohesion, but also ensures that if one of your parents was privileged with a prestigious education, you will be too. First dibs for any spaces left go to children whose parents have volunteered to help the school in some way for at least a year before primary registration, and who have committed at least 40 hours to traffic warden duties, school canteen assistance, librarian services, etc. Some schools even require parents to sit through interviews before they are accepted to be parent volunteers.

'Why does it matter which primary school the children go to?' you might be thinking. 'Surely it's not worth 40 hours of serving noodles?' Well, it matters because the score you get in your Primary School Leaving Exam (PSLE) at age 12 has an enormous impact on the course of the rest of your life. It determines what school you go to, what exams you are able to take and what kind of job you will therefore end up doing. Getting children into the best primary schools in the first place is the job of the parents, but don't assume this means that the children can relax for the first few years of primary school, safe in the knowledge that the PSLE is six years away. Even before children reach the age of 12 they are sorted into different classes, depending on their scholastic ability.

The age at which primary school streaming begins has changed over the short course of Singapore's history – in my opinion, in the right direction. To begin with, there was no streaming into different classes, but those who couldn't cope with the level of the work were allowed, and then encouraged (when progression beyond P2 at age seven or eight became conditional on passing exams) to drop out of school altogether.[104] One teacher I spoke to recalled how, as a student, she used to help her teachers at the end of each year to sort all the students' files into their new classes, and how every year there were a pile of folders that didn't get put back. When she asked about them, she was told that they were the students who didn't make it, and that they wouldn't be coming back next year.

Streaming at the end of P3 was therefore introduced in 1979 with the best of intentions; to deal with this problem of students dropping out by providing an easier curriculum for those who couldn't keep up. Unfortunately though, this meant deciding at age nine whether students would follow an academic or vocational path. Until 2008, students were put into one pathway for all their subjects, and those in EM3 (the lowest) would rarely make it to a secondary stream where they could even take the exams that might qualify them for college, barring their path to university before they even understood what university was. The plight of these children inspired the film *I Not Stupid* by Singaporean film-maker Jack Neo, about the lives of three boys in this academically 'inferior' EM3 stream. The film depicts the boys being bullied for being in the 'stupid' stream, and when one gets caught cheating in an exam, he subsequently attempts suicide.

The film was a big hit, and became the second highest-grossing film in Singapore at the time. Its criticism of the streaming system sparked national and parliamentary debate, and led to the abolition of streaming instead of setting. Now, children take tests that determine whether they will take individual subjects in their last two years of primary school at a higher, standard or foundation level, recognising that students may have strengths in different subjects.

Students in different subject bands in Primary 6 will then take different papers for their Primary School Leaving Exams (PSLEs), which is taken into account in their final score. These exams are a BIG DEAL. Parents take 'PSLE leave' from work to help coach their children through them. The government still looks to PSLE scores as cut-offs when appointing adults to certain roles in the army (or so I am told by an 'insider' – this isn't official policy). Although you can apply to six secondary schools of your choice, whether you get in or not will be almost entirely based on your PSLE results – all schools are selective.[105] Your 'PSLE T score' – which is calculated relative to the performance of the rest of your year – is also used to determine which stream you enter in secondary school. There are five potential outcomes for you, based on this number, which are listed below next to the approximate proportion of pupils admitted to each programme.[106]

Approximately 8% of students are admitted to the prestigious Integrated Programme. You won't do O levels, instead you will work straight through to A levels, allowing more curricular flexibility.

Approximately 60% enter the Express Stream, which sees you do your O levels after four years of secondary education. If you are then in the top 20 per cent of O level scorers, you can go onto junior college to take A levels in preparation for university if you so choose, otherwise you go to a polytechnic.

Approximately 20% take the Normal Academic course, in which students do N levels (easier than O-levels) after four years, and then O-levels the year later. These students are likely to go on to polytechnic, or the Institute of Technical Education (ITE).

Approximately 11% go to the Normal Technical stream, where they take a combination of academic and technical subjects, and take N-levels. If these students continue to post-secondary education, they will most likely go to ITE (sometimes unfairly referred to as 'It's The End').

Approximately 2.5% don't pass the PSLE. They have the option of repeating the year and retaking the exam, or going to a technical school where they take only vocational qualifications.

Figure 3: The Structure of the Singaporean Education System

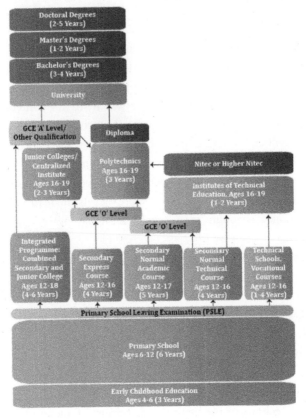

Diagram taken from the Centre on International Education Benchmarking.

The path you end up taking, at this early stage and then later on if you take further exams, affects the rest of your life – your peer group, your post-secondary education, your job prospects, even your marriage prospects. Moving 'upstream' is possible if you score high enough in regular exams during the first few years of secondary school, but it is unusual, to the extent that those who manage often make the news.[107] It seems extreme, so why separate students out into different life paths so early?

Eugenics and Population Control

Let me take you back to the 1980s, shortly after the introduction of streaming in Singaporean schools. Michelle, 31, a graduate with *good genes* and a job in the civil service, has the day off today (at the government's expense) to begin her subsidised leisure cruise to the Maldives. Peter, 34, an engineer with a top degree from the National University of Singapore, is also about to leave for the boat, and is anxiously flattening his unruly hair in the mirror. Both hope that they might meet the partner of their dreams on this cruise, the one that will put light in their life and fire in their loins. The government hopes so too; this cruise was organised by the Social Development Unit (SDU)[108] – an organisation established in 1984 with the purpose of matching up graduate singles in Singapore in the hope that they would reproduce and have intelligent babies.

At the time this wasn't in response to a decline in population, but rather, the *wrong type of people* having children. At the National Day Rally in 1983, the late Lee Kuan Yew – then prime minister and founding father of modern Singapore – lamented publically that there were too many unmarried female graduates. Graduate men were choosing to marry less-educated women, and this was a big concern: 'If you don't include your women graduates in your breeding pool and leave them on the shelf, you would end up a more stupid society… So what happens? There will be less bright people to support dumb people in the next generation. That's a problem.'

Lee Kuan Yew believed that intelligence was innate and inherited, and that eugenics programmes – such as incentives for the sterilisation of mothers without O levels and tax rebates for graduate mothers – were therefore justified by the future economic success they were sure to bring to the country, by virtue of having a more intelligent workforce. Having a talented workforce (whatever your beliefs on the origins of talent) was and is more important for Singapore than for most other countries. Singapore is a city state; an island of only 5.3 million people and no natural resources. When it got kicked out of the Malaysian Federation in 1965 after a falling out between Lee Kuan Yew's party (the People's Action Party) and the central Malaysian government, Lee cried on national television. It did seem hopeless – Singapore relied on imports, and didn't even have its own water supply. The only hope Singapore had of succeeding economically was to develop the country's human resources through education, and produce a literate and technically-skilled workforce that would allow Singapore to become a centre of industry, and later, business.

They did this remarkably successfully, as indicated by the fact that they now have the third highest GDP per capita in the world, and a top-performing education system by many measures. Since Singapore's independence, the education system has been carefully designed and adapted to meet the changing needs of the country's economy. As in any economy, there are many different roles to fill, with different levels and types of education required for each role. Some people are needed to strategically design the 'Mozzie wipe-out' campaign to prevent Dengue fever, others are needed to spray the bushes with anti-mosquito spray (this I am told is what the men with gas masks and spray guns are doing at the side of the roads – they look like lost 'Stormtroopers').

Now imagine that you are Prime Minister Lee Kuan Yew. You need a system that educates citizens for different roles to support the economy, and you believe that talent is inherited and stable – in other words, you're either born clever or you're not, and there's nothing you can do to change it. What kind of education system would you design? I don't know about you, but I would design a system which identified talent as early as possible, so I didn't waste resources trying to educate the 'ungifted' in topics they couldn't handle. I would separate children of different abilities into different groups, and teach them different things, according to their abilities and the needs of the workforce, so that everyone had the skills to fulfil a useful role. As we've seen, that's exactly what they did.

So what's the problem? Well there are several, but let's start with the most fundamental: that this model of education is based on an outdated and inaccurate understanding of intelligence. Back in 1965 when Lee Kuan Yew was Premier of the newly independent Singapore, the research on intelligence was still in its infancy, and due to an unfortunate sequence of events in the field of education psychology, it was actually rather misleading.[109] What is more, Singapore was not the only country to have an education system designed around these now outmoded ideas.

A Brief Foray into the History of Intelligence

The first man to develop a modern intelligence test was Alfred Binet: a Frenchman and a bit of a loner. His work in the early 1900s was light years ahead of its time, but he was not very good at communicating it to others. As developmental psychologist Robert Siegler puts it, 'Binet's product was strong, but his marketing was weak.' This shortcoming, combined with others' wilful misinterpretation of his work, actually led to a major misrepresentation of the nature of intelligence; a misrepresentation that persists to this day.

Binet developed an intelligence test with Théodore Simon – a young physician pursuing a doctorate – in order to help identify children in need of alternative educational provision in France. Having come up with a number of questions to test current cognitive development, they reasoned that those in need of extra help would be those who scored poorly on the test compared to peers of their own age – in other words, children whose development was retarded (in the original sense of the word).[110] They made their test available for this use with some very clear caveats.

Caveat 1: The test result was not to be interpreted as a permanent measure of a child's ability, nor should they be taken to suggest anything about the child's potential for future development. It gave a snapshot of how developed the child's intelligence was compared to his peers at the time of measurement only.

Caveat 2: Comparisons should only be drawn between children of similar backgrounds. Differing experiences of children from different backgrounds were likely to affect their scores, and therefore the scores would reflect these experiences rather than any problems with their cognitive development.

Caveat 3: Testing should not be a one-off event, as individuals' intellects develop at different rates, and a child who performed below his peers at one age may catch up with them at another, and vice versa.

In other words, they believed that intelligence was not something that is fixed but something that develops. 'With practice, training, and above all method, we manage to increase our attention, our memory, our judgment and literally to become more intelligent than we were before.'[111] This is a conclusion shared with modern intelligence researchers, including those who acknowledge intelligence to be partly heritable. For example, the geneticists Kathryn Asbury and Robert Plomin write that 'environment plays a role in influencing IQ, and IQ alone does not predict achievement'.[112]

However, this early insight of Binet's was lost to the world, and worse, his test was misused to further propagate ideas about intelligence that he completely disagreed with. Binet and Simon's test was discovered by the Director of the Vineland

Training School for Backward and Feeble-minded Children – Henry Goddard of New Jersey – on a trip to Europe. He initially dismissed the test as being overly simple, but then tried it on some of the children at his school, and was surprised and delighted by how well the scores correlated with his experiences of different degrees of 'feeble-mindedness' in the children.

Goddard believed that intelligence was 'a unitary mental process... conditioned by a nervous system which is inborn... that is but little affected by any later influences' – quite the opposite to Binet's own understanding. Whereas Binet saw the results of a test as indicating a child's current level of development compared to their same-age peers (because this is how he designed it), Goddard assumed and then espoused that the test identified something about the child that was not only stable over time, but inherited too.

This belief about intelligence being a fixed entity was not unique to Goddard but widely held at the time and, to Binet's dismay, the test became a convenient tool for categorising and labelling children. Eugenics was popular in the United States even before his test made it across the Atlantic, which may explain why the idea of intelligence testing became so widespread once it got there. By 1964 (one year before the establishment of modern Singapore) about 60,000 people were subjected to compulsory sterilisation in the United States. Just fewer than half of these were sterilised on the basis of having a mental disability, and intelligence tests informed these diagnoses.

What is the truth about intelligence, then? Is it fixed or does it develop? Is it heritable or does it depend on your environment? How does it affect the ways we design education systems? And why am I still banging on about intelligence instead of writing about the Singaporean system? Enormous questions.

For a start, there is no one agreed definition of intelligence. Traditional intelligence tests measure IQ: general verbal and/

or non-verbal cognitive ability. Some, such as the psychologist Howard Gardner, have a broader view of intelligence that includes more physical, practical and personal skills: something I will discuss in relation to British Columbia's education system when we get to Canada. But for now, we will use the narrower definition taken by most researchers of the genetics of intelligence, that it is 'general cognitive ability' as measured by intelligence tests.

Let's address the technical questions first. Here goes:

- Intelligence is not fixed, it develops. Like height, your 'general cognitive ability' changes over time at a rate that depends partly on the environment you experience; you are more intelligent now than you were when you were seven (well, we would hope).
- Intelligence is partly heritable. Like strength or height, the variability in intelligence in the population is partly explained by genes, and partly by the environment and their experiences; about half and half in the case of cognitive ability.[113]

So far this may seem to make sense. You might think (as I did) that it is the environmental influence that allows your intelligence to develop. But here's the tricky bit. Even if IQ was 100 per cent heritable, and entirely determined by your genetics, intelligence would still develop – it is not a fixed trait. It seems intuitive that if intelligence has a genetic basis then you must have a fixed 'amount' of it, and that every time you measure it you should get the same result, but that is not the case. The confusion comes from a conflation of the concepts of intelligence and IQ – even if you are to define intelligence as narrowly as 'what IQ tests measure', there is a subtle but important distinction between the two.

It was another American, Lewis Terman, who cemented the popular but false idea that intelligence is fixed and stable –

giving it legs long after the research showed otherwise. He did this by making famous the concept of the intelligence quotient (IQ) as a measure of someone's intelligence. Your IQ is not the same as your score in an intelligence test. To produce a child's IQ score, you first calculate a child's mental age by comparing their intelligence test score with the average scores for each age group. For example, if a seven-year-old, Justin, takes an intelligence test and scores 43/100, which is above the typical score for a seven-year-old and closer to the average score for a nine-year-old, Justin is said to have a mental age of nine, even though he is seven. To calculate his IQ score, you divide his mental age by his actual age, and, because Terman didn't like decimals, you multiply your answer by 100.

IQ = mental age / chronological age x 100
Justin's IQ = 9/7 x 100 = 129

Why does this matter? Because by including the 'typical' scores in the calculation, IQ stops being a measure of 'general cognitive ability', and becomes 'general cognitive ability relative to the rest of the population', or in the case of children, 'relative to your age group'. The use of IQ as a proxy for intelligence is the reason so many people still think intelligence is fixed, despite evidence to the contrary.

To demonstrate this, let's take the case of Justin's sister Julie, who is six and just starting school. If we give Julie the same type of intelligence test now, then at ages 9, 12, and 15, we would see her test score increase every time: 23, 45, 65, 83. If we converted these four test scores into mental ages, they would also be increasing – if she is an 'average' child she will most likely have a mental age of 6, 9, 12, and 15 at each point. Both measures show that Julie's intelligence, her general cognitive ability, is developing over time (though real children don't necessarily develop in such a predictable way). But if we take the step of converting these scores into IQ scores, and divide her mental age by her actual age (and times by 100), suddenly her scores at each point become the same: 100, 100, 100, 100. Suddenly it looks like nothing is changing at all.

Julie's average development:

Age:	6	9	12	15	Increasing
Scores:	23	45	65	83	Increasing
Mental age:	6	9	12	15	Increasing
IQ:	100	100	100	100	Stable

So Julie may have significantly developed her cognitive abilities between the ages of 9 and 12, she may be able to do all sorts of new things and solve harder problems than she could before, but because her rate of development was the same as the average and everyone else has developed too, her relative intelligence, or IQ, doesn't change.

In addition, psychologists now dispute the idea that intelligence develops in a straightforward linear way as the concept of 'mental age' seems to suggest, and instead believe that intelligence develops in 'intermittent bursts' (just like growth spurts), which can happen at different times for different children. This makes it difficult to assess children for their 'potential' at a young age, as some may be developmentally ahead of their peers early on but then slow down, whereas others may have a shaky start but make accelerated progress later on. Variability of IQ in young children is due more to home environment than genetics.

One final point on intelligence before we move on; IQ and achievement are not the same thing. Geneticists Robert Plomin and Kathryn Asbury use a racing car analogy to explain this: equating IQ with achievement is like saying that the top spot in any motor racing contest will always go to the car with the biggest engine, irrespective of the skill or experience of the driver.

IQ and achievement only correlate at 0.5, and 'a great big chunk of school achievement is entirely independent of IQ'.[114]

Back to Singapore

Which brings us (finally) back to Singapore. The education system in Singapore is based on the concept of meritocracy: that is, it aims to identify talent in the young and give different opportunities to different children dependent on that talent. This system assumes that it is possible to accurately identify talent at the ages of 10 and 12,[115] when the most significant streaming and selection into different schools take place, because it was built on ideas about the nature of intelligence that although popular at the time, have since been shown to be false.

Thinking and structures are slowly changing though. The downsides of streaming and school selection at this age have recently been debated in Singaporean parliament, with two MPs proposing that the government rethink the segregation of students according to their abilities.[116]

Moves have since been made to mitigate the effect of streaming, and the government is piloting a programme whereby students in the Normal Academic Stream will be able to take 'Express' level courses in the subjects they did well in at their PSLE. These moves are due to a recognition that streaming early can mean that late developers miss out on the chance to pursue dreams they are perfectly capable of achieving, because they weren't ahead of the curve at age 10. I met one such late developer, who would have missed out on his dream job of becoming a teacher if it weren't for him making a very bold move.

David Hoe is a thoughtful, passionate teacher trainee, and among many other accomplishments has set up a mentoring programme that matches current undergraduates with underprivileged children. He is passionate about all young people having opportunities, and understands better than most the effects that family life can have on early outcomes.

I'd arranged to meet David after reading about him in the newspaper. David had a difficult childhood. He lived in a one-room flat with his mother (his parents divorced when he was a toddler) who earned a living as a supermarket sales promoter. One day she went into hospital for a routine cataract operation, but became blind when the operation tragically went wrong. As Singapore has an extremely limited welfare system, she was reduced to selling tissues in public canteens, with seven-year-old David guiding her. The time David had to devote to caring for his mother had an impact on his studies, and when he took the PSLE at age 12, he got a low score, relegating him to the Normal Technical Stream for secondary school. David explained the implications of this, 'What it really means is this. If you are "normal tech" (in the Normal Technical Stream) you are set for vocational training. If you go to ITE you probably don't even think about going to university. At best, you think about going to polytechnic.'

The problem is, David wanted to be a teacher – a job for which you need to take O levels. David did work extremely hard at school, and with the help of some wonderful teachers and mentors, aced his N levels, getting some of the top scores in his year. But that still wasn't enough; as a Normal Technical student it wasn't possible for him to take O levels. So what did David do next? In a brave move for a teenage boy, he wrote to the then Minister for Education, and explained his situation. As a result, he was granted special permission to repeat Years 3 and 4 of secondary school, but in the Express Stream.

David is now on a teaching scholarship, having studied economics at the prestigious National University of Singapore, and is sure to make a brilliant teacher. But his success rather calls into question the ideas about talent that this stratified education system was built on. It calls into question the idea that a test taken at a young age is an accurate measure of your intelligence and future potential. Glass-half-full Singaporeans would say that David's example shows that anyone can succeed in Singapore, if they try hard enough – but effort and intelligence are not the only things which make a difference to your chances.

Chapter 9: Private Tutors, Public Pressure

Nobody owes you a living
Lee Kuan Yew

Many education systems are competitive, particularly Asian ones, as we shall see – but what is particularly interesting about Singapore is how the views about talent on which the system is based are at odds with the views of the population at large. The system is based on the idea of fixed intelligence, leading to early 'identification' of talent, but the largely Chinese-origin population believe that academic success is mainly down to effort and hard work, so many believe that their child can make it into that top stream, or top school, if they pull out all the stops and work really hard. Parental expectations and involvement are therefore high.

On my first trip to the local mall I saw a stall selling stacks of past exam papers from the local primary schools, going back several years. No one seemed to be behind the counter, but when I tried to take a photo, a small plump woman in a stripey dress ran out from the store next door waving her arms in front of my camera. I apologised, confused, and asked permission in advance the next time I saw such a stall in the next corridor of the mall. Once again, this was met with vigorous headshaking. I later learned that selling such tests is illegal and so doesn't officially happen. In the same mall, and in every other mall in Singapore, the bookshop had an education section which took up about 50 per cent of its floor space. Children's author Monica Lim told me over our coffee at the airport that every term, all the parents go with their children to the book store to buy practice books for all their subjects, and that it is totally normal for parents to set their children homework from these books once they've finished their school homework.

When parents have the money (even when it is scarce) they spend it on private tuition. Every day on my humid walk home from school, I walked past a tutorial centre, set up like a shop with a glass front allowing passers-by to see into the classroom. I was exhausted and sticky after a day of interviewing teachers and observing lessons, and pitied the nine-year-olds who were still studying having finished a full day at school themselves. Often there were still little people working when I came home from an evening out at 10pm. Not all Singaporean parents want to put their children through this, although some are proud of their *kiasu* status – a Singlish (Singapore English) word that means 'fear of losing'. A friend of one of the parents I chatted to told her how determined he was to not be like this, and instead to give his child the space to be a child. A few months into the school year, though, he was looking for private tutors like everyone else. When the best opportunities for a good (financially secure) life are only given to the top-ranked students, and the parents of most children are buying private tuition, parents who aren't comfortable with this model are left in a difficult position.

This means that unlike other countries that complain of grade inflation where it becomes easier over the years to get top grades, in Singapore they have the opposite problem. Exams are actually getting harder. Petunia Lee, organisational psychologist and mum of a 10-year-old son she refers to as 'Little Boy', writes in her blog:

I realized something odd about our primary school language textbooks today. The level of difficulty of the language printed in a Primary 5 textbook is about two years easier than the level of difficulty in the Primary 5 exams. After examining Little Boy's Chinese textbook in detail (something I have never done because I had never found them useful in preparing Little Boy for the exams, and therefore intuitively ignored them), it occurred to me to ask myself why today. Why don't I find school textbooks useful in preparing Little Boy for exams? Why did I spend years fighting with Grandma trying to get her to ignore the Chinese textbook when helping Little Boy with Chinese? And why was it that Grandma's stubborn focus on the textbook produced a steady downward trend in Chinese grades?

A Limited Amount of Pie

This disparity between what is taught at school and what is in the exams puts further pressure on parents to fund private tuition, and further psychological pressure on the children to study harder than their peers. And due to this increased effort and extra tuition, each cohort does better than the last, leading the government to make exams even harder to differentiate between the top performers, and so the cycle continues. This is not just abstract, theoretical stuff, this is felt by children in their classrooms and at their kitchen tables.

On Petunia's blog I also came across a wonderfully perceptive, although saddening, account of a conversation she (PL) had with her son (LB) on this topic. So, out of the mouth of babes:

LB: Mom, this happens [the exams are hard] because as different groups of students go through the educational system, children become better and better. Therefore, this forces the government to raise the standards of the PSLE.

PL: Yes... but where will it end? Maybe in 10 years' time, PSLE students will need to do research in order to get into a good secondary school.

LB: That won't happen Mom. It's just like a bubble you know. It will burst one day...

PL: Hah? What? What's that gotta do with your PSLE, eh?

LB: OK... the government will raise the standards of the PSLE. The PSLE bubble of skills and knowledge will get bigger and bigger and bigger. Then, when the students cannot take it anymore, they will all commit suicide. Then the PSLE bubble of skills and knowledge will pop and become smaller because the government will be forced to bring down standards... otherwise there would be no more children left. We would all have died. So, as long as you help me get through this, it will be ok. We can do it, Mom. And don't worry about your Grandson because I think when that time comes, the bubble will have burst.

PL: Oh!... Wow... wow... whoa!

Luckily Petunia's little boy is OK as he has a sensible mother who is an expert in child psychology to shield him from the negative effects of this exam pressure, but others aren't so lucky. A survey by Singaporean Press Holdings in 2000 of 1,742 children between the ages of 10 and 12 (when children are approaching their PSLE) found that more than a third of students were more afraid of exams than of their parents dying.[117] One in three said they sometimes thought life wasn't worth living.[118]

Of course, the Singaporean government doesn't want this either – they are not child-hating monsters, far from it. Education policy in Singapore is formed with great thought and care, with an awareness that educational changes will have their effects many years down the road.[119] But now that such a competitive culture exists, it is a very difficult situation to address. And when they have tried to change it by advocating more of a focus on character, or by ceasing to publish the names of the 'top scorers' in exams, it is not always welcomed by parents.

I met with Monica Lim, author of *The Good, the Bad and the PSLE*, and mother of two school-age (and polar-opposite) children to discuss the origins of this pressure.

'The majority of Asian parents want their kids to do really well. But for our kids to do well, it means that others will not do as well. That will always be a problem.'

'Is that inevitable?' I asked.

'Yes it's inevitable, because the Asian parent will never believe that there's enough for everybody. Somebody has got to be at the bottom, and as long as it's not my kid I don't really care, right? So long as my kid's on top. But the question is, how do you define what it means to be on top? Because the minute the Ministry tries to say, "OK, we will reduce the focus on academics and introduce other things like character", then you suddenly get these parents who will jump up and say, "OK, how do we measure that?" You know? Because then they want to make sure that their kid comes out tops, in character, or whatever it is.'

She went on: 'As long as parents don't embrace the idea that, you know, there's not a limited amount of pie, and they don't move on from that mindset that if somebody else gets it my kid doesn't get it, it's really really hard to change. Because you will find that there are always parents who are trying to get the better of the system, no matter what it is.'

'So where does that mindset come from?' I asked. 'Why do they think there's a limited amount of pie?'

'We're born into a society that embraces that idea. And I think because, historically, the government has always drummed into us this point about scarcity and how you've got to look after yourself and nobody owes you a living – I mean we heard that to death when we were kids – and because of that, somehow, they've unconsciously groomed a whole generation of Singaporeans who think that if I don't look after myself then no one else will.'

So you have a situation where, educationally, there is only a limited amount of pie – only a certain proportion of children are allowed into the Academic Stream to take O levels, no matter how well they all do – and where parents rightly believe that if their children don't get well-paid jobs, they will struggle to get on with their lives in the world's most expensive city.[120] One of the Academic Stream students I spoke to after an English class told me: 'You feel compelled. If you don't do well, you might not be able to get a proper house, you might not be able to get a car, and these kinds of things do pressurise us. I guess our parents are one of the main things that press us for greater successes.'

This is, of course, an area of huge concern for parents because they care about their children's future happiness and well-being, but there is a financial element too; someone needs to support them in their old age. I saw frail old ladies cleaning up in burger joints – if you don't have the support you're forced to keep working. Parents can actually sue their children for not financially supporting them in their later years, but this is no good if their children aren't earning anything.

The Ministry of Education (MOE) in Singapore recognise the amount of pressure on students is a problem, and have taken some steps to address it, including introducing classes and assemblies on mental health for the students. I happened to be in school for one of these assemblies, and had a chat with the presenter, Billy, afterwards in the canteen over a cup of 'kopi C' (hot coffee with evaporated milk). Billy is a psychologist, and has a clinic where he sees children that are referred to him due to stress.

He told me, 'Stress is a problem in Singapore even for the little ones, because their parents put a lot of pressure on them, and some go to tuition for a different subject every night. Some students I see are too anxious to set foot in school.' I asked him if anything could be done to address this problem, and he responded, 'I would get rid of streaming, as it affects the kids' well-being and becomes a self-fulfilling prophecy, and I would also reduce the focus on academics and make school more holistic.'

Inequality and Elitism

Coming back to the concept of meritocracy, what effect does all of this pressure have on the fairness of the Singaporean system? Petunia Lee concluded her blog on the textbook/exam difficulty gap thus:

> Hopefully, parents who read this post will realize that to get an "A" in school exams, there is a need to expose the child to reading material at least 4 or 5 years beyond that written in the textbooks. Not all parents know this. I surely did not.
>
> Does this not go against the MOE's [Ministry of Education] stated intention to use education to lift people out of poverty? Lower income parents have little means to pay for the enrichment classes to fill the gap between textbook and exams. Lower income parents also have not the skills to coach and help their children to bridge the gap between textbook and exams.

Unfortunately, but inevitably, not all parents have the same amount of time or the same amount of resource. Some children start P1 in Singapore having already had three years (or more) of high-quality, but expensive, preschool. One of my youngest interviewees in Singapore, a six-year-old girl in Primary 1, told me conspiratorially that she had Grade 5 piano and Grade 7 violin! (The reliability of this source remains questionable.) Others have not been to preschool at all, due to a lack of affordable high-quality provision, and are starting school from scratch.[121] Some children continue to get intense support out of school from private tutors, others have to go home and look after younger siblings. This makes it a challenge for teachers of P1 to cater for everybody (despite putting considerable time and effort into this), and means that some students never catch up with their peers who have enormous head starts.

This difficulty is exacerbated by the fact that, because education is a competition, out-of-school tutors are often used to 'get ahead', rather than to catch up in a subject you struggle with. I talked to a lot of the students I met about the tutorial system, and although some said they went because they struggled with certain subjects, many of them wanted to go even though they were already top of the class. At Chinese New Year the schools broke up for four days, and I asked a couple of teenage boys in the playground what they had planned for the holiday. The more confident of the two replied with a grin and a roll of the eyes, 'I want to relax, but I have to keep studying because I don't want the others to catch me up!'

The manager of one tutorial centre I visited explained to me that the children had to take a test to get in – this means some students get tutoring to help them get into the tutorial centre. And at the other end of the educational spectrum, a trainee teacher I chatted to told me she'd gone to a tutorial centre during junior college to help with her biology, but they went too fast for her to keep up. A comment I overheard in the staffroom on this topic tickled me (though wouldn't if I taught there). 'Marcus is refusing to buy the textbook because he says he's learnt it all already in tutorial'.

This reliance on the shadow education system, which is only available to some, then makes it rather unfair that a test at 12 determines your future. How well you do in that test will not only be due to how clever you are or how hard you have studied – it will depend on how much money your parents have invested in private tuition too. I went to visit the offices of a charity that works with disadvantaged communities in Singapore, at the bottom of a tower block on an estate, and learnt that 40 per cent of the children they work with (those from low-income communities) fail the PSLE. There are a few schools specifically for these failures (and yes I'm consciously calling them that because that is what defines their education), and about half of these children come from families with a monthly income of less than 1,500 Singaporean dollars.

The risk of elitism in a society that separates children of different abilities (and often of different backgrounds) at a young age is one that is often discussed in the Singapore press. Some students in the top streams look down on those who haven't made it, believing their success to be all of their own making (and not recognising the help they have often received from family and tutors). Raffles Institution, one of the most prestigious schools in Singapore, has had unwanted publicity recently due to the blog rantings of a student (also the daughter of an MP) who wrote, 'we are a tyranny of the capable and the clever' and described a man she disagreed with as being from 'the other class'. When her father intervened due to the ensuing uproar, it was to say that 'some people cannot take the brutal truth'.[122]

This is an extreme case, but Associate Professor Irene Ng

from the Department of Social Work at the National University of Singapore (NUS) explains that 'As you put students into finer and finer categories, their social circle becomes more and more isolated... Even if they have good intentions to do so, their social circle is just so limited they will have limited empathy and understanding to help effectively people who are different from themselves.'[123] It is in response to this phenomenon that David Hoe has set up his mentoring programme – not only to help disadvantaged students, but to help the privileged undergraduates that are mentoring them to understand some of the issues these students face before they go on to become the next policymakers of Singapore.

If we come back to PISA results, we can see that in 2009 and 2012, Singapore did extremely well overall, with average scores for maths, reading and science that put them at second, third and fourth in the world for these subjects respectively. If we look at the impact of socio-economic background on the scores, though, Singapore performs at or below the OECD average (depending on the measure), with a one-point increase in socio-economic status being associated with a 44-point rise in PISA score (which puts them in the bottom ten countries in this measure). This suggests that despite the MOE's best efforts to mitigate the effects of background by offering a financial support to poorer parents for their children's education, the structure of the system is not meritocratic.

And Yet...

Even though Singapore's educational system does not produce equitable outcomes, they do very well at getting a high proportion of their young people to reach baseline levels in reading, maths and science. Fewer students score very poorly in the PISA tests here than most other places. So although how well you do compared with your Singaporean peers does depend to a significant extent on your background, even those at the bottom of the PISA scale by Singaporean standards outperform many other students internationally, and those who are socially disadvantaged by Singaporean standards often do better than disadvantaged students elsewhere. The latter have been dubbed 'resilient students' by the OECD.

Lovely as this measure is for politicians who have evidence of many 'resilient students' in their countries, I'm not sure this would particularly comfort the 'resilient students', were they to ever hear that they had earned this moniker. Resilience as defined by the OECD does not necessarily mean that you've come from a disadvantaged background and scored higher than your advantaged peers in your own country. It doesn't even mean you've scored higher than more advantaged students elsewhere (although some of the poorest in Singapore do). It just means you've done well compared to children of a similar background internationally. So because students in Singapore generally score significantly higher than many other countries in PISA (more on this in a minute), many teenagers in the bottom quarter of the Singaporean socio-economic spectrum will score in the top quarter in PISA when compared with similarly disadvantaged teenagers elsewhere, and be classed as 'resilient'. But it doesn't mean they have better academic opportunities, as their advantaged peers in their own country are still ahead of them, filling the places in the junior colleges and forcing them onto less academic courses.

However, although the Singaporean system doesn't necessarily overcome the difficulty of getting those from poorer backgrounds to perform as well as their more affluent peers, once children are streamed, it does make sure nearly all reach a certain minimum standard. And despite the fact that sorting into different streams and schools is based on an academic test and therefore some routes are specifically for people who have failed this test (in the most extreme cases), the subsequent response is to train them up in genuinely useful vocational skills, and recognise the 'many peaks of excellence' (albeit with some peaks much bigger than others), rather than to continue to put them onto 'faux academic' courses or vocational courses that don't lead to employment opportunities.

The Singaporean government recognised in the 1990s that 'Singapore will be poorer if everyone aspires to and gets only academic qualifications but nobody knows how to fix a TV set, a machine tool or a process plant.'[124] They took steps to tackle the negative perception of vocational and technical training as a 'dumping ground', and put a huge amount of money into vocational education, into developing their polytechnic courses and their ITE and ensuring they had cutting-edge facilities. The courses at ITE are designed in collaboration with businesses to suit their needs, which contributes to Singapore's enviable youth unemployment figures (just over half the global average).[125] These courses are still not as respected as A levels by the population at large – or by elderly aunties interrogating their nieces and nephews at Chinese New Year family gatherings – but perceptions are changing, with some students who qualify for junior college choosing to study at polytechnics instead. Due to the money put in and the careful development of courses, they give genuinely useful qualifications to students that are respected by employers.

I met Alan, a polytechnic graduate and youth activist in a very noisy hotel lobby in town, where they charged us 24 Singaporean dollars for two cups of herbal tea (that's a lot). He too believes that academic qualifications are not everything.

'People develop at different paces at different life stages. Many of us are late bloomers. Bill Gates? Steve Jobs? Ray Kroc? Sim Wong Hoo? These are famous personalities who have made it big in life despite not having a university degree. They made many mistakes but they did not give up. They worked hard. They persevered. Each and every one of us are born with unique strengths and talents. When someone is not good in academic studies, it does not mean that he is also not good in other areas. And so in my opinion, academic grades are just one way of measuring a person's ability or knowledgeability.'

The Singaporean system seems to recognise this, even though academic routes are considered the most prestigious. Let's take NorthLight, the school for the children with the lowest marks, as an example of how Singapore's education system treats those at the bottom of the educational hierarchy. I met the deputy head of this school at their school sports day, in a huge stadium complex filled with excitable teenagers. We sat across from each other on a picnic bench, and she gave me her take on the children's outlook. 'Look, these kids are the lost, the last and the least. They've failed their exams, they've been the bottom of the pile in their primary schools. But here they have a fresh start, with friends that are like them, where they won't be looked down on.'

Unlike other teachers in Singapore who are placed in schools by the government, NorthLight directly employs its own teachers, and they are employed because they are passionate about turning these young people's lives around. Some of them teach the children the academic skills that they need (though these don't lead to any particular qualifications), some come from the ITE and teach them a variety of technical skills to prepare them for technical college, and still others are employed directly from industry to train students up in skills that are useful for the world of work. All final year students complete an eight-week Industry Experiential Program where they work in retail, hospitality, mechanical services or facility services before they graduate. In a similar school, Assumption Pathway, there is a fully-functioning restaurant on site run by students studying catering. I'm told they do excellent fish curry.

Selection at the age of 12 into more academic and more vocational schools and streams has benefits as well as drawbacks. In Singapore, it interacts with an already competitive culture to lead to intense pressure on children at a young age, as parents try and ensure their progression into academic tracks at 12. It leads to the reinforcement of social class groups and a lack of understanding between them. But, although it increases the inequality of educational opportunity, it does prepare people well for the labour market. This is not just the case in Singapore – recent research by Dutch researchers Bol and van de Werfhorst carried out an analysis on the extent of selection into different courses, the vocational education provision and youth employment situation in 29 countries, and found that there seems to be a trade-off between educational equity and youth employment.[126] Selecting early into academic and vocational streams leads to greater inequality but, in countries where the vocational education was work specific, also appeared to lead to greater youth employment.

However, a choice between equity and high employment figures is not inevitable. Bol and van de Werfhorst suggest that there might be a 'sweet spot' that would allow countries to both reduce educational inequality and unemployment. The extent and specificity of a country's vocational programmes – its vocational orientation – is not what drives inequality; the age and extent of its selection onto different courses does. But it is the vocational orientation of a system, not the early selection, which leads to high youth employment. Is it possible to reduce the extent of selection in a system and simultaneously increase its vocational orientation? You bet it is, because these different features come into play at different times.

The authors explain that the extent of selection is something which distinguishes education systems from one another in the early-secondary phase, whereas the extent and nature of vocational education is usually something that distinguishes systems at the advanced stages of secondary and tertiary education. So although few countries do it (hence the overall appearance of a trade-off) you can have the best of both: limit selection in the early stages and benefit from reduced inequality, and enhance strong vocational education in upper-secondary and tertiary education to reduce unemployment. Singapore has the latter down to a tee – this analysis suggests that other countries can learn from their expertise in this area at the upper secondary level, without having to make a compromise on equity by introducing selection onto different courses at a young age.

Chapter 10: Attraction, Career Ladders and Working with the Psychology of Motivation

A strong sense of purpose or belief in what you are doing is a powerful motivating force.
Gan Kim Yong

Excellent Teachers for All

What do we think might help explain the relative PISA success of lower attainers in Singapore? It cannot, of course, be attributed to any one factor. The high value that Asian cultures place on education surely plays a part, insofar as parents from varying backgrounds still push their children to aim high and study at home; many teachers go above and beyond and do remedial classes after school for children who are falling behind, and the Ministry of Education (MOE) has recently put more and more 'levelling-up programmes' in place to address the needs of these learners. Having a reason to continue in school even when you're not academically inclined must help with students' motivation too.

The most significant thing the MOE has done to make a difference to all students, though, the lower performers included, is to attract and develop a high-quality teaching workforce. I saw an advert for teachers in the paper one day as I was riding the spotlessly clean metro. I assumed at first that it was advertising some designer or other – six good looking men and women, all wearing stylish outfits entirely in black – posed across the second page of the paper. I looked more closely at the lady in the middle, with a sleek bob and a silk scarf flying out behind her, and saw written above her head:

Ng Hui Min
Teacher, Catholic Junior College
MOE teaching scholarship (overseas)
London School of Economics, UK (Economics)
Master of Science, University of Oxford, UK

It was advertising teaching scholarships. In order to attract 'high flyers' into the profession, the government offers top-scoring 18-year-olds the opportunity to apply to have their degrees paid for (in Singapore or overseas) in exchange for a four- to six-year 'bond' or return of service, teaching in the nation's state schools. This is an extremely popular route, for obvious reasons (another scholar on the advert had been to university in France; an exotic adventure for a Singaporean teenager) but also because it comes with additional career opportunities such as sabbaticals working in the Ministry of Education on policy (which would be an exotic adventure for someone like me.)

Teaching isn't 'naturally' an attractive profession in Singapore – in the 1980s there were significant teacher shortages, which were plugged by employing expat teachers from New Zealand, Australia and Great Britain – but the Singaporean government has worked hard and does work hard at making teaching attractive with scholarship programmes, decent pay and salaried training. Nevertheless, they can't offer scholarships to every trainee teacher, and they don't currently have enough graduates applying to ensure that all of their teachers are graduates; some enter a two-year teaching diploma straight out of junior college or polytechnics. This might seem surprising – that in such a high-performing country they take in teachers who don't have even undergraduate degrees – but they approach the challenge of forming an excellent teaching force using a different model from many countries. According to Ho Peng, former Director-General of Education:

> I think we are a deep believer of lifelong learning. At the pre-service level, we cannot teach our pre-service teachers everything that it means to be a good teacher. We have to encourage our beginning teachers to come by and be involved with continual learning and in-service courses, and there's plenty of professional development opportunities for them, and I think the access and the support is... an envy of many countries.[127]

Chris Husbands of the Institute of Education in London recently contrasted Singapore's approach to initial teacher training with England's, which is going through a period of deregulation where schools can take the leading role in preparing teachers. 'In Singapore, the government is clear: the improvements in teacher training since a low point of low morale and shortages in the 1980s have been driven by improving teacher training through the National Institute of Education,' he says. 'I was in Singapore working for the government a few weeks ago and no one could believe what we [in the UK] are doing in terms of deregulation.'

I was privileged to be able to attend a lecture at the Singapore's National Institute of Education with 'Prof. B.', a kind and indomitable lady who modelled the kind of 'tough love' demeanour that all teachers aspire to achieve. The class of teacher trainees was small, no more than 20, and they were learning about teaching maths to early primary-school children. I learnt that in teaching young children the concept of number, you should start with the concrete, then move to the pictorial, before finally representing numbers in the abstract. I learnt that children should be encouraged to articulate their processes, and feed back to each other on whether they are right or wrong, and why. And I learnt that this is so that children understand number concepts, not just procedures, because (though not only because) the PSLE tests understanding, not just memorisation. As I was chatting to the professor in the car as she gave me a lift to the station, she also expounded on the importance of teacher–student relationships – 'you can't touch their brain until you have touched their heart'.

Let me elaborate a little on the teacher–student relationships that surprised and tickled me, and then I'll get back to explaining how Singapore has a different model for developing great teachers. Singapore is a top-performing East Asian country, so I suppose I went in with certain stereotypical expectations – that teachers would be authoritarian, stern, scowling at children for interrupting their lectures. Many of the classrooms I visited were actually full of laughter. One primary class I observed were presented with the question, 'Sally has lost 5 kilograms, and is now 60 kilograms. What was her former weight?'

One boy's hand shot up. '55 kilos,' and he explained why he thought so.

The teacher paused and considered. 'What do we think?' she asked the class.

'Not right,' a few called out.

'But what was good about his wrong answer?' (expecting a point about his approach).

Another student quipped, 'She's lost more weight!' Cue teacher and children collapsing into giggles.

In another classroom, the class rules were stuck up on the

wall in a child's writing. The offenses and subsequent sanctions had been agreed on as a class under the guidance of the teacher. The last offence on the list read: 'No playing with paper balls' punishable by 'Mr Lieu will throw a paper ball at the person'. In the next classroom, the motivational sign made by the pupils and stuck above the blackboard said, 'Study Hard, Play Harder, Eat Hardest'. But I digress...

Career Ladders

I was telling you how Singapore develops great teachers despite not all of them having degrees. Unlike the many systems where you have the same status of 'Qualified Teacher' after your initial teaching qualification as you do after 20 years in the classroom, the Singaporeans recognise in the structure of their system that initial teacher training is only the first step. After a one-year induction period where you are mentored in your school and evaluated to ensure you are up to scratch, you are considered a qualified teacher. But you do not yet have the skills required to be a Master Teacher, or a Specialist Teacher or, for that matter, the Director-General of Education for the whole country (the pinnacle of the teacher's career structure). Your pay increases annually for the first three years of your career, but after that, the only way to get a pay rise is to move up one of the available ladders – the Teaching Track, the Leadership Track or the Specialist Track.

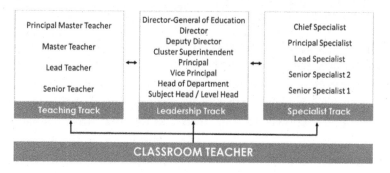

Teaching Track	Leadership Track	Specialist Track
Principal Master Teacher	Director-General of Education Director	Chief Specialist
Master Teacher	Deputy Director Cluster Superintendent	Principal Specialist
Lead Teacher	Principal Vice Principal	Lead Specialist
Senior Teacher	Head of Department Subject Head / Level Head	Senior Specialist 2 Senior Specialist 1

CLASSROOM TEACHER

Figure 4: Singapore's Teacher Career Structure

The positions in each of these ladders require different skills, expertise and knowledge, and there is a comprehensive teacher development structure parallel to the career structure, run by Yoda-like experts who have reached the heady peaks of 'Master Teacher'. So you can't achieve a certain position without having completed certain training: some of which anyone can undertake, some which you have to be accepted onto. This means that despite there being different routes into teaching initially with varying levels of prestige, anyone can move up the ladder and have a successful career if they have the talent and put in the effort.

Moving up the career ladder also brings you extra responsibility, which is reflected in the higher salaries. Depending on the stream, you may be mentoring less-experienced staff, running pedagogy-focused committees, or running training across schools in your area. This works because there is much more going on in a teacher's day in Singapore than teaching and individual planning/marking. Teachers work extremely hard but, just like Japanese teachers, they have less actual teaching time than the OECD average, so more of their time can be spent planning with other staff and learning from each other.

I was privileged to meet three of these Master Teachers at the Academy of Singapore Teachers (AST), one of the many centres for professional development in Singapore. The AST is housed in an old school building, which has now been entirely given over for the purposes of teacher development. The Master Teachers hold many of their workshops here, and some of the teacher networks meet here too. It was established in 2010 to build a teacher-led culture of professional excellence; a mission that it seems to be achieving. Some teacher networks, I was told, exist without the AST's knowledge – teachers just get together to discuss particular pedagogical topics and share best practice across schools. Even the networks that are led by the Master Teachers are not instigated by them (with the exception of the networks of school principals). Teachers approach them after workshops they have attended and ask them to come and share their expertise, based on their own development needs or the needs of their colleagues. And of all the workshops offered at the AST, none are compulsory, but they are still in demand.

I can hear policymakers in other countries thinking, 'how the hell do they do that?' Why aren't more teachers in all countries voluntarily forming networks and seeking out training opportunities? Are Singaporeans naturally conscientious? Perhaps, but the system helps. It removes all barriers to teacher learning, allowing teachers' intrinsic motivation to drive these positive effects, and is also structured so that it adds a little external nudge for those that need it (i.e. you don't move up the pay scale unless you've put the effort in to improve your teaching).

Working with the Psychology of Motivation

This would be a good time to revisit the psychology of motivation. When discussing teacher conditions in Finland, we heard about intrinsic motivation, and three things that have been found to support intrinsic motivation: autonomy, mastery and relatedness. Intrinsic motivation is the motivation to do an activity because you find it inherently enjoyable or interesting, and has been associated with all sorts of positive things, such as creativity, problem-solving, cognitive flexibility and persistence.[128] The 'opposite' of intrinsic motivation is extrinsic motivation, which for a long time was defined as the motivation to do an activity in anticipation of an external reward, or to avoid a punishment. This was seen as unhelpful to productivity, as although the promise of an external reward might lead to an initial increase in effort, it was found to lead to a decrease in intrinsic motivation, making the activity less inherently enjoyable even after the rewards had stopped.[129]

Type of motivation	Definition	Associated with
Intrinsic motivation	Acting because the action is inherently interesting or enjoyable	Creativity, problem-solving, cognitive flexibility, persistence
Extrinsic motivation	Acting because the action leads to a separate desirable outcome, like a reward	Initial increase in frequency of action, but leads to longer-term decrease in intrinsic motivation

Table 1: Intrinsic and Extrinsic Motivation – the original theory[130]

Over time, this theory was refined when it was realised that there are other types of extrinsic motivation which don't have the same negative effects. Let's take the case of a teacher who is marking some Year 8 exam papers on her sofa after dinner. Take it from me – marking is not inherently enjoyable to the vast majority of teachers. Therefore, she is not performing this task because she finds it inherently enjoyable or interesting, so it cannot, by definition, be intrinsic motivation that is causing her to do it. But neither is she doing it because someone has promised her a reward, or threatened her with the prospect of extra lunchtime duties if she fails to complete it. She's doing it because she cares about the children and their education, and recognises that her marking their work will advance their learning. So what kind of motivation is it?

Ryan and Deci's more recent research suggests that there are actually four different types of extrinsic motivation, which fall along a scale, ranging from autonomous to controlled.[131] At the controlled end is the external 'carrot and stick' type, which would include rewards and sanctions, and at the autonomous end, right next to true intrinsic motivation, is 'integration' – where the goals of the activity (helping the children learn) are the same as the individual's goals. Between these two lie 'identification' where the individual consciously self-endorses the goals of the action, and 'introjection', which is motivation due to the desire for approval from others (see Table 2).

Type of motivation		Reason for action	Source of motivation
Intrinsic motivation		The action is inherently interesting or enjoyable	Internal (autonomous)
Extrinsic motivation	Integration	The goals of action are the same as individual's goals	Internal (autonomous)
	Identification	The individual consciously self-endorses goals of action	Somewhat internal (somewhat autonomous)
	Introjection	Desire for approval from others	Somewhat external (somewhat controlled)
	External regulation	Compliance with external rewards or punishments	External (controlled)
Amotivation		Non-compliance	No motivation present

Table 2: Intrinsic and Extrinsic Motivation – the updated theory[132]

Where schools or education systems can find individuals who are already intrinsically motivated to do the work required, or who already have a strong sense of purpose and belief in the importance of education (and who have therefore internalised the same goals as the school), good things come of it: positive work-related attitudes, effective performance, job satisfaction and psychological well-being.

In order for this to happen, teachers need to feel that they are autonomous, and they are performing certain actions, like professional development, because they want to, not because they are being forced to. This is what makes Singapore's teaching career structure so clever. With the exception of countries with the benefit of high selectivity on entrance to the profession (like Finland), there will always be some teachers in a system who aren't quite as motivated to improve their teaching practice as others. Until recently, the English solution to this has been for senior teaching staff and management to run observations of teachers which end in a grading from a scale of 1–4, where 1 is 'outstanding' and 4 is 'unsatisfactory'. Whether these labels lead to further reward or sanction has depended on the school, but the result is that many teachers feel externally controlled and externally motivated to prepare for or respond to these observations. This affects all teachers, the ones who would be working on developing their practice anyway, and the minority that wouldn't.

By building in a career structure which is tied in to high-quality training, teachers' observations in Singapore become something that helps them to make the next step forward in their career. For already intrinsically and internally-motivated teachers – those who will work their socks off to provide the best education possible – this structure recognises their efforts and provides a framework to help them with something they'd be seeking to do anyway. For those who care but are not quite as fired up, it gives them an extra nudge to put in the effort for the sake of their career development. For those few who are in the profession for entirely the wrong reasons, and don't make an effort to improve their teaching over the years, it prevents them from receiving salary increases past a certain point, and in some cases from continuing in the profession at all. These few bad apples are dealt with, without the imposition of a controlling system that makes everyone feel rotten.

Professional Development

The way in which the career ladder is structured and worked through allows for teachers to make autonomous choices too. Teachers in Singapore are entitled to undertake 100 hours of professional development a year. They use this allocated time to address their personal development needs, which are identified by the teachers themselves in partnership with their line manager. They can go to workshops and courses during the school day, and the schools both organise the necessary cover and pay for it; each school is given a ring-fenced 'manpower grant' every year specifically for this purpose. As I said, teachers also have more non-teaching time during the school day than the OECD average, and there is designated timetable time for professional learning and discussion.

The courses and workshops on offer are varied and intelligently designed. They aren't all given by Master Teachers at the AST (even in a small country, 16 people delivering all the training would be a stretch); the Institute of Education runs professional courses and degrees, there are the Curriculum Planning and Development Divisions at the MOE that run training on curricula for different subjects, and the AST is the biggest of seven academies with varying subject specialisms.

The Master Teachers told me that they never run one-off workshops – all are part of a series of at least two, allowing for teachers to apply what they learn and feed back. This avoids the common problem where professional training is seen as a day to sit back, drink tea and let someone else do the talking (if you are being cynical) or even the problem of people having excellent intentions but then not implementing what they learnt in their classrooms. If they know they'll have to feed back on it, they are reminded to practise, and also have the support of other teachers and the trainers in working through any unexpected issues they face in their implementation.

If other countries had free, high-quality professional development courses that teachers could get cover to go to (as they do in Finland too), lots more teachers would be clamouring for it. Even those that aren't naturally so enthusiastic would become more so if this professional development was effective at getting you the knowledge and skills required to move up the career structure (and therefore pay scale), as it is in Singapore.

So the teachers come into the classroom after one year at the National Institute of Education, and they have many years of training and improvement ahead of them. But what about now? What about when they aren't actually very experienced yet? And what about the teachers who just aren't that great, who haven't progressed up the career ladder after several years? Isn't that a bit risky?

Well, all these teachers have a mentor and have colleagues to work on their planning with them in weekly planning meetings. But what they also have – which seemed to play a role in making sure all lessons were of at least a minimum, decent standard – are teachers' guides. Students have good quality textbooks too, of the same high quality as those found in Finland, but many of the teachers also have accompanying books that contain a whole host of useful information and advice, which are crafted by individual schools and subject departments, and contain:

1. Objectives for the lesson
2. Common misconceptions children have about this topic
3. Suggested questions to get them thinking
4. Assessment questions to help figure out what they've understood
5. Suggested activities

Having a book like this when I was teaching secondary science would have saved me so much time. Even if you were to follow these tips and utilise the student textbooks, and not do any planning, your lesson would be boring but well-constructed. If you were to use these tips as a springboard, allowing you the time to make the lesson your own and modify it to suit the particular needs and interests of your children it could be well-constructed and exciting. As an experienced, veteran English teacher of 20 years, Madame Ng does the latter. 'I don't use the textbooks that much – I make my own resources based on trial and error over the years.' The teachers' guides act as a catch-all, catering brilliantly to the lowest common denominator, but not limiting great teachers to a set lesson structure.

Singapore's education system got me thinking harder than anywhere else. I puzzled, I read up, I even went back and conducted additional interviews when my flight stopped over there on my way back from China, before it all clicked into place. The system produces spectacular results in reading, maths and science, the policies are ever so sensible and carefully thought through and the teacher training provision seems excellent. Vocational education is well-funded and leads to low unemployment rates, and introducing sophisticated career structures that offer teachers incentives, time and support in developing their practice could suit countries in which professional development is ineffective, or only available for the most dedicated of teachers. Offering teachers sabbaticals in which they work in the civil service designing curricula and education programmes is also an idea that might transfer well to a Western context, and might ensure that such programmes are workable and beneficial when implemented in the real-life context of a school. In these ways I found the Singaporean system to be very well run.

However, when you spend a bit of time in this system, and you also see the less shiny side. Children's futures are decided at a young age based on results that are heavily influenced by private tutoring, and an intensely competitive structure piles pressure on students at all levels. Would you want this in your country? Perhaps you would; you could certainly do worse than a system that ensures all its young people graduate with useful skills. But you can't simply implement the same policies elsewhere and recreate the Singaporeans' success, because some policies will most likely have different effects in different places. If a Western country were to introduce streaming or school selection at such a young age, for example, they may not find that it incentivised all children to work harder and raise their game, as it seems to in Singapore. This is because more people in Western countries believe intelligence is fixed, and would therefore be more likely to assume that failure in tests and allocation to bottom sets was something they had little control over, rather than something they could change through putting in more effort. Let's look at this important psychological difference in more detail in the country that has had the most cultural influence on Singaporean attitudes to education – China.

Chapter 11: The Confucian Mindset

笨鸟先飞早入林
A clumsy bird that flies first will get to the forest earlier.
(Chinese proverb)

Aside from a faltering chat in Mandarin with the taxi driver from the airport (during which I reached the heady heights of communicating that I was a teacher, and he asked me for a tip), my first encounter with a Shanghainese resident was with a six-year-old in a Snow White outfit singing 'Let it be' from Disney's *Frozen*. Her mum Michelle, a portrait photographer, had been happy to have a Brit to stay for a few weeks to help teach her daughter English. I sang along, and we bonded. She seemed just like a six-year-old girl anywhere else; making friends on the swings, enjoying English games like 'find me a... shoe', but getting bored after 20 minutes and letting me know about it. The only obvious difference between Angel's life and that of a middle-class British child of her age was that Angel had not yet started school; she did, however, attend kindergarten, as well as other private classes, including piano and painting.

The differences in home life became more obvious when I was invited to stay with Jenny – one of the teachers I had the pleasure of meeting – and her wide-eyed 14-year-old daughter, Angela. On the day of my arrival Angela showed me her room, which she'd kindly given up to let me stay in. We'd discussed our shared love of Adele, and in her broken, but very impressive English, she was talking me through the ending of *Sherlock*, Season 2, when

149

Jenny's sing-song voice called out from the other room: 'Angela, it's time for your homework!'

Angela had to do a maths paper that night, in addition to her English homework. These took her three-and-a-half hours, which Jenny told me quietly in the kitchen was typical of an evening's homework. Sometimes, it was four hours, but Angela got on with it diligently. This hard-working approach was typical of the students I met in Shanghai. Sophie, now a graduate student studying pharmacology, was just a little older than Angela when she left China for Toronto in Canada to attend high school, so she was able to draw out some of the differences between Chinese and Canadian students: 'The work ethic is different. In China it doesn't matter if you have a good grade or not, you are expected to put a lot of effort into your study. You also treat people who have good academic grades as being your role model, and you try and get to the same standard as well.'

Now, there are obviously school-based reasons why children in China have so much homework, and I will come to these later on. But in this chapter I want to share with you the more fundamental origins of the Chinese work ethic, which exist to this day but go back thousands of years. This work ethic goes above and beyond the competitive Chinese school system; it crosses borders. Chinese immigrants in other countries take it with them, and set their children extra homework when American or British schools don't provide 'enough'. Chinese graduation and encouragement cards even have more of a focus on the importance of hard work and continued self-improvement than American cards do ('Congratulations on your hard work' versus 'celebrating your exceptional brain'[133]), suggesting that in part, at least, this focus is cultural rather than being solely a product of the education system.

This work ethic extends to other East Asian cultures too – Taiwan, Singapore, Japan – and I believe that this additional effort made by East Asian students, and the way in which they apply this effort, is a significant contributor to their PISA success. But despite the deep-rooted cultural causes of this approach, I believe some of it (as much as we'd want of it) could be adopted or learnt by Western families, schools, and even education systems.

Failure is the Mother of Success

Let's go back to Sophie's statement, 'You also treat people who have good academic grades as being your role model, and you try and get to the same standard as well.' This is something that came up in other conversations I had during my time in China – the identification of students that are doing particularly well and everyone else's aspiration to be like them, either through the use of particular strategies, or through working harder. The point is: they believe it is possible. The Chinese students believe more than the Americans do that 'studying hard' contributes to success, and academics have argued that it is this belief in effort that accounts for the achievement gap between those of Asian and American descent.[134] This emphasis on effort over ability is something that's associated with Confucian philosophy, and its influence is felt not just in China, but all over East Asia.

It isn't just studying hard that helps, though; it is the *way* in which they study hard. I had some students in England who were very proud of themselves for copying out pages of the textbook, or who would revise only the things they found easy and skip over those they found tough. East Asians tend to do the opposite; they use more self-regulated learning strategies such as rehearsal ('I practise repeating things to myself'), elaboration ('I try to understand how the things I learn in school fit together with each other'), monitoring ('I check to see if I understand the things I am trying to learn') and planning ('I try to plan out my schoolwork as best as I can),[135] and they persist for longer when they are faced with a challenge.

Stevenson and Stigler – psychologists who studied Japanese and Chinese education in the early 1990s – recount an experiment they attempted to carry out on persistence in Japanese and American children. Their intention was to give students from each country a maths problem that was unsolvable in order to see how long they would keep attempting it for.[136] However, Stevenson and Stigler weren't able to complete their study, because the Japanese teachers convinced them to drop it after trying it out with a few children. They'd found that the children refused to give up, and had carried on attempting to solve the problem for far longer than it was fair to let them try for.

Other studies have shown that not only do East Asians persist longer in the face of challenge, they are also more likely to seek it out.[137] Not only that, they are actually spurred on to work harder in the face of failure – the opposite reaction to typical Western students. Heine and colleagues conducted a study on this strange phenomenon, by giving Japanese and Canadian students a test of creativity called the RAT, in which they had to come up with a word that connects three words they are given (for example, the word 'dream' connects the words 'day', 'fantasy' and 'sleep').[138] The difficulty of the test was deliberately altered so that some students received an easy version and some received a harder version, and after taking the test, the students were asked to mark their own test against a mark scheme, which also contained information about how other students had done. The students with the harder tests therefore believed that they'd done significantly worse than most people, whereas the students with the easier tests believed that they were really rather good at it compared to the rest of the population.

The interesting bit was what followed. As often is the case in social psychology experiments, there was an element of deception.

Students were told that the next task was to complete a test of emotional intelligence using the computer, but a few minutes into the task, the computer 'crashed'. The experimenter pretended to be distressed by this, and said they'd go and sort it out, but that the students could work on another RAT test if they liked, as they may be a little while fixing the problem. The length of time the students worked on the new RAT test (this time containing a mixture of easy and hard items) depended on whether they'd succeeded or failed the first time – but in opposite directions for the Japanese and the Canadians.

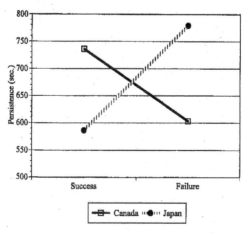

Figure 1. Study 1: Persistence time.

Figure 5: From Heine et al. (2001)[139]

Canadians who had done badly in the initial test spent less time on the new test than their peers who had succeeded. They spent more time on the task if they believed they were good at it – they were motivated by success. But for the Japanese students, doing badly at the first test meant they actually spent longer on the new test than their more successful colleagues – they seemed to be motivated by their failure. This is likely to be the case for

153

Chinese students too. In a study measuring performance rather than effort, Ng, Pomerantz and Lam found a parallel effect – Chinese students' performance improved after failure; Americans' did not.[140]

A Clumsy Bird that Flies First Will Get to the Forest Earlier

What can explain these underlying differences? Why would students from one country be consistently trying harder in the face of challenge or failure than students from another? The expert in this area is a woman called Jin Li, who wrote a book (more than 10 years in the making) about cultural learning models in the East and the West.[141]

Many years previously, before she completed her doctorate at Harvard's Graduate School of Education, Li arrived in the United States from China and signed up to be a substitute teacher in Vermont, and then Pennsylvania. As someone who had been educated in Chinese schools, with peers who worked hard at their studies, what she discovered in American classrooms initially shocked her: 'What struck me the most was that they were not the least bit interested in learning the content of the already minimal English tasks... My perplexity deepened; the idea of the richest nation on earth inhabited by so many students not wanting to learn really threw me for a loop.' This led her to spend many years studying the question that we are interested in: what could explain these differences?

According to Li, the way we think about learning in the West is based on a long-standing intellectual tradition that began with the ancient Greeks. Three of its central ideas that are particularly relevant to our question are that:

- human curiosity about the world is the inspiration for knowledge,

- the individual is the sole entity for inquiring, discovering, and ultimate triumph, and
- learning privileges those who have superior ability.

It follows that if one isn't curious about what one is learning, one will lack motivation to learn; that the reason for learning is primarily individual benefit and that whether or not you are good at learning will depend on your individual attributes, which are relatively fixed.

Research on American children and adults' conceptions of intelligence and ability give support to the existence of the latter idea – and these ideas about ability being fixed become stronger as children grow older.[142] However, the same suppositions are not found in East Asian cultures. East Asians are less likely to view people as having innate differences in abilities and more likely to view achievement as a product of effort rather than ability.[143] Hess and colleagues found that Chinese mothers were most likely to attribute their children's failure at school to a lack of effort more than any other factor, whereas this option was selected the least by American mothers when asked the same question.[144] Heine and colleagues designed a questionnaire asking Japanese and American students what percentage of intelligence was due to effort, and what was due to talent or innate ability. They found that, on average, European Americans saw effort as accounting for 36 per cent, Asian Americans saw it as accounting for 45 per cent and the Japanese saw it as accounting for 55 per cent.[145]

You can see then that the Asians do still recognise that there are differences in innate ability between people; they just don't see it as being as important, because they don't think it contributes to performance as much as effort does. The title of this section, 'A clumsy bird that flies first will get to the forest earlier' is a traditional Chinese proverb, meaning that even someone that is naturally clumsy or stupid can perform better than others, if they try hard enough.

Those who are familiar with the work of psychologist Carol Dweck might recognise the parallels between East Asian educational culture and what Dweck calls 'growth mindset'. Growth mindset describes the beliefs that people have when they think that intellectual abilities can be cultivated and developed through application and instruction, and it can be contrasted with a fixed mindset, which describes the belief that intellectual abilities are basically fixed – that people have different levels of ability and little can change that. Which mindset children have has huge implications for how they behave when faced with challenge.

Dweck has found that those who believe that intelligence is fixed are therefore motivated to avoid challenging tasks, lest it show that they are not intelligent – something that they don't believe they can do much about. On the other hand, those with a growth mindset are motivated to seek out challenge, as they believe that their intelligence can grow through taking on challenges and working hard at them.[146] Remember the differing responses of the Japanese and Canadian students to 'success' and 'failure' in Heine's study? They mirror the behaviours one would expect from those with a growth and a fixed mindset almost exactly.

People with different mindsets are also prone to think about effort and practice differently. If you think that intelligence is something you have a certain amount of, and that's that, you will want to appear naturally smart, which means that you won't want people to see that you have to put in effort to achieve something. This is an attitude I'm familiar with, having grown up in England and been a teacher there. On the other hand, if you think that intelligence can grow, there is no shame in being known to make an effort, as you perceive this as making you smarter, not as evidence of your stupidity. Pualiengco and Chiu investigated these attitudes in European American and Asian American students by giving them a challenging task to do, and a practice task beforehand.[147] After the practice, they were given two opportunities to publically report to their peers on how much effort they'd put into the practice; only the European Americans played down the amount of effort they'd made on the practice task, which the authors suggest was to protect their self-image should they then do badly.

Dweck has developed scales to measure these mindsets, and within her American samples finds that about 40 per cent of students have a fixed mindset, about 40 per cent have a growth mindset and 20 per cent are somewhere in between the two.[148] This raises an important point about all the cross-cultural research hitherto described; while there are marked differences between students of different cultures, these mask the differences *within* cultures. Not all Westerners believe that intelligence is fixed. Not all Chinese believe that intelligence is malleable, but far more of them do, and this is likely due to the culture they've been brought up in.

Confucian Learning Culture

I met Nancy in a Parisian-themed coffee shop in the basement of a Shanghai shopping complex. Like many Chinese people I met, she insisted on paying for my coffee, even though she was the one helping me out by talking to me about her education. Nancy is a university student with a cheeky grin and a love of the English language, who lived in a different part of China until her parents moved to Shanghai, bringing her and her little brother with them. We were chatting about essays, as you do, and she described how a common type of essay they'd write at school would be a personal motivational pitch, about how they had big goals, and would work really hard to achieve them. They'd often draw on famous role models to illustrate their drive to succeed – like Kuang Heng, a scholar from the Han dynasty.

Kuang Heng was from a poor family, so couldn't afford lamp oil to aid his study at night. He felt this was a waste of good study time, so he bored a small hole in the wall of his house, letting through the light from his richer neighbours. By this light he studied through the night, and became an outstanding scholar. Nancy told me another favourite of hers was Li Bai, a renowned poet whose poems include *Waking from Drunkenness on a Spring Day* who read extensively as a young boy, and was able to compose poetry by the time he was 10. Chinese children are brought up on these stories and others like them, which encourage the virtue of working hard.

The origins of this idea come from Confucius, an ancient and highly-influential philosopher who lived in the sixth century BC. According to Confucius, the path to virtue included self-improvement through knowledge. Learning is a goal to be achieved through personal striving to perfect oneself. So working hard and persisting through challenging times are important not only because of what one can gain through doing this, but are a fundamental part of being a moral or virtuous individual.

This came up quite accidentally in a conversation I had with Rony, an extraordinarily insightful young man who was educated in China but now runs a tutoring business in Canada. We were in a noisy café talking about moral education, and how approaches to it differed in different countries, when I asked Rony, 'What does it mean to be moral, to be a good kid, in China?' His reply surprised me: 'Self-discipline, hard-working, smart for sure. Then you're the model student.'

At the time this left me confused, as this is not what I understood by the term 'moral' at all; I thought of morality as being mainly about how you treated others. But I then came to realise that the Chinese have a different, broader way of conceptualising morality. According to Jin Li, the Confucian intellectual tradition holds that 'Learning enables one to become a better, not just smarter, person. The ultimate purpose of learning is to self-perfect and to contribute to others at the same time.'[149]

It would be a bit unfair if self-perfection was the goal of morality, but only some were able to achieve it due to their innate learning ability. But another notion about learning held in the Confucian tradition is that 'Learning does not privilege anyone, and neither does it discriminate against anyone. Everyone is capable of seeking and achieving knowledge regardless of one's inborn capacity and social circumstances.'[150] It seems likely that growing up in a Confucian culture contributes to Chinese children's growth mindset.

Parents and Teachers

How does this reach them though? We've heard already that children are told stories about famous scholars who work hard, and that greetings cards in China focus on the journey and the process of working hard rather than the pride of achievement once you reach your goals. Two more immediate sources of the messages about the roles of intelligence and effort come from the adults that children spend the most time with: their teachers and parents.

There were two occasions on which the Chinese teachers I was speaking with became visibly awkward when they began telling me about their impressions of English and American education systems, as their impressions were not universally positive. Wendy, a maths teacher, had been to England to teach maths for a few weeks as part of a UK government programme to learn from the

Shanghainese, and Lina had spent a year teaching in the United States. I asked them what they thought about these foreign systems, and after commenting on how the teachers made a great effort to make the lessons engaging, and how they'd enjoyed this, they appeared a little uncomfortable and both made similar comments. 'One thing I found strange though, is that the teachers in England gave students different levels of work. Some students only did very easy maths. How can they keep up if they don't do the same standard?' This reminds me of a comment made by Bart Simpson in one of his more astute moments. 'Let me get this straight. We're behind the rest of our class and we're going to catch up to them by going slower than they are? Coo coo!'

In China, all of the lessons I saw had all the students attempting the same work. Though some raced ahead, no one was given an easier worksheet, or told to work on a separate task with a teaching assistant. Of course some found it trickier, and the teachers would help these children during and after the lesson, but they were still attempting to help them reach the same level as the rest of the class. They were given challenges rather than concessions, and were expected and supported to rise to them, promoting the idea that all can achieve if they put in enough effort.

Praise is used differently by teachers too. Jin Li writes about this from her own experience: 'In all my school years, when we had a quiz or exam in class, the teacher frequently asked the most hard-working student, not the highest-achieving one, to stand up to receive applause from peers for his or her great learning virtue.'[151] This praise for effort rather than achievement is one of the most effective methods of promoting a growth mindset in children, according to the marvellous Carol Dweck.[152] Like many ideas in this book, this doesn't mean I'd advocate a sudden switch to these approaches in British schools. For a class in which some children have fallen further and further behind each year, and others are recent learners of the English language, giving the same tasks to all children would be inappropriate. And if children have already spent years in a system which promotes a fixed mindset, getting a hard-working student to stand up for applause might well embarrass him or her as, in such a system, having to work hard is a sign of a lack of natural ability. These approaches need to be taken right from the beginning.

That is what is happening in China through the messages they get from their parents. Chinese parents tend to play down their children's successes, because they see it as their role to promote effort in their children, and fear that emphasising their achievements might lead to a lack of motivation to learn. For similar reasons they are more prone to highlight their children's failures, but this isn't always as harsh as it sounds to the Western ear. When British or North American parents point out a child's failures, if they ever do, it is seen as particularly crushing or damaging to a child's self-esteem, because they tend to believe that traits are fixed, and so whatever caused the child to fail will remain with them permanently, making them a failure. So we tend to praise children's positive traits – 'Aren't you clever!' – rather than acknowledging their weaknesses. Rony tickled me with a deliberate exaggeration of this from his experiences tutoring maths in Canada. 'When an Asian student does a maths problem wrong, he is told that it is wrong. When a North American does it wrong, he is told he is creative.'

When parents from Eastern cultures point out a child's failings or mistakes, its whole purpose is to allow the child to grow and improve. Ng and colleagues asked children themselves about how their parents responded to their successes and failures at school. They found the Chinese children didn't report their parents as being more negative, but did report that they got involved after failure – supporting them to learn from those mistakes, and being more involved in their children's education than American parents were.[153] They don't lack warmth,[154] but they are not as concerned about boosting their children's self-esteem through unearned praise.

Sometimes, when I'm talking to people about my work, they ask, 'How can you learn anything from China when the culture is so different?' Most of the time I reply that there are some practices that are culturally dependent and others that are more transferable, but here I want to make the case that there are things we can learn from the culture itself. Parents of young children and primary-school teachers could help children by teaching them the importance of learning virtues – hard work, perseverance, resilience – along with more traditional virtues such as kindness and honesty. They could avoid praising children for being smart or clever (hard to do, I know), and instead focus on their efforts and strategies. And they could be less afraid to point out children's current weaknesses, so long as it was in a supportive context and combined with advice on how they might go about improving themselves.

Chapter 12: Chinese Legends, *Guanxi* and Migrant Workers

千军万马过独木桥
Thousands of troops on a single log bridge.
(Chinese proverb)

Not only did Angela have three to four hours' homework a night; she also spent most of her weekend attending extra lessons in Chinese, English, maths, opera singing and basketball. She had very little time to herself. Of course I'd heard the stories about tiger mothers – Chinese parents who force their children to take all sorts of extra classes and make them practise these activities in the extreme – but Angela's weekly schedule still surprised me because Jenny was the complete opposite of how I expected a tiger mother to be. In my mind, tiger mothers are overly strict, unsympathetic to their children's hardship, wear stilettos and threaten to burn their children's cuddly toys. Jenny wore pumps and Alice bands, told Angela what a good girl she was and didn't want her to go to university abroad because 'I would miss my baby'. On the way home from school one day, she stopped at the entrance to the compound to retrieve something from the post box – two Taylor Swift T-shirts as a surprise gift for Angela. She was clearly not a tiger mother. Why didn't Angela have any time off then? Jenny explained this to me as she was preparing the dinner: 'Everyone is going to these classes. If Angela didn't go too, she would feel anxious because she would fall behind her classmates.' She shut the fridge door. 'But this isn't the only reason – it is also so that she can get into a good high school, so that she has a better chance of doing well in the *gaokao* and getting into a good university.' She shook her head. 'There is so much pressure though, the students in Shanghai are very, very poor (by which she meant "unfortunate").'

Thousands of Troops on a Single Log Bridge

The *gaokao* is the exam that Chinese students take at age 18 to get into university. It is a series of papers that together take nine hours over two days, and test the students' knowledge of Mandarin, English, maths and either sciences or arts. To say that this exam is a big deal would be an understatement. Apart from those students that manage to gain entry to university based on 'exceptional talent' (the ultimate goal of extracurricular classes), your *gaokao* score is the only thing that determines whether you get into university, which one you get into, and which subject you can study. The university you get into determines the kind of job you will be offered on graduating, and hence the salary you command and the kind of lifestyle you can have.

It even indirectly affects your marriage chances. I stumbled across a marriage market in the People's Park in Shanghai, known in Mandarin as the 'People's Park blind-date corner'. Parents lined the sides of each path with information about their offspring – their age, job, income, education and Chinese Zodiac sign – looking to arrange introductions for their grown-up children. If you do poorly in your *gaokao*, your chances of finding a marriage partner are severely reduced. Due to these high stakes, attempts at cheating are common; in Henan province last year, officials were driven to flying drones above the students in the *gaokao* examination hall to check for radio signals from smartphones, and every year some students attempt to pay professional test-takers to sit these exams for them.

More than nine million students sit this exam every year, and though it has long been seen as the only route to success, fewer than seven million make it to university, and only a few thousand qualify for the most coveted places at the most prestigious universities; hence the *gaokao* being oft described as 'thousands of troops on a single log bridge'. The *gaokao* itself has only been around since 1952, but is part of a Chinese tradition of high-stakes exams promising a leap to fame and fortune that goes back thousands of years – since the civil service examinations became a major path to office during the mid-Tang dynasty. The scholarly heroes that Nancy learnt about at school were drilling holes in walls and studying the classics in order to take this life-changing exam. The Confucian focus on effortful learning exists in a culture where exams have been of the greatest importance for over a thousand years, and where they remain so; it is no wonder Chinese students are under a lot of pressure to study hard.

This pressure comes from their parents, who typically set extremely high standards for their children's school performance, sometimes manifesting as dissatisfaction with whatever their current performance might be.[155] It can also come from their grandparents, who often play a significant role in Chinese children's lives, looking after them while their parents are at work. While this is, in many ways, a positive thing, it can add to the already intense pressure on the children to do well at school; particularly as China's one-child policy means that four grandparents' and two parents' hopes can all be pinned on just one child. While I can't imagine what this pressure must be like, having been brought up as one of five by relatively laid-back parents, I was saddened by a poem I saw stuck up on the wall of an English reading and writing club that I visited. It was written by a 10-year-old girl, and was titled 'Exams'.

All exams are significant,
And I am going to FAINT!
For my poor mid-term scores
Which drive grandma dizzy
And make my grandpa crazy.
My world is not fantasy,
And my mind is in vacancy.
My teachers are getting chilly,
And thinking if I am silly.
My classmate is not a bully
Just making unfriendly raillery.
I am so afraid of the terrible shouting
And endless moaning.
How I wish I have nubility,
To improve my ability.
From now on I get to know
That life isn't interesting
And I must be hard-working.

We Have No Choice

Despite the impressive academic achievements of students in Shanghai being supported by the intense competition for a few top university places, none of the parents I met wanted this pressure for their children. In fact, I had an email from Jenny, Angela's mum, while I was writing this chapter, and her second paragraph read, 'It is very cold in southern China this winter. Today is the coldest day in Shanghai in 30 years. Luckily, we are in the winter holidays, but Angela had to attend an extra maths class. Chinese students are very, very poor [unfortunate]. We have not the power to change it.'

I was invited to stay with a friend of Michelle's one weekend – a lady called Raye who had a six-year-old son – and she told me of her own experiences of this pressure, and how the dissatisfaction from her parents continued even into adulthood: 'I know my pressure from my parents to me, really really, it's very big. When I was in Shanghai working, the salary was much higher than before, but still my parents weren't satisfied.' Raye didn't want to pass pressure on to her own child, nor did Michelle, Jenny or Raye's friend Erin, but all were aware of the context in which their children were being educated.

Raye's son, Alexander, played the ukulele, so while we were chatting about this topic in a local coffee shop with Erin, I asked her a slightly tongue-in-cheek question to try and understand her motivations. 'Would you be happy if Alexander became a famous ukulele player, and was very successful at music, but failed all his school exams?'

She laughed. 'For my own opinion, I don't care about that. Most parents, when their kids are very small, they don't care. But I don't know, if he really got into that situation, when the teacher pushes the pressure on me, I don't know if I can hold out! Many parents, their pressure comes from the teachers. Schools put pressure on teachers, and then the teachers transfer it to the parents.'

'How?' I asked. 'How do the teachers transfer the pressure to the parents?'

'SMS!' Raye's friend Erin now started talking in Mandarin, and I waited while Raye interpreted for me. 'SMS [text messages] every day. Like, 10 messages. Your child did bad. You have to check his homework.'

She leaned over the table, moving my coffee to one side, to show me the texts from her son's teacher. Although I couldn't read the script, I could see that she'd been in regular correspondence with the teacher, and I was told that these messages were mainly the teacher telling her that she needed to supervise her son's homework better to make sure he did it properly.

Even without this pressure from the teachers – the reasons for which we'll return to in a minute – the existence of the *gaokao* as the sole measure of success and sole pathway to university and highly-paid jobs is reason enough for parents to focus heavily on their children's academic attainment. I wondered aloud to a few people during my time in Shanghai about why there had to be such a singular route to success: such a narrow bridge for all of those troops. Why couldn't they conduct interviews for at least the most prestigious courses to allow for an understanding of the students' thinking processes or passions in addition to high scores, or have broader criteria for university entrance to include a range of different types of exams or student achievements?

It turns out, the Chinese government are thinking along the same lines, and a few weeks after I returned to England, the Chinese Communist Party announced that there would be reforms to the *gaokao*, to try and reduce the pressure on young people.[156] Rather than having to select arts or sciences, students in the future will be allowed to choose three out of seven elective subjects, in addition to the core subjects of Chinese, maths and a foreign language (which no longer has to be English). Students will be able to take their elective exams twice, and choose the best score out of the two. And university entrance will also take into account high-school performance in other areas, such as morality standards, art cultivation and social practices. While having a greater choice of subjects and a chance to retake will reduce the pressure, some are concerned reducing the significance of the *gaokao* scores could lead to unfairness in admissions.

This was Rony's take on it. 'If the government really wants to give more of a say to the universities, they need to ensure transparency. This might be harder in some provinces than others; in some inland provinces it would be terrible, and it would be the rich kids, the mayor's son, who would most easily get in.'

Essentially, the reason that a single exam has remained the only route to university for so long, despite attempts at reform, is because it is incorruptible in the current exam-determined system (providing the drones are effective and exams are policed properly). Unfortunately, Chinese universities are prone to corruption; 52 members of senior management were reprimanded for violating laws and regulations in 2015 alone, and that is without the possibility of them taking bribes for letting students in. If university entry becomes more nuanced, officials will most likely be called upon to do favours, in the same way that they are for school admissions, due to a cultural practice called *guanxi*.

Guanxi and School Access

Guanxi is commonly translated as 'relationship' or 'connection', but neither of these terms really cover its pervasiveness and complexity. *Guanxi* is fundamental to Chinese culture, and describes a network of mutually-beneficial relationships that can help you in your personal life or in business. In a country where the official governmental bodies will not necessarily support you financially or legally in times of need, networks that might offer this support are all the more important. Extended family ties form part of *guanxi*, as can people you went to school with or people you've worked with, and these ties are maintained by the giving and receiving of favours and gifts. Once someone has done you a favour, failing to reciprocate leads to a major loss of face, and is considered unforgiveable. Hence if an admissions official at a coveted university has received help from a school friend in the past, it puts him in a very difficult position if asked for special consideration for his school friend's niece.

If you have a primary-school-aged child, *guanxi* can be very helpful in getting them into your chosen school. While officially there is no longer a system of 'key schools' – schools which used to be given priority by the government in the assignment of teachers and resources, and permission to pick the 'best' students – some schools are still considered to be better than others, and different types of school are subject to different regulations. Officially, children in Shanghai are supposed to go to a local junior high school once they finish primary, and schools are supposed to select on locality alone. However, a well-timed gift to a teacher or expensive dinner with a principal can give your child a better chance of getting into the most desirable schools.

There is also a more official process of selection by financial means (not forgetting the ability to afford a home near a prestigious school). While ordinary schools can only accept students from their district, 'municipal exemplary schools' are allowed to select students from all over Shanghai. They are also allowed to charge these out-of-district students a 'school choice' fee – up to 30,000 yen, which at about $4,400 American dollars might still not be enough to get your child in if you can't afford the gifts required for *guanxi*.[157] You can now see an additional, slightly cynical reason why teachers put pressure on parents to get their children to study: the schools' continued reputation, exclusivity and ability to charge 'school choice' fees depend on their students' grades, which they advertise to parents.

These official and unofficial policies combine to form a system where the schools with the best resources are only accessible to those whose family have the money and the contacts. It is no surprise then that in Shanghai, the percentage of variance in PISA results explained by student background is significantly above the OECD average, bigger than any other country in the top PISA 15 except Singapore, and greater than the variance explained in both the UK and the United States. And that is just Shanghai; these figures would likely be worse were they to take into account student performance across the whole country.

Shanghai is not at all typical of China as a whole. We are going to hear from Rony again, because he was educated outside of Shanghai, in Inner Mongolia (an autonomous region of the People's Republic of China), but then moved to Shanghai for university, allowing him to observe some of the major differences. Without being prompted, he warned me: 'I really want you to think of Shanghai as an exception; it's really different to the rest of China. They have a lot more resources from a very early stage. There are good schools. The GDP is a lot higher, and that's related to exam results. It's a hugely international city compared to a lot of other places in China.

'A lot of people would misrepresent the result and think that Shanghai represents China, and think 'Oh look, China is doing so well. Yes, in part, if you look at a few big cities, but there's huge disparity as well. I had some friends who moved from north-eastern China to Shanghai in the middle of their schooling, at 13 years old. They experienced culture shock; it took them many years to get used to it. And they were so impressed by how developed the Shanghai school system was.'

'How did they manage to get into public schools?' I asked. I asked because there is a system in China called *hukou* where people are registered according to their family's hometown, and can only access public services in that area. 'Was it *guanxi*?' I asked, trying out my new vocabulary.

'Exactly. These are not migrant-worker kids, they would be the kids of business people or professors, so I guess they had *hukou*, or an arrangement where the parents' employers would make sure their kids were educated in Shanghai public schools.'

Hukou and Migrants

The first time I'd come across the idea of *hukou* was during my chat with Nancy in the Parisian coffee shop, where she'd explained that her parents had originally moved to Shanghai without her and her little brother, leaving them with grandparents. Because her family are not originally from Shanghai, they do not have a Shanghai *hukou*, so Nancy would have had trouble getting into a regular public school in Shanghai. Parents who want to migrate to the cities in China are therefore often faced with a choice – leave their children behind, or bring them along and send them to a low-cost private school in the city. To their credit, the Shanghai government has recently admitted many of these migrant students into local public primary schools, but a few migrant schools remain in the outer regions of Shanghai where there isn't capacity in the public system.

I spent a week in one of these migrant schools, teaching English to Classes 4 and 5. It wasn't terrible – the teachers seemed to care and certainly worked very hard, and they had textbooks and large TVs in each room on which they could show PowerPoint presentations. But it was of significantly worse quality than the public schools I'd spent time in.[158] The toilets, for example, were just three long channels dug in the floor; no cubicles, and used by both staff and students, which meant I drank as little as I could during the school day to avoid having to use them. When chatting to the teachers I learned that many of them didn't have the same qualifications as teachers in public schools would, and those that did were hoping to leave and get a job in the better-paid public sector. The standard of English was also far below the level that was expected in the curriculum. I'd been given the Class 4 and 5 textbooks to prepare my lessons, and completely abandoned my plans after the first 15 minutes of class when it became clear that the children barely knew any verbs, let alone tenses.

I was told by one of the teachers that these were the children of Shanghai's migrants with 'residency permits' only – granted to those who can demonstrate a stable job, accommodation and social security payments for at least six months. There are also migrant workers in Shanghai who are only on 'temporary residence permits', who may have been working in the city for many years, but in part-time or unstable jobs or housing. I can only assume that these are the workers that leave their children by themselves or with grandparents when they come to the city for work, adding to the 60 million 'left behind children' in China.

Children of migrant workers with residence permits who come to the city with their parents can attend primary school there – either in public schools or registered private schools. However, no one without a local *hukou* was allowed to take the high-school entrance exam in Shanghai – residency permit or no residency permit. This meant that young people who wanted to attend high school would be forced to go back to their 'hometown' to take the high-school entrance exams, and because these exams differ by region, they would most often go 'back' for at least the last year of junior high school to prepare for them, if not for the whole of junior high.

Zhan Haite is one of these migrant young people. Although she's been in Shanghai since she was four, her parents don't have a Shanghai *hukou*, so at age 14 she was faced with a choice: go back to your parents' hometown for high school, or don't go to high school. Zhan didn't like the idea of going to school miles away from her family, in an area she didn't know, so instead she made quite an unusual move; she stayed in Shanghai, self-studied some high-school courses, and took it upon herself to draw attention to migrants' rights on Weibo (the Chinese equivalent of Twitter). On 8th June 2012, Zhan posted a photo of herself holding a sign that read, 'Where is my right to the high-school exam?' and later requested a debate with those who were against migrants attending high school in front of the Shanghai Education Commission. She hadn't been the first to raise these issues, and in a move to make the system more equitable, the government responded by bringing in a change of policy, allowing certain 'qualified' migrant students to attend high school in Shanghai. But this only came into place in 2013, after Shanghais' wowed the world with stellar PISA results in 2009 and 2012.

As a consequence of the original policy, many migrant students, the least educated in Shanghai society, had to leave the city by 13 or 14; just before the age at which students sit the PISA test. This makes sense of the strangely low number given by Shanghai authorities as the total student population of 15-year-olds in 2012; 108,056 out of a population of 23,019,196. Tom Loveless of the Brookings Institution in Washington, DC, points out that this is a similar number of 15-year-olds to countries with just half the total population of Shanghai. While migrant residents account for approximately 40 per cent of the total population, 43 per cent of five-year-olds and 63 per cent of 20-year-olds, in the 15-year-old age group they make up only 27.7 per cent.

Having a significant proportion of your poorest and least-educated students leave the city just before the age at which they'd take the PISA test is likely to have a positive effect on the results of those PISA tests, but a negative effect on the students who are forced to leave. This is not cheating – the Shanghai authorities are still including a representative sample of all the 15-year-olds who are in the city at the time of the tests – but their results may well be artificially inflated by this counter-educational (though arguably practically necessary) policy. An analysis by faculty members at the Indiana University School of Education suggests that the exclusion of migrant students from the PISA tests could exaggerate Shanghai's maths results, to the extent where if Massachusetts were to exclude the same proportion of low-performing children, it would cut Shanghai's lead over them by half.[159]

The recent government changes to include more migrant children in public schools and allow 'qualified' students to attend high school in the city show that they are taking steps to address this challenging problem, but the current reforms do not go far enough to make the system fair (or to make their PISA score representative of the true make-up of the city). Only those whose parents have a residency permit and at least 120 points – based on age, education and type of profession – are allowed to stay in Shanghai for high school. Low-paid, less-educated workers – without whom the city could not function and grow as successfully as it has – are still forced to send their children hundreds of miles away if they want them to attend high school and improve their lot in life. Zhan Haite still does not qualify for high school in Shanghai.

Chapter 13: Memorisation, Deep-Fried Chicken and the Paradox of the Chinese Learner

井底之蛙
A frog on the bottom of a well.
(Chinese proverb)

I could hear it before I saw it. As I approached from the back of the school, a loudspeaker piped out lively classical music, with chanting played over the top of it – '*Yī èr sān*' ('One, two three!') I rounded the corner and walked into the school yard, and was met with the sight of hundreds of primary school children in bright orange tracksuits, lined up in rows and dancing in time with the prefects, who high-kicked and spun their arms on the stage at the front. This was morning exercise, and there was definitely more enthusiasm coming from some children than others.

When the music stopped, the students 'marched' back to their classrooms, swinging their arms wildly, and got ready for their lessons. In Grade 2P they sat in rows, facing the front of the room, where the class prefect directed the class in their singing of English nursery rhymes ('There was a man who had a dog... ') as they waited for their English teacher. She arrived and greeted the children, and started the lesson by playing them a recording of a story about a frog who lived in a well.

Frog's friend, Bird, came to perch on the side of the well one day, and asked him, 'Oh Frog, what do you see?'

Frog replied, 'I see the sky. It is very small.'

'Oh no, no, no!' said Bird (in a terribly posh English accent). 'The sky is very big!'

Having spent some time watching lessons in China, and speaking to Chinese teachers about their practice, I've come to think that the common Western perception of Chinese education is similar to the perception of the frog. He saw the sky, and it really was the sky that he saw, but he didn't see the whole sky, so he didn't have a full understanding of what the sky was. In the previous two chapters, we've looked at some of the cultural and contextual factors that might explain Shanghai students' success in international tests; here we'll look in more detail at what these children actually do in school, how it differs to the stereotypes and how their teachers contribute to their studies.

Timetables and KFC

The English lesson about Frog and Bird was 40 minutes long, in common with all of the students' other lessons, and was followed by 'eye exercises' set to music, where students rubbed their eyes for five minutes to improve blood circulation and relax ocular muscles. The beginning of my lessons were interrupted a couple of times by music coming on over the school speakers, with the familiar chanting 'Yī èr sān', in time to which the students rubbed their eyes. Primary students typically start school at 8am, and have four lessons each morning, followed by lunch in the canteen, and then three more lessons in the afternoon. In junior high they start half an hour earlier, and fit in five lessons in the morning, and four in the afternoon, and in high school where students are preparing for their *gaokao*, the school day can stretch to be as long as twelve hours in some schools.

The work doesn't finish there though – as mentioned previously, students in Shanghai receive a huge amount of homework every day, compared with their peers in other nations. And there is no getting away with not doing it. Sophie explained, 'If you don't finish your homework you have to do it three times in class, so stay late, maybe till seven. And if you forget it they assume you haven't done it, so you have to do it again after school.'

Teachers, on the other hand, do not attend that many lessons. Although class sizes are large compared to elsewhere – up to 50 in one room – teachers have much more time for planning and marking than their Western counterparts, as they teach just 12 to 15 classes each week. To put that in perspective, I was teaching ten additional lessons per week on top of that when I was still a trainee teacher in London (and my lessons were longer too). Like teachers in Japan and Singapore, Chinese teachers use some of this time to plan together with colleagues who teach the same subject. They also spend a lot of time observing other teachers, in their own school, and in other schools in the district and across the city.

One Thursday afternoon, I was invited to go with two English teachers from the school with the orange tracksuits to another school about 20 minutes drive away, where a 'demonstration lesson' was taking place. We pulled up in the school car park, and filed into a classroom which was already full of 20 or so other teachers. 'Where are the students going to sit?' I thought. I then turned to face the front of the classroom, and saw that there was a large screen in the wall which was transparent, allowing the visiting teachers to observe all that was going on in next door's classroom. There were also TV screens along the front; one projecting the board, one with a close-up of the teacher and one from a camera that faced the students, allowing us to see their activities and responses.

The lesson itself was not as exciting as the set-up – the students were studying a passage from *Tom Sawyer*, in which Tom tricks a friend into painting a fence for him. They read it out together, they repeated sections after her, she asked them questions about each section, and they then answered comprehension questions. Having sat through a lot of English lessons during my time in Shanghai, including the lesson about Bird and Frog four times, I'd say this was fairly typical of a primary/junior high school English lesson, with the level of difficulty of the comprehension questions changing depending on the age group.

Science lessons seemed to be a bit more active, with students trying out experiments that demonstrated the concept of the lesson, like rubbing blocks of wood on the desk to demonstrate friction, or trying out the magnetism of different metals. Chinese lessons included a lot of recitation of the texts being studied, with the teacher asking students why the author had used particular turns of phrase (or particular Chinese characters), and explaining why if they weren't sure. The main subject I'm going to focus on though is maths; partly because this is a subject Shanghai did extra-specially well in (with an average score 119 points above the OECD average in 2012, equivalent to nearly three years of schooling),[160] and partly because there has been much more research on how Chinese teachers teach maths than on how they teach anything else.

In maths and other subjects, there seems to be more consistency amongst different lessons with different Shanghai teachers than there is in England or America. In their teacher training, teachers are taught to teach in a particular way – to consider the order in which they teach concepts, to think about how appropriate connections can be made between classroom activities and the content being taught, and to reflect on how that new content relates to things that students have already learnt.[161] They talk through this together in their planning sessions, and some of this knowledge is contained in the structure of the textbooks they use. The logic behind this was explained to me by a renowned head teacher, whom I shamefully overlooked when I first came into his office as he was sitting on a sofa wearing jeans and a grey North Face fleece.

'In teaching style, individuality is fine, once you're experienced. But you need to reach a certain standard first. You need to know about the best order of the content, the big problem then the little, the major then the minor. It's like KFC!' His eyes lit up. 'Why does all their chicken taste so good? They don't have amazing chefs in every store, but they have certain procedures in place. Once teachers have mastered these procedures and skills, they can be more experimental.'

Demonstration and Intuition

The most obvious difference between mathematics lessons in England and lessons in Shanghai is the amount of time spent in 'whole class teaching' – i.e. directed by the teacher from the front of the classroom. This includes carefully planned lecturing, but it isn't all one-sided; teachers actually ask the students huge numbers of questions (on average 50–120 per lesson) during this demonstration period, making it highly interactive.[162] Some of these questions are deliberately very easy, so that teachers start where the children are, and build up their explanations and questions, gradually moving to more difficult mathematical concepts.

Schleppenbach and colleagues compared Chinese and American teachers' responses to children's answers in class, and found that Chinese teachers were more likely to ask follow-up questions when a child got an answer wrong, in addition to explaining their error – whereas the American teachers tended to move on after pointing out the error.[163] Expert Chinese teachers will also bring other students into the conversation when responding to answers in class, by asking them, 'Is that right? Do you agree? How would you do it?' and then getting the original contributor to respond. Novice teachers don't do this as much however, and are more likely to simply comment on a student's answer.[164] Perhaps this is something they pick up in their numerous observations of demonstration lessons.

In Chinese mathematics lessons, the demonstration and modelling is followed by practice. Luke, a teacher from Yorkshire who visited Shanghai on a study tour, described the process as 'ping pong' style – you do, I do, you do, I do. Students don't work for extended periods of time on independent work in class (apart from in their 'study lessons'), but they do a huge amount of practice on each topic as part of their homework. The textbooks guide this, offering progressively more difficult questions for the students to tackle.

The benefits of this extensive practice came up in my discussion with Rony when we were discussing the differences between the Chinese and Canadian students that come to him for private tuition in preparation for their college entry exams. There is a particular type of maths question that gives you some facts about a number (e.g. x is a prime number, x is a factor of 56, etc.) and asks you to find what the number is. Rony finds that the most effective way of teaching his Canadian students to answer this kind of question is to give them an acronym – Zone F – as a checklist of all the types of number it could be: 'Zero, one, negative, extreme numbers, Fractions. They don't have the instinctive awareness about all these different categories, so they like having the checklist, they like doing one thing at a time, they like having a structured frame going to a question.'

'When I try to teach the same concept to a Chinese student of roughly the same level, they find the idea of 'Zone F' and the idea of having to check through everything a little too... hm... they find it strange, they're uncomfortable doing it, they find it dogmatic. What they feel more comfortable doing, and what they prefer, is to have an intuitive understanding; when you think of a number, that number could be anything. And out of the ocean of numbers I'm going to start picking them.' I asked Rony why he thought they had a more intuitive understanding of number. His answer surprised me.

'For the Asian teacher, before they help their students onto that level, they actually use a more systematic approach… you know, a massive amount is drills, exercises and homework, to make students master things, to feel the intuitive side of it, but this comes from a massive amount of homework and practice. Whereas the typical Canadian student has so much less experience practising with numbers, that they're still on the stage of following the structure, and partly because they didn't have enough of the structure at school, they still appreciate how their tutor has this secret weapon of "Zone F", so that they can solve the puzzle. So they're still on that stage.'

This was echoed in a conversation with Sophie, when she complained that she had to follow all the structured steps to come to an answer in her Canadian mathematics lessons, even though she could just 'see' the answer so was able to do it in just one step.

'They just require you to do it the way they taught you. They give you an example assessment question in class with some numbers plugged in, and then you have to use your calculator to find the answer. In the exam it would be exactly the same question, except the numbers are changed, so as long as you memorised the way to do it and plug in the numbers you would get it right.' The Chinese were accusing the Canadian approach to mathematics of being dogmatic and of being based on memorisation rather than understanding. I was flummoxed. Isn't that what Westerners accuse the Chinese of?

Tennis

I was very grateful to Rony; as a man who has spent a lot of time thinking about and analysing the differences in pedagogy between the country he grew up in and the country he now lives in, he was able to sort through this muddle with a clever analogy.

'An analogy I give about learning math, is that it's like learning any sport. Take tennis. A tennis coach teaches you how to serve. You toss the ball, you practise tossing the ball 100 times until you reach that consistency, then you practise pulling back your racket, and you pull back your racket enough times, and you try to smash it, you try to smash it again, and your coach gives you feedback. And they break it down into steps. Thing is, when Roger Federer serves, he doesn't think through those steps, it becomes so a part of himself, it's in his blood, and he has that natural instinct to do it. So now, translate this to learning anything, or learning, for example, math. You need to have a massive amount of practice until you forget those steps. But the thing is, the Asian system is good at giving students so much practice, that they forget about the steps. They think this is just an intuition, or they perceive it as intuition, but of course it's not natural intuition. But then again, you know, for students who are not used to doing that much practice, they still need to do that practice.'

There are two more things to pick up here about how Chinese students get to this stage. Yes, they have lots of homework, and this might not be something we'd want to introduce to the same degree in the West (remember Nancy? She had a callous on her finger from writing so much...). But this isn't the only reason they get more practice – they also spend longer on each topic. According to Sophie: 'The most significant difference I find is the depth of material covered. In Canada they do a little bit of everything, and they do it really fast, before you really get the essence of that part, and then they jump into something else. Whereas in China they go on about some knowledge for quite a long time, maybe several weeks before they move to the next topic, so you get a lot of practice, and you really know it.' Like the Japanese, the Chinese have a narrower but deeper curriculum.

The other important point to emphasise is the feedback. Practising at length is not useful, and can even be harmful, if you're practising in the wrong way. Chinese teachers make the most of their extra non-teaching time to offer feedback to pupils in three ways. Firstly, they will often mark the students' classwork and homework on the same day it's handed in, using a set of symbols to indicate what the students got wrong so that students get immediate feedback.[165] This doesn't always happen; in some schools I saw students in the staffroom marking their peers' work using the mark scheme, but this still gives the teacher an idea about the distribution of mistakes, which they can use in their planning.

Secondly, they discuss common mistakes or misunderstandings at the beginning of the very next lesson, and ask students who got the tricky questions to demonstrate how they did it on the board to the rest of the class. On one occasion a maths teacher was hesitant to let me observe her class because, she said, 'we're only going over homework', yet this is probably where the most learning gains happen.

Thirdly, they also have one-to-one or small group sessions during and after the school day with pupils who need extra help – so although the lessons are mainly directed to the whole class, and don't have much individualised instruction, students who need it get this extra help later on.

The Paradox of the Chinese Learner

Repetition in Chinese schools is not limited to the practice of mathematical procedures; it is a fundamental part of Chinese education. Part of the reason Erin was 'in trouble' with the teacher for not supervising her son's homework was that his homework was often to recite something five times, and there was no evidence of him having done this if she wasn't there to hear him. I saw several Chinese lessons in which the whole class would recite a poem several times, and English lessons in which the whole class, sometimes in two halves, would repeat the English text after the teacher, then again, then again (so although I only saw the lesson about Bird and Frog four times, I heard the story at least twelve times). This focus on repetition (and consequently memorisation) goes back to the times of Kuang Heng and Li Bai, who had to memorise huge swathes of classical poetry for the civil service examinations.

Herein lies the paradox. In the West, we tend to think that rote learning is unhelpful and old-fashioned. To us, hearing someone repeat something again and again suggests that they don't understand it, and that they're just doing it for the sake of a test where they will regurgitate what they've learnt onto the page. It doesn't allow for true understanding and use of the information, and doesn't allow for enjoyment or appreciation of the subject matter. Yet students from Asian countries that take this approach consistently outperform Western students on PISA – which is a problem-solving test. PISA doesn't allow for regurgitation – it requires the intelligent use of what you know to solve a given problem. How can this be? Biggs coined this puzzle 'the paradox of the Chinese learner' in 1992, and has since also suggested its solution.[166]

Our mistake is in our assumption that memorisation and repetition necessarily imply only shallow, surface-level learning. Watkins and Biggs distinguish between two types of learning strategies that outwardly look the same – rote learning and repetitive learning. Rote learning is what I just described; shallow, mechanistic, with no attempt at understanding. Repetitive learning, on the other hand, involves deepening your understanding through deliberate repetition, paying attention to the features of whatever it is you're repeating. Unlike rote learning, repetitive learning can lead to deeper understanding of the subject content.[167]

The second time I met Rony, it was with his girlfriend Sophie too, and I asked them, 'Why is it considered useful to read something over and over? I saw this in a number of classes.'

'Great question; why is it not?' Rony turned the question back on me, and I felt momentarily taken aback. 'If someone from Asia comes and visits a school in England, that's going to be one of the first questions they ask: "Why don't you make your students repeat the Shakespeare verses so that they truly make sense of it?"'

'Umm…'

Luckily I was rescued by Sophie's interjection. 'I guess it's about knowledge consolidation, the more you repeat it the more you get it.'

That gave me time to recover. 'The Western conception is that if you're just repeating it over and over, you're not understanding it any better each time.'

'In China, when we repeat ancient poems the fundamental assumption is after we memorise a certain amount of input, you become intuitively familiar with each Chinese character, the meaning behind each character, and also the rhythm of it. It comes naturally to you,' said Rony.

Sophie nodded. 'It really does.'

Although I didn't think it at the time, this reminds me of what they'd previously said about maths – that after lots and lots of practice, they forgot the steps and it became intuitive. There is some memorisation in maths too – not of individual steps to solve a problem, but of times tables, and basic number facts. This means that when they are solving more complicated problems that require these facts, this part of the problem comes easily to them, and does not take up more of their working memory – the psychological concept we came across in the Japan section.

Even if you acknowledge that the Chinese approach to teaching and learning can lead to deep understanding and an advanced ability to problem solve, two important concerns remain. Sure, Chinese children are (on average) good at learning, but can they really be enjoying it when it is so repetitive and they are under so much pressure? And what about the skills of the 21st century – critical thinking, personal skills and creativity – doesn't all the drilling squash these important traits out of them?

Motivation – a Surprising Finding

With this amount of pressure coming from external sources, such as parents, one might think that while most Chinese students are motivated to study hard, this is entirely extrinsic motivation, and driven by fear of punishment or promise of reward rather than interest in the task. It would be easy enough to pick out examples of Chinese students being bullied by their parents and hating school – but would this fairly represent the 'typical' Chinese experience?

It wouldn't be unreasonable to assume so. At the very least, given that British and American parents are more concerned with making learning interesting and fun than their Chinese counterparts, you'd think that their children would be more intrinsically motivated than Chinese children.[168] Another reason for thinking so would be that Chinese teachers have been described as more 'controlling' than Western ones: putting more pressure on the children, giving them more tests and demanding more conformity.[169] According to Ryan and Deci's well-evidenced finding that autonomy is a key prerequisite for intrinsic motivation, it ought to follow that Chinese children have, on average, very little of it.[170]

This is not actually the case. Wang and Pomerantz gave Chinese and American adolescents questionnaires that asked them to say how much (from 1–5) they agreed with various statements about their motivations for studying, which corresponded with the different types of motivation identified by

Ryan and Deci on their taxonomy: intrinsic motivation (e.g. 'I do my homework because it's fun'), identification ('I work on my classwork because it's important to me to do so'), introjection ('I work on my classwork because I'll be ashamed of myself if it doesn't get done') and external motivation ('I do my homework because I'll get in trouble if I don't'). They found that Chinese students actually had a higher index of relative autonomy – i.e. they gave more intrinsic and identified reasons for studying than American students. While this index declined over the course of junior high school (a period where the pressure intensifies in China due to the high school entrance exams) it remained higher than American students of the same age.[171]

This is surprising – Chinese students are under lots of pressure from parents and teachers, and are taught in a way that doesn't give students much freedom, and yet they report that they enjoy learning more than Americans do and that they work hard because it is important, rather than because their parents force them to. However, it is consistent with research carried out in the 1990s which found that Chinese children reported liking school more than American children.[172] More recent research was carried out by the OECD in 2012 in which 85 per cent of Shanghainese 15-year-olds surveyed agreed with the statement 'I feel happy at school' compared to 80 per cent of American 15-year-olds and 83 per cent of British 15-year-olds (not a big lead for the Chinese, but they are not behind on this measure as you might expect).[173]

How can we make sense of this? There are two potential explanations, one from some Chinese researchers and one from a tiger mother. Zhou, Lam and Chan suspect that the answer to this paradox lies in the different ways that students from different cultures interpret the apparently 'controlling behaviours' of their teachers (and I would argue this extends to parents and grandparents too).[174] Zhou and colleagues tested their hunch by giving Chinese and American fifth graders various scenarios involving teachers, such as a teacher keeping a child behind in class to finish some homework they hadn't handed in, and asked the children to say how they would feel if their teachers did the same to them (choosing from 12 emotions). They found that American students were more likely to interpret the teachers' actions as being controlling, and to say it made them feel sad or mad, whereas the Chinese students interpreted exactly the same scenarios more positively, indicating that they felt looked after or cared for. In addition, they found that for students from both countries, feeling controlled led to less motivation in that teacher's class, whereas feeling cared for led to more motivation, and that students were less likely to perceive an action as being controlling if they had a good relationship with that teacher.

If you've been brought up in a Confucian culture, where fulfilling your role within the family is very important, and where parents impress the value of learning upon you from a young age, you are likely to have internalised these values and goals. When an adult then acts in a way that will benefit your learning, you are less likely to perceive that behaviour as being controlling, and more likely to see it as evidence of your teacher or parent's concern for you and your future; especially where that relationship is a loving one. In other words, Chinese students have higher levels of autonomous motivation because they have internalised the cultural and familial goals, and made them their own. They are less externally motivated despite the pressure from parents and teachers because the pressure is to pursue goals that they themselves believe in.

Another explanation for why Chinese students have, on average, more autonomous motivation by early adolescence than their American peers is articulated by the original tiger mother, Amy Chua, author of *Battle Hymn of the Tiger Mother*. She explains: 'What Chinese parents understand is that nothing is fun until you're good at it. To get good at anything you have to work, and children on their own never want to work, which is why it is crucial to override their preferences. This often requires fortitude on the part of the parents because the child will resist; things are always hardest at the beginning, which is where Western parents tend to give up.'[175]

This sounds very much like external motivation to me. However, Chua continues: 'But if done properly, the Chinese strategy produces a virtuous circle. Tenacious practice, practice, practice is crucial for excellence; rote repetition is underrated in America. Once a child starts to excel at something – whether it's maths, piano, pitching or ballet – he or she gets praise, admiration and satisfaction. This builds confidence and makes the once not-fun activity fun. This in turn makes it easier for the parent to get the child to work even more.' So although Chinese parents may be getting their children to work hard against their will initially, the children may then develop genuine intrinsic motivation once they get good at the activity in question, and begin to enjoy it and pursue it for its own sake.

The bottom line however, is that even though Chinese children seem on average to be more intrinsically motivated than their Western counterparts, in those cases where they lack this intrinsic motivation or enjoyment of study, they still continue to work hard – whether they like it or not.

Critical Thinking and Creativity

Based on their analysis of a survey completed by 479 Chinese university students and lecturers, Pratt and colleagues suggest that the Chinese think of basic knowledge as the first step in a four stage learning process:

1. Memorising and mastering the basics
2. Understanding

3. Applying the knowledge to problems and situations
4. Questioning or critical analysing[176]

We know from the PISA tests that Chinese students are good at getting as far as stage 3, but what about questioning or critical analysing? Are they able to do these too or is this where their system of whole-class demonstrations and structured practice falls down? This is certainly something the Chinese government have been concerned about, along with a number of prominent Chinese commentators. In 2010, the then Premier of the State Council, Wen Jiabao, announced that: 'Students don't only need knowledge; they have to learn how to act, to use their brains. We must encourage students to think independently, freely express themselves, get them to believe in themselves, protect and stimulate their imagination and creativity.'[177]

In recognition of this perceived problem, the Chinese government introduced a new curriculum in 2001 that emphasises the cultivation of independent and critical learners, and a reinforcement of inter-subject connections. They are moving away from *tiányāshì* (force-feeding the duck) – a concept used to describe the pressurised system of preparing children for high-stakes exams which was first explained to me in the migrant school by a teacher who mimed the force-feeding of a duck as she said it. Increasing numbers of Shanghai schools are aiming to foster innovative thinking in their students through their curricula, which are now partly designed by the schools themselves.[178] Some are including 'explorations' in their lessons, during which students are encouraged to discuss and express their own ideas. Only time will tell whether their new efforts will pay off and result in greater creativity and critical thinking, or whether the threat of true independent thought will be too much for a government that recently told universities to 'shun Western values'.[179]

In the meantime, the West should not be complacent. Students from Shanghai and other Chinese regions don't only score highly due to their intensive work ethic. Their lessons are highly structured, with a stated aim, clear explanations and modelling as a result of careful planning, and opportunities for students to practise and get prompt – lesson features which have consistently been found to correlate with high student performance.[180] The Chinese fondness for memorisation is also aligned with research into 'what works' – committing certain facts to memory aids problem-solving by freeing up space in the working memory and illuminating contexts in which existing knowledge can be applied.[181] And even the culture-soaked Confucian approach to effortful learning is something that schools in different countries can begin to embed by using the right language and instilling beliefs about the importance of perseverance from an early age. While we might not want to put our children under the kind of pressure that Chinese children are under, it would be a mistake to assume there is nothing we can learn from them.

Chapter 14: Diversity, Relationships and the Limits of Individualism

Diversity is Canada's strength.
Justin Trudeau, Canadian Prime Minister

I got off the plane in Vancouver feeling groggy, and wondered for a moment if I'd ended up in the right country. The billboards and signs that greeted me as I walked through the airport were in some kind of East Asian script – Japanese or Chinese, I couldn't tell. Once I'd seen a Tim Horton's Café and Bake Shop and realised that I must at the very least be in North America, I made my way through customs, into town on the train shuttle, and went straight to bed in the first hostel I came across.

Jetlag woke me up early the next morning, so I went and sat in a coffee shop while I waited for the rest of the city to wake up. As I nursed my latte in the window, I watched people of all shapes, sizes and colours passing by and I felt at home. Like London, Vancouver is a hugely multicultural city. British Columbia (BC), the province Vancouver is in, welcomes more than 40,000 immigrants every year,[182] and Canada as a whole takes in about 250,000 annually,[183] meaning that about one in five of the people living in Canada were born elsewhere, mostly in Asia or Europe.[184] Mary Jean Gallagher, Chief Student Achievement Officer and Assistant Deputy Minister of Ontario – the most diverse province in Canada and the second that I visited – does not see this as a barrier: 'It's seen as an opportunity and a challenge.' In a presentation I attended at the ministry in Ontario she described how they think it's an advantage for their children to grow up in a diverse environment as it will help them to understand other cultures, preparing them to solve global problems, and do business with the rest of the world.

This diversity is partly why I chose to come here. If you were to take averages of different systems' reading, maths and science scores, Canada would rank seventh in PISA 2009, and eleventh in PISA 2012,[185] so had I been just visiting the top five PISA countries in the world I wouldn't have been to Canada; I would have added Korea to my itinerary instead and gorged myself on *kimchi*. But Canada is impressive and unique in that it gets these relatively high scores, while being a geographically dispersed and hugely diverse country, with a culture that is in many ways similar to the lower-scoring UK and the US.

I found the Canadians to be welcoming, and polite but easygoing; there were none of the formalities that I'd got used to in Japan and China (let alone the stares and requests for photos). One of the families I stayed with exemplified this openness to experience, described by Mary Jean Gallagher in her talk at the ministry, by having a Chinese exchange student stay with them for a semester, and then welcoming me into their home in addition. Loree and Randy went out of their way to include their Chinese guest in the conversation at dinner (despite his English being elementary) which was no doubt helped by the fact that Loree also worked as a teacher for children who had English as their second language. In British Columbia, these students participate in the regular curriculum, but the ministry provides funds for additional language support if a series of criteria are met.

Box 4: Does Canada's immigration policy explain its PISA results?

Having 8.4 per cent of Canadians identify as South Asian or Chinese doesn't sound like many, but immigrants to Canada are not spread evenly across the country. Most settle in the four biggest provinces – Ontario, British Columbia, Quebec and Alberta – which are also the provinces which get the highest PISA results. British Columbia, where Chinese Canadians make up 10 per cent of the total population, got the highest average PISA score of all the provinces in 2012. It does make you wonder doesn't it? You've just read about the kind of attitudes Asian students have towards their studies, so you might just be thinking, 'Does the presence of immigrants explain Canada's PISA success?'

Canada's immigration policy of welcoming people who are likely to make an economic contribution to society means that they do have an educated and relatively affluent immigrant class. In 2008, 49 per cent of PhD holders in Canada were born elsewhere (and you'd imagine that their children, if they have them, would be doing pretty well at school), and the average 'International Index of Socio-Economic Status' of parents of teenagers taking the PISA test in 2000 was slightly higher for immigrant parents than for the 'native' parents (as it was in England).[186] But they don't only take in the educated and the affluent; about 9 per cent of the immigrants to Canada are refugees, who are less likely to score well at school, having spent their time enduring famine or conflict in their homeland, rather than at their books. And when you separate out the PISA scores of the first and second generation immigrants from the native population, and compare Canada's average 2009 score with and without them, you can see that, overall, immigrants have a slightly negative effect on Canada's PISA results. Without them, the score is 533, with them it is 527 (you find a similar, marginal difference between natives and immigrants in the UK and the United States).[187] Of course, there is far more to immigration than its effects on PISA scores, but I'm spelling out the stats in case anyone is under the misapprehension that Canada's generally high PISA scores are simply the result of their immigration policy.

Canada is made up of 10 provinces, and three vast but sparsely-populated territories in the North. Each province and territory runs its own education, so Canada is effectively made up of thirteen different education systems, 10 of which contribute to the PISA data.[188] These provinces have a surprising amount in common.[189] They share approaches to comprehensive education, they have similar textbooks, they all have strong teacher unions, teacher training is based on a common model (with an important exception) and most of them have similar assessment approaches.[190]

Overall, these approaches, and the rest of the Canadian context, result in a system in which fewer children than average fail to meet the baselines in reading, maths and science, and in which there is a relatively weak link between family background and PISA scores. What are the factors that might help explain the stronger performance of those that are usually the educational underdogs?

Catering for Struggling Learners

Let's start at the beginning, before educational factors come into play. Canada has traditionally had a pretty decent welfare system, born of their response to the Great Depression, meaning that pregnant mums (along with everyone else) are guaranteed free healthcare. This welfare system includes low-income support, so these mums and their young children are less likely to be malnourished than mothers and children in countries without this social safety net. This net has holes, and Canada is some way from eliminating child poverty, but the percentage of Canada's PISA-taking students who have an index of economic, cultural and social status below -1 (one measure of coming from a poor background) is one of the lowest in the world.

Compared to other OECD countries, not many children are enrolled in preschool before the age of five (which some suggest could be an area of improvement for Canada),[191] although some provinces such as Alberta and Quebec offer free preschool places to younger children from disadvantaged backgrounds. You'll remember the research discussed when we were looking at Finland – the early years are an important time when learning gaps between children from richer and poorer backgrounds can be widened or narrowed, and good quality preschools help to make sure it is the latter (though poor quality preschools can have a negative impact on everyone).[192] By the time they are five, the vast majority of children in Canada attend kindergarten.[193] And my goodness it looks fun.

I spent a morning with the kindergarten in one of the elementary schools I visited. All the displays were at child height – something that seems obvious to me now but that I'd not considered as being important before. Around the room were different stations where the children could choose to do different things – painting, building, play-acting, thinking. The thinking station had a laminated picture of a spider on it, with a question at the top (which was read to them) asking, 'Is a spider a good guy or a bad guy?' Six Post-its had been stuck on the laminate by the children: two said 'good guy', one said 'googuy', one said 'good', and two just had pictures of spiders on them.

The kindergarten teacher, Melvyn, explained to me that they spend most of their time choosing what they want to do, but they do have prescribed learning outcomes including goals around physical activity and pre-reading and writing skills such as speaking and listening and letter identification. A lovely example of their attempts to support these skills is that children are encouraged to track words with their finger while the teacher is reading, and to 'hug' words, meaning they put one finger at the front and one at the end to develop their understanding of the concept of words.

Once they start school, at age six, the resources available to them don't differ too widely based on the average income of the area. This is as a result of one of the major policy shifts that happened across Canada during the 1980s; all provinces except Manitoba and Saskatchewan negotiated with local school boards to implement equalised funding. This means that rather than schools being funded by local property taxes like they are in the US (meaning schools in richer areas have more money), most of Canadian schools' funding comes directly from the province, based on number of students, with additional money for those in poor areas to match their funding to that of schools in richer districts (in the cases where additional funding is still raised by local government), or beat it where there is more need. So even the primary school I visited in a run-down area outside of Toronto seemed pretty well equipped, with interactive whiteboards and a well-stocked library. The provinces also fund some programmes directly, such as special education programmes, early intervention programmes, and a wilderness camp for young offenders.

I met a mum at a bus stop in this slightly dodgier part of town, pushing a buggy with her two-year-old son. We'd been waiting at the bus stop for 15 minutes already, and then the bus we needed drove by without stopping. There was collective anguish amongst the folk at the bus stop, and it opened up that space that only happens (at least, in England) when public services let you down; it became acceptable to talk to strangers. She picked up on my accent immediately.

'Is that a British accent?'

'Yep. Yeah. It is.'

'What brings you to Ontario? You on holiday?' She looked a bit unsure as to why I'd be in this part of town if I were.

'I'm doing some research into the world's best education systems. Do you have kids at school?'

'Yeah, Molly, she's seven, she's just started Grade 2.'

'How does she like it so far? Do you think the school system is good here?'

'Yeah, I do actually. Molly was struggling with her reading, she finds it quite tricky, so they said she could go to this summer catch-up class at the school. It seemed to help her out, and it's cool that they offer that for free.'

Catching children up on their reading in the first few years of elementary school seems to be a big focus here, as it was in Finland. Teachers spend more time in small reading groups with these children during class, while the others are getting on with independent work (and instructed by one teacher I met not to interrupt her unless it was for one of the '3Bs' – bathroom, bleeding or barfing). This is necessary because children do come into school at different levels, and some pick things up more quickly than others. According to Janet, a Learning Support Teacher, this partly has to do with the month in which they're born.

'Quite often they're the late birthdays, November, December, and they're just not quite developmentally ready to learn to read, and be sitting and working as much as our system expects them to. Most of the kids do OK, they start to pick up the reading, but the ones that I work with are the ones that are struggling with that. So I explicitly show them pieces that the rest of the kids are picking up on their own.'

Janet works with these children that are falling behind, both in class, and in small groups out of class. In Canada, Learning Support Teachers like Janet are fully-qualified, certified teachers, often with additional qualifications in special educational needs. At a secondary level too, I was shown learning support rooms, manned by a number of qualified teachers, where students could book in or pop by during their free periods to get additional support. Rather than leaving the difficult job of helping those that find learning the hardest to well-meaning but less-qualified teaching assistants, school and district leaders in Canada, like in Finland, recognise that this is a job that requires additional expertise. This is not to devalue the role of teaching assistants in other areas – I have worked with some brilliant ones – but it does seem sensible that those children with the most complex educational needs receive additional input from those with the most specialist training.

After describing to me how she helped the children catch up, Janet went on to include a strategy that I wasn't expecting. 'I also try and explain to them why we're doing things. I think, if they don't figure it out on their own, they need somebody to point them in the right direction. Why we're learning the sounds of the letters. Why we're learning to recognise the sight words. I think that's an important part. Most kids just absorb that from the atmosphere in the classroom, but the ones I work with that are struggling maybe just don't get it at all.' The motivation of children plays a huge part in whether they succeed, and Janet's focus on children's motivations and their experience of school was echoed in many of the conversations I had across the two provinces I visited – British Columbia and Ontario.

The Canadian Approach to Motivation

One of the first things an Ontarian primary school principal said to me when I asked her what her responsibilities were, was 'Making sure there's an entry point for each child. You know, how can we engage the kids so that they feel valued at the school and like they're part of a community?' That sounds lovely, I thought, but how do you actually do it?

'There are many layers. One is obviously the relationships you build in the school. Listening to the children and asking them what kind of things they'd like to be a part of. And, pretty much, we don't say no to *any* initiative that the teachers or parents want to bring in, whether it's that we've got a hatchery (chickens) because the kids are interested in that, or they're going to go and release the salmon because a parent got on that and the kids enjoy it and we want it to be part of their experience. Or they want to do chess club or a craft club – we put money towards that, so that's what we fundraise for, the money we fundraise all goes to student activities. What are *they* interested in?'

I've mainly focused on primary school so far, but this concern extended to middle school and high school, and was evident not only in what the teachers and students said, but in the way the system was structured. High schools offer an impressive array of extracurricular activities – tennis, anime, Frisbee, Amnesty International, debating, rugby – you name it and they've either got it, or plucky students can set one up. One of the counsellors – professionals who support the personal, social, academic and career development of students through one-to-one and small group sessions – explained to me that one consequence of the array of activities is that 'Everyone has a stake in school. Like this kid Joey for example,' she gestured to the notes on her desk, 'even though he's finding his courses hard, he doesn't want to drop out of school because then he'd have to leave the basketball team.' In British Columbia, some activities like taking part in musicals even count towards your credits for high-school graduation (alongside core academic requirements), and at one high school I visited, the principal proudly told me that 600 out of 1,000 students played on some kind of team.

You'll find counsellors in every high school. But they aren't just there to support students with mental health needs; their role includes chatting to all the students about how everything is going, how they're finding their studies and about what courses they want to choose. Another counsellor explained to me, 'All students are worthy of learning, but until they feel loved and cared for, they aren't going to care about *Hamlet*.' In both the counsellors and the teachers that lead the activities, there is an opportunity for the young people to form a meaningful, positive relationship with a responsible adult who cares about their education. This is especially valuable if for any reason they've not been able to form such a relationship with their parents or regular teachers.

This is important because while those who find academic study easy are often already motivated by being good at it, the ones who don't find it as easy – the ones most likely to fail – need a reason to keep coming to school; a reason to put in the effort. The Canadian strategy seems to be to get them involved by making them feel part of a school community, using extracurricular activities and stressing the importance of human relationships to do this. Not only is this intrinsically valuable, but there is research to suggest that it has further positive effects too.

Cornelius-White did a meta-analysis of 119 studies of teachers' personal attributes (such as empathy and warmth) and their relationship with student outcomes. He found strong correlations between person-centred teacher variables and students' critical thinking, maths and reading scores, and concluded that teachers facilitate children's development when they demonstrate that they care for each student as a person.[194] Ontario has also recognised the power of relationships in their 'student success' strategy, by employing student success teachers whose job is to work directly with students at risk of school dropout.

Another more structural element that makes a difference to student motivation is the Canadian approach to grouping students. There is no selection into different schools, selection into different tracks within a school (streaming) or selection into different classes for different subjects (setting), until at least Grade 9 (age 14–15), when it commonly begins with the introduction of an advanced math class. This hasn't always been the case: Canada, like everywhere else, began its education system on the assumption that only a small minority of the population was suited to an academic education, and used to operate 'bilateral' schooling – i.e. separate vocational and academic schools. After much discussion and heated debate, this model was gradually replaced across the provinces by a comprehensive school system, with some leading provinces making this transition in 1968, and others following throughout the 1970s, with the final province implementing this system in 1982. Whether or not this change was related to the improvement in Canada's international test scores that took place throughout the remainder of the 1980s is an open question.

In Canada, even high schools are comprehensive in intake, but have different levels for different subjects which students can choose to take, supported by chats with the counsellors. So one high-school student I met, for example, let's call him Mike, was taking foundation math, advanced English and advanced social studies. This is in contrast to most countries where students are tracked into more academic or less academic programmes across all subjects by this age. In fact, student choice is so important in Canada that a school across town from Mike's only recently brought in cut-off grades required to take 'advanced math' in Grade 10 – previously anyone could take it who wanted to, even if they weren't a mathematical top performer.

There is also choice in the range and type of subject students can take, so if Mike had wanted, he could have been taking genuinely academic courses alongside vocational courses like metalwork and mechanics, without having to even leave the school building. This is true right across Canada, as found by *Learning to School* author, Jennifer Walner: 'Across of all the provinces, secondary education is underpinned by a commitment to extend flexibility to students; it affords them considerable time to determine where their strengths and skills lie before sending them down a particular path.'[195]

This delay in pushing students into particular courses has been found to be internationally associated with higher student motivation. The OECD paper that outlines these effects explains that 'there is a strong negative association between the levels of students' motivation and the degree to which school systems sort and group students into different schools and/or programmes.'[196] In other words, students in systems that separate students into different schools based on their perceived ability are less motivated than students in systems (like Canada's) that don't. Singapore's motivated students seem to be an exception to this trend, perhaps because of their Confucian learning culture.

The Limits of Individualism

In this way and others, the Canadian approach to education goes further than any other country I visited to meet children's individual needs. Partly their hand is forced by the fact that Canada is also a more diverse country than most, with children from different cultural backgrounds and with different first languages all being educated in the same classrooms. Partly it is due to the fact that they can't rely as much as schools in Asia on parents motivating their children to study, so have more need to find a way to motivate children based on their own interests. Of course, they could still ignore these factors and ignore individual children's needs, and it is a testament to the teachers of Canada that they don't. This was impressive. However, based on what I saw, I believe that there is also a limit to the amount of individualisation that is good for children. So here are my caveats.

I heard a number of teachers in Canada talk about meeting children's needs by catering to their learning styles. The theory goes that children (and adults) have preferred ways of learning – some prefer visual input, some like to hear about the topic, some would rather learn by doing. Therefore, if teachers match their teaching style to the learning styles of their students, by providing a diagram for one and a hands-on task for another, the children will learn better (this is called the meshing hypothesis). This approach is common in England and I was taught it too when I was doing my teacher training. It was known as VAK, which stands for visual, auditory and kinaesthetic, and I was encouraged to apply it in all my lessons.

The problem with the theory of learning styles however, is that there is almost no evidence that it works. A review of the evidence by four respected professors of psychology from three different universities found that while children and adults will, if asked, express preferences for the ways they like to learn, there is 'virtually no evidence' for the idea that teaching people in their preferred learning style leads to better learning outcomes. 'Although the literature on learning styles is enormous, very few studies have even used an experimental methodology capable of testing the validity of learning styles applied to education. Moreover, of those that did use an appropriate method, several found results that flatly contradict the popular meshing hypothesis.'[197]

This doesn't mean teachers shouldn't use different ways of explaining concepts, but that the appropriate way to explain something has a lot to do with the concept or idea that is being taught, rather than the person learning it. The structural features of mountain ranges in Canada might be best taught visually for example, whereas getting the students to consider what it's like to be new to a country might be better taught by conducting some of the lesson in an unfamiliar language. Sometimes for particularly tricky topics, the children may benefit from having them explained in more than one way, and I'm sure this is the approach that many Canadian teachers take too.

The issue I would like to draw attention to though goes deeper than whether something is a waste of teachers' time or not. Sometimes, a well-meaning attempt to adapt the educational environment to the student can lead to low expectations of that child in the short term, which puts them at a disadvantage in the long term. Though this problem isn't limited to learning styles, it serves as a clear example of how it works.

Let's say Joe in Year 5 doesn't like reading, and prefers to build things and paint things. It might be said that he has a 'kinaesthetic' learning style, and so his teacher might ask him to paint a picture of the Roman baths based on the other pictures in a history book, rather than reading up about them like his desk-mate Sarah is doing. In the next class, he sorts and matches some cards with the names of poets and their most famous poems on them, while she reads some of those poems. Quite apart from the question of who will learn the most about Roman baths or poetry, he is not getting any better at reading, and she is not getting any better at painting. Their differences – their strengths and their weaknesses – are being exaggerated and encouraged, and all Joe's future literary possibilities and Sarah's artistic possibilities are being closed down at an early age, rather than being worked on and expanded.

Let me give you a real-life example from my trip of where individualism went too far. I visited one school in Vancouver, where I met a really passionate, enthusiastic Grade 12 history teacher who invited me to come into her school and talk to her students. She'd recently set the group a task to watch a video for homework, so that students could get straight to making use of that information in the lesson. Here is a conversation she had with one of her students who hadn't watched the video that he was supposed to watch, about how he found that type of homework.

'Did it work for you?'

'No.'

'Why not?'

'Because I'm lazy.'

'So you were lazy and you didn't get it done. But my hope is that next time we do it, you and I can have a one-on-one lesson, while the other 29 students who have watched it get on with the essay reflection or whatever the task is. So what you thought was a failure, like "it didn't work for me" is in fact like a huge educational victory. I'm like, well I'm glad it didn't work for you, because now I can work with you, does that make sense?'

This teacher is being lovely; supporting the student to learn and involving him in the lesson even though he admits it was his own laziness that means he's not prepared. Perhaps that young man had been having a tough time at home, and so she was making exceptions for him in order to include him in a class that he might otherwise drop out of. There might be really good reasons for this approach. But on the surface, it looks like the teacher is accepting that 'laziness' is an inherent feature of this student, that he won't do his homework next time either, and that therefore she should adapt the educational environment to suit the student by teaching him in class what he should have done for homework. If this is the case, then this student is never going to work hard because he knows he doesn't have to. That might be great for him at school – he's getting the teacher's undivided attention after all – but he won't last long in any job if he tells his boss that he didn't do the paperwork because he's lazy. Sometimes, rather than adapting the environment to the child, the adult needs to support the child in learning to adapt themselves to the environment.

Chapter 15: Universal Standards, Answerability and Streaming Up

You may have a fresh start any moment you choose, for this thing that we call 'failure' is not the falling down, but the staying down.
Mary Pickford, Canadian actress and producer

I spent an enjoyable week in a small town outside Vancouver with Marilyn, a second-grade teacher who not only hosted me but generously invited me to join her and her family for Canadian Thanksgiving and fed me three types of pie (pumpkin, chocolate and pecan). As in other countries, I offered to help out at school in any way I could, and Marilyn asked me to take her Grade 2 students out of the classroom one by one, to run through a basic, one-to-one assessment with them. This involved me asking them to count as high as they could (but stopping them once it was clear they could get past 110), to read certain words and to point to various body parts as I said them.

Now, one of the little boys decided to have a bit of a joke with me. As you can imagine, as I'm from England, I have an English accent. And the word 'ear' sounds different in an English accent, compared to its Canadian pronunciation. So when I first said 'ear', he said 'Huh?' – at this stage, genuinely confused. When I then said 'eearrrr' in my best Canadian accent, he smiled and pointed to his ear. From then on, though, any word I said in an English accent was met with 'Huh?' and a cheeky giggle, so I had to say all the body parts in 'Canadian'.

This type of assessment, and the colourful charts and graphs outside the staffroom displaying the proportion of children at 'grade-level', illustrate a broader point about expectations for children in Canada. British Columbia has developed 'BC performance standards' for teachers' use in classrooms. These describe what it is expected of children at each grade level, and provide detailed descriptors of what counts as 'not yet within expectations', 'meets expectations' (minimal level), 'fully meets expectations' and 'exceeds expectations' for each descriptor.[198] For example, the Grade 3 writing standards include 'Literary Writing' (writing stories and poems). A snapshot of the criteria to meet performance standards for the latter are shown in the table below, although in the official documents it is then further broken down into different aspects: meaning, style, form and conventions.

Aspect	Not Yet Within Expectations	Meets Expectations (Minimal Level)	Fully Meets Expectations	Exceeds Expectations
SNAPSHOT	The writing is often very brief, disjointed, or illogical, and flawed by repeated basic errors. The student needs ongoing support.	The writing presents loosely connected events or ideas, with some detail; parts may be hard to follow or flawed by frequent errors.	The writing is a complete, easy-to-follow story or poem with some interesting detail.	The writing is an engaging story or poem with some originality.

Table 3: A section of the British Columbia Performance Standards for Literary Writing, Grade 3.

These standards are accompanied by real examples of what work looks like at each level. This is a particularly important addition, because humans aren't naturally very good at comparing work to descriptors – what counts as 'interesting detail' for example? How about, 'My favourite song was *The Simpsons* because I didn't know they knew *The Simpsons*' about a trip to a concert, or 'I felt a bit scared when Mrs Schimdt said the people that painted the pictures above the Orpheum laid down on a high board'? Having the examples allows teachers to compare their own students' work with the different exemplars, and decide if each piece is relatively better or worse, a skill our human brains are much better at.[199]

This outcomes-based approach to the curriculum and the assessment of what children should be able to do was introduced in the 1980s, after a period in the late 1960s and 1970s in which the curriculum had been decentralised to local school boards and even individual schools, to allow more flexibility for individual children.[196] The more flexible approach had originally been brought in to challenge what were perceived as 'inflexible programs, outdated curricula, unrealistic regulations, regimented organization and mistaken aims of education' (as told by a report on Ontario's education in the late 1960s), but less than 20 years later, the curriculum shift was back in the other direction, with policymakers specifying what outcomes students should meet in what grades – an approach that has survived to this day. It was also in the 1980s that Canada's international test results began to climb.

Canada's performance standards are mainly used in the classroom by teachers, who create their own assessments that help them decide if the students have met the criteria and report on students' progress to parents. They can also use resources such as the BC exam bank to help them, which provides curriculum-linked multiple-choice questions for those subjects that are assessable in this format, like science and maths. However, there are also provincial skills assessments in Grades 4 and 7 in reading comprehension, writing and numeracy – which are externally marked, go beyond multiple-choice questions and give a snapshot of how different students are doing against the Performance Standards – and also a smattering of provincial exams in Grades 10–12. Ontario has the same set-up, with standards that students are expected to meet at each grade level, but they give their students the external assessments in Grades 3 (general), 6 (general), 9 (maths) and 10 (literacy) instead. In a similar pattern to the one for the existence of provincial standards described above, these provincial assessments had been abolished in the 1960s and 1970s, but were brought back in throughout the late 1980s and 1990s in response to mounting criticism that standards were slipping and there was a glaring lack of accountability in schools.

Canada's outcomes-based approach to assessment is known as criterion-referenced and grade-based, and differs from the way some other countries approach assessment. Singapore's Primary School Leaving Exam (PSLE), for example, is cohort-referenced (as opposed to criterion-referenced), meaning that rather than measuring students' performance against set criteria, they are measured against each other. Their actual mark in the PSLE is adjusted to give a PSLE T-Score, which takes into account how well everyone else did. This creates a situation where if you do badly, but everyone else does worse, you get a high mark, whereas if you do brilliantly, but everyone does even better, you will get a low mark (remember Little Boy's explanation of how this leads to increasing difficulty in the exams in Singapore). It only matters indirectly whether you've mastered the curriculum, because the main determinant of your grade is how you score compared to your classmates. In contrast, in Canada, it is theoretically possible (though practically unlikely) that the whole Grade 4 cohort in a province could fully meet the provincial expectations for Grade 4.[200]

It sounds technical (and it is), but it also demonstrates something quite fundamental about different philosophical approaches to education. Is the assessment designed to distinguish between children, to divide the smart from the less smart, the worthy from the unworthy, and allocate opportunities accordingly? Or is it to establish whether or not, and to what extent, children have succeeded in learning the knowledge or skills that society has decided they ought to have? Both have their place, and it surely ought to depend to some extent on the stage of education. But if you've decided that all students are capable of meeting common standards and attending common schools until the age of 14 or 15, as Canadian legislators have, then there is no need to cohort-reference pupils' assessments and rank students against one another; comparing their performance to criteria and exemplars gives you all the educational information you need. The results don't need to be as fine-grained as you are able to get with cohort-referenced assessments if you are using them as a basis for a conversation about how to teach better or what individual students need to work on, rather than as a basis for which student should go to which school, or which teacher should be paid more money.

Facing the Facts about Intelligence

I had a long chat with the principal of a comprehensive high school, an articulate man with a big oak desk and a blonde moustache, about the philosophy behind this idea that children should be aiming for common standards until aged 15. Bob told me, 'In a perfect world I'd never stream kids. The intellect is not the issue any more – it's interest, it's passion, it's how people want to work – and I think as you divide by ability you're setting the stage for identifying where someone can go, and what they're able to do. I'm very aware of trade teachers I have in this building, outstanding educators, who were pushed towards a non-academic career when they were at school because they weren't ready at that time, not because they weren't able. So I'm not about to dictate a person's life on the basis of readiness.'

He paused and shifted in his chair, considering his next point.

'At some point you may have to do that, but you certainly don't have to do that when someone's 13. In fact, to me that's almost abuse. It's saying, you know, "you're not going to be able to because you're not smart enough", whereas what we really should be saying is, "you know what, you're not able to right now, but we don't think it's because you can't, we think it's because you're not ready". I have those conversations in this room all the time.'

Bob makes a point about intelligence not being the only trait of relevance in the modern workplace (a point that we will return to), but he makes two more implicit assumptions about intelligence too. One assumption is that intelligence is not a fixed entity, but something that develops (so you might not be ready, but that doesn't mean you are unable). The other is more subtle; in acknowledging that different children are ready at different ages, he is recognising that talents and abilities develop at different rates in different people.

These assumptions about the nature of intelligence are well supported by scientific research. More so, in fact, than the assumptions underlying either the Singaporean system (which is structured around the idea that intelligence is fixed) or the Japanese system (which is structured around the idea that everyone begins equally intellectually capable). I'm not implying Bob's comments represent the views about intelligence held by all Canadians, but the way that education is structured in Canada takes both of these points into account.

Intelligence does develop, even if IQ doesn't (as was discussed in Chapter 7). It doesn't develop in a steady linear fashion – it develops in fits and starts, with children making great progress in one month and then plateauing for the following two, just like children's height develops in growth spurts. As articulated by Janet, the Canadian approach to identifying children who are struggling with reading and catching them up is based on this idea that all children can achieve with the right input. As expressed by Bob in his office, the pan-Canadian decision to delay even setting (let alone streaming) until high school means that no one's options are closed down at a young age due to them not having reached the required stage of development yet.

But the Canadian system recognises and caters for the other half of the story too – not everyone's intelligence develops at the same rate. Some do find learning harder than others. And this is partly heritable, suggesting that some people are born with brains that make academic learning easier, and others with brains that mean they'll have to work extra hard to reach the same level. We've seen that they cater for the latter in the same way that the Finns do – they don't lower the level expected, they support them to meet that challenge with qualified teachers like Janet who give extra time and support to enable them to keep up with their peers. But the Canadians cater to the top end too.

Janet invited me to join her for one of her pull-out groups for children who aren't finding regular classwork that challenging. One of the other teachers told me, 'In primary school we encourage them to help their friends, and this helps them to understand stuff too. But sometimes it can be quite repetitive.' To make sure they have the chance to be stretched too, they are often taken out in small groups to work on additional projects. The class I attended was made up of seven students from different grades, and the students were reporting back on their progress researching a famous Canadian. The older children were delivering short talks to the rest of the group on the best way to go about researching a topic based on what they'd learned through their previous projects – such as which online sources you could trust, and how to use search terms to retrieve relevant results.

This approach of getting the students together with intellectually equal peers and equipping them with the skills and time to follow their interests through independent work is in line with the guidance given for educating gifted children on the British Columbia government website, which is based on feedback from 33 academically-gifted students at Vancouver's University Hill Secondary School. They were asked, 'If we as teachers could provide the very best learning situation for you, what would you have us do?' Common responses included 'Provide independent study opportunities – let us study something we are interested in', and 'Let us work with older kids. We can fit in.'[201]

John Hattie's meta-analyses of research into programmes for 'gifted' students suggest that the most effective form of intervention is acceleration – putting particularly able children into classes with students in the grade above. This approach has an effect size of 0.8 (which is high) when students are compared with others their own age, but no effect compared with the students in their new class – possibly putting them at a disadvantage in important tests later in their school careers. Hattie looked at two types of ability grouping – one in which the gifted children follow a different curriculum specifically designed for them (0.3 – low to medium), and one in which children are selected into different classes where they follow the same curriculum but at different speeds (which I've been calling 'setting' throughout this book). The latter only has an effect size of 0.14 (low) on those in the top set. The other common approach of enrichment classes, as exemplified by Janet's small research group described above, has an average effect size of 0.39 (medium) on the students that take part, although the effectiveness of these programmes varies depending on the experience of the teacher.[202]

The extent to which more able children are given these opportunities, and in what way, differs across provinces in Canada.[203] No provinces make these programmes mandatory, but neither do they forbid their implementation. And while none of the provinces select children into different streams or classes before the age of 14, once they are at high school they make use of the type of 'ability grouping' based on providing some more able children with a different curriculum. Since reading about the negative effects of selection into different schools and classes on equity, I'd been wondering whether it was possible to group students in a way that was to the benefit of everyone, without one group's gain being at the expense of another's. It was a question that had been playing on my mind, and so I was particularly interested to hear about the approach taken in one high school I visited on Vancouver Island, which I learned was typical of many high schools in Canada.

I met Marie in a chemistry lab which was full of stuffed toy moles (I believe in reference to the 'mole', which is a unit of measurement for chemical substances). She'd invited me to watch an Advanced Placement Class of hers, who were working in groups to design their own experiments investigating factors affecting the rate of a reaction. Advanced Placement (AP) classes are for the 'top' students only, allowing teachers to teach more advanced material to those who can handle it, in preparation for university. But rather than dividing students into several sets of different abilities, this was the only 'ability group' they had. There was the AP class, and then there were mixed-ability classes made up of everyone else; no one was placed in a bottom set.

Marie explained to me after class, 'We stream up rather than down. We think a rising tide lifts all boats, but if you stream down, you have students giving up or thinking they're dumb. Some people think this is bad for the other kids who aren't in the top stream, but we find that those kids in the normal set that used to be too scared or slow to put up their hands when the more advanced kids were in the class with them now get more involved.' Food for thought.

Expectations and Accountability

You might be surprised, given what we were saying about the focus on individualisation in Canada, that the performance standards for students are still grade-based (i.e. by the end of Grade 4 pupils should be able to...). This means that up to the age of 14 or 15, everyone in the same grade is working towards the same thing, as they are in Finland, Japan, Singapore (at primary) and Shanghai. This contrasts with the more individual approach used until recently in England: students were judged against performance descriptors, as they were in Canada, but these matched up to 'Levels', which didn't necessarily go hand in hand with school years. You would start at a Level 1 when you started school and, at your own pace, work your way up through the levels as you progressed through the years. Most students were expected to reach Level 4 by the end of primary school, but if you didn't: well, here's where an approach with grade-based expectations (Canada) and individualised expectations ('old' England) differ.

Let's take two identical twins, Conor and Edward, separated at birth and brought up in different continents. Neither have special needs, but nor are they natural academics. Let's say that Conor in Canada is 'not yet within expectations' at the end of primary school (despite the early intervention from qualified teachers). He gets extra ongoing support to help him meet those expectations, but even if he doesn't reach them now, he'll be in the same class as his friends at middle school. He will still be expected to work towards the standards set for the first year of middle school, and be exposed to the same content and teaching, like everyone else, but he will get extra support to help him reach them. When he goes to high school, he might take one less elective subject, allowing him to spend that extra time in the support room to ensure he keeps up with his friends in class. I should add at this point that there is no need to tell Conor that he is 'not yet within expectations' in a certain subject – especially while he is in primary school – but to acknowledge as teachers and parents that he is below where he should be so that he gets sufficient support in keeping up, and doesn't fall further behind.

On the other side of the Atlantic, Edward hasn't got to Level 4 by the end of primary school, despite extra input from teaching assistants. But his secondary schooling experience will be quite different. His secondary school might look at the level he achieved in his end of primary school exams, see that he has achieved a Level 3, and on his first day at his new school, put him in a lower set in a class with other students who are at Level 3. These children will most likely be given easier tasks, rather than extra support to complete the same tasks as their peers. They will cover less content, putting them at a further disadvantage when it comes to exams. And they often will be set lower targets, sometimes visibly marking them out from their friends who managed to score a Level 4 at age 11. A lot less is expected of Edward.

This isn't the fault of identifying students' 'levels' per se, but of using them to project what students are capable of. In one school I used to teach at, the students were given 'target grades' which were based on their level at the end of primary school, and had to stick these on the front of their exercise books. The first lesson of the school year, when the students come back, perhaps thinking they might make a fresh start, children are given a grade to stick on their brand new book before they've even written anything in it. Some students were given 'As', some 'Cs'; I even had one girl whose 'aspirational' target grade was to achieve a D in science. Think of the messaging that's giving to these teenagers – if you try really hard, you could achieve a grade that you've been told in assemblies isn't good enough to help you find fulfilling employment.

Bizarrely, this practice stems from attempts to make the education system in England fairer. Schools in England are judged on their exam results. If their exam results aren't good enough, the school is publicly branded as 'inadequate', and often taken over by new management. The school principal is at risk of losing her job, which as you can imagine, generates a large amount of stress and fear in schools that are at risk of failing, as all but the best principals pass on that stress and fear to the staff. Given that schools are in different settings and have different intakes (some might have students coming in at Level 6, others with many at Level 3), a 'progress' measure was introduced, whereby 'good enough' included having your students make certain amount of progress rather than needing to reach some absolute level. Hence the target grades, which are based on students' previous performance.

While the intentions behind target grades are good – to make 'floor standards' fairer to schools with a more challenging intake – there are all sorts of reasons why they are unhelpful. They lead to lower aspirations for students who begin at a lower starting point, and when shared with students, contribute to the fixed mindset idea that intelligence is something you either have or you don't. Even when shared only with teachers, they affect teachers' expectations of students, which as we saw in the Japan chapter, can have a negative impact on students' prospects. There is no strong evidence that setting goals is helpful at all,[204] and that's when the goals are set by the individual pursuing them, let alone when the goals are imposed by others. So how does Canada get around this tricky issue of holding schools accountable, when they have differing intakes?

Answerability and Responsibility, or Liability and Culpability?

What does accountability actually mean, and why is it necessary? While pondering upon the former question, I right-clicked on 'accountability' in my Word document to look at its synonyms, and four alternatives came up: 'answerability', 'responsibility', 'liability' and 'culpability'. This is rather handy, as they can help me neatly explain the difference between school accountability

in England and the United States, and school accountability in
Finland, Canada, Japan, Singapore and Shanghai.

In all the countries that I've been to on this trip, school
accountability has meant 'answerability' and 'responsibility'; each
head teacher or principal is held responsible for the running of
their school, and has to be able to answer for him or herself in
explaining why they do what they do to their local educational
body. If they don't fulfil their responsibilities, or they can't provide
good reasons or answers for why results are dropping or why
parents are complaining, then they might well lose their job. But if
results are dropping and they demonstrate that they are aware of
it, that they are investigating the causes and that they are putting
into place new programmes or training to help address it, then
they have nothing to fear. More likely, they will be offered support
from experts or other schools in making these changes.

In England and the United States, school accountability too
often means 'culpability' and 'liability'. As I described earlier, if a
school in England falls below a 'floor target' in terms of results,
or if the inspectorate looks around the school and deems it to be
'inadequate' or 'requiring improvement', then the government's
response is to look for someone to blame. At the moment,
schools in such circumstances have their management changed,
and the head teacher is often let go. In some states in US schools
are actually fined for getting poor results. The approach is to
punish those who run the struggling school, rather than to look
into potential causes and solutions, or offer the schools much-
needed support.

Canada takes a different approach. They most definitely hold
schools accountable – you'll remember that many provinces
brought back provincial tests in the 1980s in response to the
claim that they didn't – but these test results are used in quite
a different way to the way they're used south of the border. I
had an extended roundtable discussion (with pizza) in Ontario

with six amazing educators who work at different levels in the provincial education system. One of the teachers described the EQAO (the province's standardised tests) as a snapshot. 'It's a dipstick. I don't think anyone feels threatened by it any more. *Any more.*' She made a face. 'If you had Grade 3 when EQAO came in you died. But people know what it is. It took a while to get to this point, but people now realise that it's not something that reflects on your practice.'

School principals don't hold individual teachers to account for their class results, as 'it's not one person's responsibility, right? The Grade 6 results are the responsibility of teachers in Grades 4, 5 and 6, so that's us as a collective, not each person as an individual teacher.' Instead the results are used formatively, to help the staff as a whole reflect on the school's strengths and weaknesses. 'Standardised testing is not our driver, but it is our driver in a way. We did not do well in Grade 6 this past year and we wanted to know why. So we looked to see where the gaps were, for example, in fractions. What do we need to do as teachers to reduce those gaps?'

It's not just up to the individual schools to improve themselves; in Canada, no school is an island. At the roundtable discussion, I met Lucy, a school superintendent responsible for a family of 18 schools, educating 15,000 students. I was curious about the role of superintendents, so I asked Lucy (in front of the principals and deputies that she works with), 'What would happen if you weren't there?' She replied, 'There would be no one monitoring the schools, and they would be a lot happier!' at which point, everyone laughed.

This wasn't a forced laugh, like a 'ha ha, my boss made a joke' laugh; these educators all seemed really comfortable in one another's company, and when we'd initially arrived there had been hugs and exclamations about how good it was to see Deirdre – their former superintendent who had kindly organised the meeting. Similarly in British Columbia, superintendents and principals appeared to have a fairly informal relationship. For example: I heard one principal say to his superintendent, 'If you've got news for me about a shop [technology] teacher I'm gonna kiss your feet and bring you presents.' Now, I'm sure he wasn't speaking literally, but this is not the kind of relationship you'd expect if superintendents were seen as inspectors who were there to pass judgement on whether the principal was doing his job. Canadian schools aren't formally inspected, although the superintendent role in British Columbia grew out of the 'Inspector of Schools' role when the Schools Inspectorate Branch was dismantled in 1958.[205]

As the current superintendent of the school I visited outside Toronto, Lucy is the representative of a school board (of which there are 72 in Ontario), and it is her job to ensure that schools are following provincial policies, and have those tough conversations with school principals where necessary. Most of her role, though, is more about supporting schools to continually improve, and to learn from one another. She and other superintendents are constantly in schools, talking to principals, watching lessons and observing students. This has quite a different feel to it from a school inspection, because it is regular and informal, and the consequences of them seeing a need for improvement are that they speak with the principal and vice-principal about next steps, and might suggest that they go and visit another school in the family who is dealing well with a similar problem, rather than publically shaming them or cutting their funding.

But what if the school board and superintendents are failing themselves? This is the kind of question that someone with a 'culpability' or 'liability' mindset might ask. Well, they usually aren't failing, because there is thorough training and careful succession planning. Superintendents who are selected for the role are ex-principals who themselves have a successful record in school improvement. Before that, teachers only get to be principals if they've been through a training and selection process run by the board, and have shown that they have been effective as a vice-principal (those at the school board level make a point of developing leadership capacity at all levels of the system). But, in the unusual instance that a school board isn't doing well, as shown by their data, here is what happens (in the words of a superintendent): 'If the board does badly, the ministry would call them in and ask why. The board then has to develop a plan for how to move schools forward. What pieces could we put into place? They'd then put in place those strategies with lots of support, and see what happened the following year, and ask, "is there an improvement?" But it's gradual, no one expects a school to change by 40 per cent in one year. What we do want to show, though, is that we're on a continuous improvement path.'

Chapter 16: Beyond Knowledge

He who studies medicine without books sails an uncharted sea, but
he who studies medicine without patients does not go to sea at all.
Sir William Osler, Canadian physician

Remember Bob, the moustachioed principal? His first point about intelligence – that there are other important traits required for the workplace – is not one that rests on science, but one that rests on common sense. While tests of general cognitive ability are good predictors of overall job performance, very few HR managers would employ someone based on the results of these tests alone.[206] Many jobs require people to work well as part of a team, to present their ideas clearly and confidently, and inspire confidence when leading others to achieve their vision for an organisation. Traits that are often referred to as 21st-century competencies for 21st-century jobs (but that were also required in many jobs before the 21st century) include critical thinking, creativity and effective communication skills.

What's more, students don't only go to school to get jobs. Many would argue that various other traits should be developed by schools to get the children ready to be citizens of whatever country they find themselves in. What these desired traits are depends very much on the culture, and on the views of those in charge. In Japan, for example, students are taught, alongside other characteristics, to get along with others in a group, to follow the rules, to be polite and helpful, and not to be a bother to other people. The four major goals for Canadian education are 'generally defined' as: 'cultivation of mind; vocational preparation; moral development; and individual development'[207]– and in Ontario, the mission statement reads: 'Ontario is committed to the success and well-being of every student and child. Learners in the province's education system will develop the knowledge, skills and characteristics that will lead them to become personally successful, economically productive and actively engaged citizens.'

Of course what governments intend and what they are able to make happen are two entirely different things, but I did see a focus on non-academic skills amongst the teachers I met – alongside more structural features of the system – to an extent that I didn't experience in the other four systems I spent time in.

Other Important Skills

During my drive to school with Marilyn one foggy morning she was telling me about her new Grade 2 class, and dropped in, 'What's a shame, though, is that they're quite weak in leadership skills, we'll need to work on that.' I was surprised – these children were only seven, and she was talking about leadership.

We pulled up outside the red-brick, one-storey building, and I popped in at reception to get a visitor's badge. I followed Marilyn through the colourful corridors to her classroom, and busied myself looking at the impressive displays while she prepared for the day. Sure enough, as soon as the children had hung up their coats, she was creating opportunities in her classroom for these little children to practise leading others. There was a routine they went through every morning, where they would look at the weather and put an appropriate picture on the weather chart, and do the same with the date. Children took it in turns to lead the class in this activity, and say, 'today it is...' for the others on the mat to complete 'Wednesday!'. 'Yesterday it was... ' 'Tuesday!' 'Tomorrow it will be... ' etc. Then they would instruct the class to go back to their desks to begin the day's lesson.

Leadership was a focus at high school too, to the extent that it was an elective subject that students could take, which counted towards their credits for graduation. On the day I went in, they were split into different groups, each working on the organisation of a different event; some were organising a BBQ for the local homeless population, others were organising a school dance (Halloween themed), and others working out the profit made from a previous event they'd sold tickets to. They'd delegate within their groups, they'd do budgeting, they'd speak with relevant people, they'd make posters, they'd follow up; the kind of skills that even some adults I know are lacking.

Martin, who ran the leadership course, set them their tasks and then let them get on with it, so was free to have a chat with me on the green sofa in the corner of the room. 'I had this kid come in, in the ninth grade last year, and she was a real quiet type. Not very confident, she cried when we went on a leadership residential one time because she was homesick. I've really seen her confidence grow this year as she's been involved in organising various events, and she's now taking charge in some groups and leading other less confident kids.'

Apart from a leadership focus, British Columbia has social responsibility performance standards. This doesn't mean that 'social responsibility' is a standalone lesson, rather, these skills and attitudes are supposed to be developed and encouraged through other lessons and activities. I was listening back to a group interview I'd recorded with a group of middle schoolers, and right at the end, just before I switched the tape off, it picked up the teacher saying, 'Thank you for actively listening to each other and showing respect for each other's opinions' – bringing the children's attention to the skills they were practising. Things like, 'Solving problems in peaceful ways' and 'Valuing diversity and defending human rights' are part of the curriculum for all children, and teachers assess how well each child is meeting these objectives.

The difference in approach of the Canadians to these non-academic skills compared to the other countries I visited was not just in the amount they were mentioned, but also in the fact that there was more of an attempt to assess them in Canada. Other things that I saw assessed were presentation skills – when students were feeding back the results of their independent research into the causes of the First World War to the class – and creativity, which was included in a marking metric for how students presented their understanding of Marxist theory.

Just to clarify, I am not pointing out these features of the Canadian system to suggest that they in any way lead to high PISA results – there is more to education than this. Nor am I suggesting that the way the teachers I observed were going about teaching and assessing these non-academic skills is the best way of doing it – I'm afraid that has not been my focus in this book. I do think it is important, though, that these conversations and attempts are happening, and are not getting swallowed up in the quest for higher test scores. It is a sad but unavoidable truth in most developed systems (though Finland seems to be an exception) that unless desired outcomes are measured in some way, they are not prioritised by governments. There are logical reasons for this (I hesitate to use the word 'good'): that when taxpayers' money is spent on public education, they have a right to see that their money is being used effectively. But when important things are left out, we either need to move away from such an audited system, or embrace the attempt to measure these skills so that they don't get sidelined.

Problem-Solving and Discovery Learning

So far the qualities I've discussed – leadership, organisation, presentation skills, valuing diversity – have been non-academic skills and traits. Of course, you can do a presentation about academic things, but you could also present on the time milk came out of your nose, and it would still require the confidence to stand in front of people, some sort of organisation to what you are saying and a clear, measured delivery. There are other skills, though, that are more closely related to academic subjects, but that go beyond knowledge and understanding of subject content; skills that are highly prized by employers and politicians, and have been floated as playing a major role in explaining differences in economic growth between countries: critical thinking and problem-solving skills.

Advocates of the importance of these 21st-century skills point out that the world has changed since education systems were first designed, and that technology is taking over most manual and routine jobs. Consequently, the kind of skills that are needed for employment are those that can't be done by computers, such as solving complex problems as a team; problems which don't have step-by-step method to arriving at a solution, and to which there might be more than one answer.

In recognition of the importance of these skills, there has been a move across Canada since the late 1990s and throughout the 2000s to teach them to children in school. One conversation I had with a school principal reflected many other similar comments in Ontario – 'Our philosophy as educators is that students are talking, communicating with one another, collaborating with one another, that they're working in groups, they're using manipulatives [physical models used in maths], they're taking a real-world problem and working through it. So if they don't understand they can find something to help them understand, they can use those resources.' The philosophy is based on getting students ready for the real world outside of school by giving them the same type of experiences that they may be faced with in the future.

Reflecting this shift in thinking, new curricula have been introduced across several provinces that stress that these skills must be taught in schools. They also stress how these skills should be taught. For example, the 2006 'Common Curriculum Framework for Math' designed by the Western and Northern Canadian Protocol and implemented by Manitoba, Saskatchewan, Alberta, British Columbia, Yukon Territory and Northwest Territories states that '*Learning through problem-solving* should be the focus of mathematics at all grade levels' and 'Problem-solving, reasoning and connections are vital to increasing mathematical fluency, and *must* be integrated throughout the program' (my italics). They later specify that, 'In order for an activity to be problem-solving based, it must ask students to determine a way to get from what is known to what is sought. If students have already been given ways to solve the problem, it is not a problem, but practice.'

This gives the impression that new maths content should not be taught to the students, but rather they should be encouraged to discover the solutions for themselves, based on what they already know. There is also a focus on children then continuing to use personal strategies for solving mathematical problems rather than being taught one correct method, and on a downplaying of learning by rote.

This is not uncontroversial. In fact, I wouldn't be exaggerating if I told you that debates over whether teachers should be guiding students to discover things for themselves or teaching them what they need to know have been happening for centuries over several continents, and have been referred to as wars. Once back from Canada I met Canadian mathematics professor Robert

Craigen at an education conference, and cornered him in the pub afterwards. Over ginger beer, he started telling me about his concerns with discovery-based learning being expounded as the best way to teach maths, and he pointed me to an article written by a colleague of his, Anna Stokke.[208]

Anna makes a very interesting speculation about Canada's maths performance in PISA and TIMSS. She points out that maths scores in Canada have dropped between 2003 and 2012. All but two provinces have shown a significant decline, with Alberta dropping the most by a worrying 36 points (bear in mind that 42 is equivalent to one year's schooling). In TIMSS too, the three provinces that took part all saw a fall in eighth-grade maths scores between 2003 and 2011, with students performing on the fraction questions only slightly better than they would do if they were guessing.

Anna draws attention to the fact that this countrywide decline coincided with the move towards discovery-based curricula, discovery-based textbooks and discovery-based professional development sessions, and through an analysis of the research into the effects of discovery-based learning compared to more traditional approaches, suggests that changing the training and curricula in favour of the latter (though without doing away with the former altogether) would halt the decline in scores.

What does the research in this area suggest? Essentially that problem-based learning,[209] where the new information students receive is through self-direction rather than from teachers, is not as effective at getting children to understand new knowledge and new concepts (I will come to its other effects later on).[210] John Hattie synthesised the results of eight meta-analyses, including 285 studies on the effectiveness of problem-based learning which involved 38,090 children, and found an average effect size of only 0.15.[211] And a recent study by the OECD based on PISA data found that while most teaching strategies have a role to play in the classroom, students in all but one of the top-15-performing countries reported receiving teacher-directed instruction at or more than the OECD average on this measure.[212] What is more, there is also a sound psychological explanation as to why this might be, which is explained in Box 3 in the Japan section (p93).[213]

Despite my initial scepticism, I therefore found Anna's suggestion that a change in pedagogy might halt Canada's PISA decline convincing: the introduction of more discovery maths across Canada correlates with the decline in Canada's math scores; experiments and meta-analyses at a sub-national level find that less guided approaches are not very effective for student learning, and there is an explanation for why this might be.

The case of Quebec clinched it for me. Quebec also introduced a new discovery-based maths curriculum, six years before the provinces in the Western and Northern Canadian Protocol. The impact of this reform on children's scores on a standardised maths test was analysed by economists from Université du Québec à Montréal (UQAM), who found that it had negative effects on students' achievement at all points of the skill distribution: i.e. for children who find maths easy and children who find maths hard.[214] What is more, the negative effects grew the longer the students studied under the new curriculum, and these negative effects were more significant for children at the lower end of the skills distribution. The latter impact may explain why in 2003 – after Quebec had implemented this type of reform but before other provinces had – Quebec had greater variance in maths PISA scores than any other province.

Box 5: Didactique de mathématiques

Although Quebec's TIMSS scores have been declining, they remain high internationally, and both Quebec's maths PISA scores and their TIMSS scores remain higher than any other

Canadian province. In her essay, Anna Stokke points out that unlike every other province in Canada, pre-service elementary and middle-school teachers in Quebec have to complete at least two three-credit-hour maths courses at university, with many completing even more. In Ontario, by contrast, pre-service elementary teachers are recommended to complete a maths course, but it isn't compulsory, leaving them trailing in the wake of Quebec teachers' superior mathematical understanding.

I had a chat with Annie Savard, a mathematics professor from Quebec who is taking part in some exploratory research into differences in pedagogy across the provinces, and she built on this idea. 'There are differences... For me it's training: teacher training. Just to give you an example, Quebec doesn't have Grade 7 and 8; it's Secondary 1 and 2. But in many provinces, Grade 7 and 8 are taught by elementary-school teachers. In Quebec they have expert math teachers, so they have two extra years with strong teachers, which might make them more prepared for this PISA math test. I'm not saying that the others aren't good, or that they aren't doing a good job. I know teachers want to do their best, and do the best for their students. But when teachers don't have the knowledge, you know, you can't.'

While she also believes that Quebec's superior maths performance might be due to teacher training, she went on to make a distinction not only between the quantities of training prospective teachers were getting, but between the types of training they were getting. As part of her research, a small sample of teachers from different provinces were filmed, and then teachers from other provinces watched the videos and discussed their contents. Annie noticed a difference in what was being discussed. Teachers from Quebec focused much more on the mathematics: 'they really talked about the concepts'. She explained that this was because teachers in Quebec get more training in 'didactique'. Annie described this as hard to

232

define, but summarised, 'it is really pedagogy and mathematics together'. Whereas teachers in other provinces get taught pedagogy (how to teach in general) and mathematics (as a subject), in Quebec they have many courses in 'didactique de mathématiques', where they learn to analyse student mistakes and deconstruct each mathematical concept, considerably more so than in other provinces.

In a recent review of research into what makes great teaching (defined in this case as teaching that leads to improved student outcomes), Robert Coe and colleagues from Durham University in England concluded that one of the two most effective features of great teachers sounds very similar to what is known in Quebec as 'didactique': 'As well as a strong understanding of the material being taught, teachers must also understand the ways students think about the content, be able to evaluate the thinking behind students' own methods, and identify students' common misconceptions'.[215] In English, the latter is known as 'pedagogical content knowledge'.[216] Coe and colleagues found strong evidence that this has an impact on student outcomes, adding credence to the idea that the additional teacher training in this area received by Quebec teachers might explain why they get higher maths results than all other provinces.

Pedagogical content knowledge would be a fantastic addition to any teacher's repertoire, whether they were teaching students directly or guiding them to discover it for themselves.

Have I Missed the Point?

I would have missed the point, had I stopped there. I started by talking about the importance of skills such as independent problem-solving and creative thinking, and then I switched to looking at outcomes of traditional academic tests only. But *je ne regrette rien* – it is important I looked at academic outcomes for two reasons. Firstly, this book is about 'top performing' education systems, so the potential causes of significant drops in international test scores are relevant, even if they may appear to some to be unimportant. Secondly, as we saw in the Japan chapter, you can't have advanced problem-solving and critical thinking without good subject knowledge, so the excessive use of any method that is not effective at getting students to understand academic content will reduce the range of topics about which they can think critically and in which they can solve problems.

Do these methods have positive effects on anything else, despite their limited effectiveness at developing children's basic knowledge and understanding? Yes they do, so it would be a waste to drop them completely. Problem-based learning can have a positive effect on deeper knowledge and understanding, *'when students already have the surface level knowledge'*.[217] Once students have been taught the basic content, problem-based methods can then be used to help children deepen their understanding through application. The mistake is to try and get them to learn the content in the first place through problems, as this limits their understanding of even the basics, precluding them from ever getting to the stage where they can apply and solve problems in a particular domain.

Knowing and understanding content is necessary for children to be able to solve problems or think creatively in an area, but it is not sufficient. Surely the case of China and Singapore have shown us that. In the more traditional classrooms in these countries at the secondary level, teaching to the test with little room for questioning or alternative interpretations has led to children having significant knowledge, but also in many cases, a mindset that there is only one right answer. This is not good for the world – all of us need to be able to think critically about issues in ways that acknowledge that not everything is black and white. There is a huge range of teaching practice though between this rigid approach – which surely limits children's creative thinking – and the other extreme of getting the children to discover everything for themselves, without teaching them anything at all.

The practice described in Finland, for example, involves teachers leading class discussions which encourage children to give their opinions, and challenge one another's ideas. In Japanese primary schools, we heard about teachers setting up a real-life problem to engage the students, before teaching them what they needed to know to solve the problem (though not how to solve it), and then letting them try it out in groups. In Singapore, I saw teachers demonstrate an experiment, and then encourage the students (as a class) to come to an explanation of what was going on through intelligent questioning. And in the classrooms I visited in Canada, I saw much more of a combination of teaching approaches in practice than are being encouraged in their curricula. In each of these settings, the learning was highly structured by the teacher, who had a goal in mind of what the students should be learning, and gave the students enough information that they were able to handle the levels of uncertainty they were being presented with. Call this traditional or progressive – it makes no difference to me. Although it may seem counter-intuitive, you don't get to be an independent problem-solver by learning everything independently; but then again, you don't get to be one either if you never get to try problem-solving for yourself.

Of all the countries I visited for this book, Canada would be my choice for where I'd like to send my own children to school. It is far from perfect – the over-emphasis on discovery learning would worry me as a parent as I know it worries some Canadian parents, and some provincial governments are cutting educational funding, which might take away from the things I was so impressed by. But in the main I found the Canadian education system to be one that had a good balance. There was a balance between the teaching of academic content and broader cognitive, social and moral skills and traits. There was a balance between having the same high expectations for all children, and catering for individuals by offering support to the less able and challenge to the more able. And at the level of the school system, there was a balance between holding schools accountable and providing them with the advice and support to improve.

Chapter 17: Five Principles for High-Performing, Equitable Education Systems

One summer evening after an education conference in London, I was enjoying my second glass of Pinot Grigio in a nearby pub garden, catching up on the latest educational goings-on in the UK with similarly keen beans. I saw a man come into the garden with a pint – a friend of a friend who at the time was an advisor to the Secretary of State for Education – and waved my free hand in a greeting. He came over.

'I see you're back from your educational travels, Lucy.'

'I am indeed.' I smiled.

'So, what are the three things that we ought to do in England to improve our education system?'

My smile froze on my face. I'd only recently got back from Canada, and my brain was still processing all the things I'd seen and the conversations I'd had. I hadn't yet consolidated what I'd learned, let alone applied them to the complex and political muddle that is the English education system (I was also one-and-a-half glasses of wine down, on an empty stomach). Yet here was someone with influence asking what I thought.

'Well, I suppose we could start by reducing the number of teacher training providers and ensuring their quality like they did in Finland.' I reasoned.

'No I don't think that would work, we're committed to School Direct and… '

I'm slightly ashamed but also delighted to say that our conversation was interrupted at this point by a friend calling over that she needed a hand carrying the drinks. I was only too happy to oblige.

This book is not about England; it's about education in Finland, Canada, Singapore, Japan and Shanghai. I'm tempted to leave it there – after all, no one knows with any certainty 'what works' in designing quality education (and if they think they do then they are unduly confident). At the level of systems, it is difficult to run controlled experiments; occasionally system leaders make decisions that allow for proper evaluation of education reforms, but often all we have to go on are correlations between particular policies and outcomes, and case studies of systems that appear to be successful. Yet despite all this uncertainty, politicians and system leaders have to keep on making educational decisions. And these decisions are influenced by the beliefs and desires of the society that they represent, and mediated by the beliefs and desires of the teachers that work for them; so to a degree we all have to work with this uncertainty, and do what we think is best, given the available evidence. And so – although I'll not attempt to offer specific policy suggestions for any one country – I won't leave it there. I want to share with you five principles that I believe underlie high-performing, equitable education systems.

The countries I went to are very different places – they vary in size, culture, diversity and history – and yet during the months since I returned home and started working on this book, I've realised that there are some underlying approaches that they have in common.[218] This does not mean they all use the same methods to achieve them – these approaches, or principles, are applied in different ways in different countries, based on the context and politics. In the main they are not specific enough to be empirically tested (few things which are that specific will work across culturally diverse systems), but the types of policies that arise from them are, and I have included links in the footnotes to the high-level evidence on these where it exists. Of course – these principles are those that I believe bring about high performance and equitable outcomes in educating children in the application of maths, reading and science at age 15, and there is more to education than this alone. So after I've shared the five principles with you, I will address a very important question: is the pursuit of high PISA scores through the application of these principles at odds with other important goods in education? But first, let's go back to preschool.

Principle 1: Get Children Ready for Formal Learning

Children come to school at different stages of readiness. In England, children from more advantaged homes already have a head start with their vocabulary, compared to children from homes with fewer books and less conversation.[219] In Finland and China, five-year-olds already have a better mathematical understanding on average than five-year-olds in England (despite the fact that the former have not yet started school).[220]

Common sense might tell us that the best way to help disadvantaged students catch up with their peers, and the best way to help English children catch up with the Finnish and the Chinese, would be to start teaching them to read and to count as early as possible. That might be why there are higher academic expectations of six-year-olds in England than six-year-olds in Finland,[221] and more academically oriented mathematics education for preschoolers in England than in Korea[222] or Japan.[223] America seems to be getting in on the early-academic action too; according to recent research,[224] kindergarten and preschool are becoming more academic and teacher directed, and a quarter of the teachers surveyed reported that there was no time for free play in their kindergarten classrooms.

In this instance, though, 'common sense' is at odds with early-years experts, economic and psychological research, and the practices of top-performing education systems. Early-years education is extremely important, but focusing heavily on specific academic skills at the expense of broader development and child-initiated activity can have long-term negative effects on motivation, social behaviour, emotional health and self-esteem,[225] without having a lasting positive effect on academic outcomes.

While those children who start formal learning early sometimes outperform their later-starting peers in the first few years of school, this difference disappears,[226] and occasionally reverses,[227] by the time the children get to late primary school. Researchers who conducted a study on the differences in mathematical understanding between five-year-olds in England, Finland and China concluded: 'The data also suggest that the approach implemented in English early childhood education at the time of data collection (i.e. focusing on specific number skills quite narrowly) was not necessarily the most beneficial approach for young children's early numeracy skills development in general.'[228]

Children in Finland, Singapore and Shanghai don't start formal schooling until the age of seven, and in Canada and Japan it is six. This means that children are not required to demonstrate specific academic outcomes such as reading or adding before this age, nor are early-years teachers expected to push them to get there, ready or not. By the time these outcomes are expected of the children, most have had the time and input they need to develop the skills, attitudes, knowledge and understanding necessary to achieve them, allowing the class to progress together.

However, children don't necessarily develop these skills and attitudes by themselves, so waiting to start any educational provision at all before age six would be a mistake. Developing accessible high-quality early-years programmes is well worth the investment in the long-term.[229] The most effective programmes seem to be the ones that build motivation and character alongside cognitive skills;[230] where there is a balance between social and cognitive development. And this cognitive development is based on developing children's pre-academic skills, through playful learning.

To prepare children for reading this means building up their vocabulary and knowledge across domains to enable their comprehension, getting them to understand the correspondence between letters and sounds, and familiarising them with the letters of the alphabet through games and songs. There are also two types of pre-mathematical skills which children need before they start learning formal mathematics: relational skills (i.e. classification, comparison, seriation and one-to-one correspondence), and counting skills (i.e. primary understanding of amounts, counting, counting with an understanding of what the numbers correspond to, and counting on).[231] Chinese and Singaporean children are better than English children at both of these,[232] and are taught them in preschool through playful teaching activities (by matching, ordering and comparing different colour toy cars, for example[233]). Japanese teachers also arrange the environment and activities to encourage an interest in quantity and informal mathematics, and Finnish children have exposure to mathematical concepts through play-based activities in preschool too.

Preschool in all of these countries is also used as a time to get children used to being in a social environment, and to develop other important skills that come about through play – self-regulation, planning and language development. The latter is particularly important for the children of immigrant parents, who benefit the most from preschool, but are less likely to attend than their native peers.[234]

Lest 'get children ready for formal learning' be too vague, let me attempt to sum up what I am suggesting so far in a single recommendation:

> *Enhance children's social and pre-academic skills through rich environments and playful learning before age six, rather than requiring specific academic outcomes from them.*

But this is not all that I mean by 'get children ready'. Once they are in school, teachers in East Asia spend a significant amount of time teaching the children routines that allow for smooth transitions between activities, such as handing back books or getting into groups. I saw a great example of this in Canada too. Every morning I spent with Marilyn, the children lined up in the playground at the sound of the bell and stumbled into the classroom. I know how hard it is to get a bunch of seven-year-olds to organise themselves having once covered a Year 3 class in England, and asked them to pack up at the end of the day; there were tears. Not so in Marilyn's class – the children efficiently hung up their coats, unpacked their bags, handed their homework to that day's homework monitor, and sat down unruffled and ready to start the day's learning. This prevents the emotional disturbances that can occur during classroom transitions, and saves precious time during the subsequent weeks, months and years which can instead be spent on the objective at hand, whether that is learning about the kings and queens of England or learning to manage themselves in a group.

Take the time early on to teach children the routines.

To get children ready for learning during the day, throughout primary and lower secondary school, four out of the five systems I studied had 10–15 minute breaks between every lesson, during which the children could let off steam. In contrast to the quiet focus I observed during lessons in Japan and China, I had to step over those same children as they wrestled on the floor during their breaks, seemingly unacknowledged by their teachers (if they were there at all). As well as being good for their social development and reducing cognitive overload, it provided opportunities for physical activity too. In Finland children were outside in all weathers, (a number of Finns told me, 'There is no such thing as bad weather, only unsuitable clothing'), and in China and Singapore they also did their morning exercises to prepare for the day.

Give children (and teachers) a 10–15 minute break between each lesson.

Finally, something that seemed effective at getting children ready for learning in Finland and Canada was the presence of multi-disciplinary teams of professionals on site (though not necessarily full-time in small schools) that would meet to discuss all children (in the case of Finland) or those in need of additional support (in Canada). Teachers and policy makers I spoke to in both places recognised that sometimes social or emotional problems were preventing children from making the most of school, but rather than using this as an excuse, they took the steps (and had the resources) to address these issues, making the most of the skills of the professionals on the team.

Resource schools with access to professionals who can address children's non-academic needs.

Getting these foundations right, with social skills practised, pre-academic skills developed and early issues identified, sets these children up for the rest of their education, and their life.

Principle 2: Design Curricula Concepts for Mastery (and Context for Motivation)

How can George, aged 10, understand what his teacher is telling him about multiplying fractions, if he didn't really 'get' fractions the last time they were taught? And how can Annie, aged 13, retain her childhood fascination with science when she's being taught what an atom is for the third time, since half the class hasn't covered it at primary? Avoiding these kinds of situations is just one of the reasons for having a defined sequence of knowledge and skills children ought to be taught at each grade. In Finland, Japan and Singapore this exists at the national level, and in China and Canada – so much more diverse and distributed – at the level of the province.

Of course, having a national or provincial curriculum is not an unqualified advantage; if it is of poor quality – too full, in an illogical order, overly-prescriptive – it can be harmful to children's learning and teachers' sanity. But if it is carefully designed and of high quality – and aligns with examinations and curricular materials – it can ensure that all children under its remit have access to key content that can help them enrich their lives, and at each stage, that they have an understanding of the concepts without which they cannot address the next topic.[235] So what does this actually look like? I'll admit now that I have not personally pored over curricula from five different countries in four different languages, but some of the features drawn out by educational researchers who have looked at what the curricula of top-performing systems have in common concur with my

244

own conversations and observations in classrooms around the world.[236]

A good national/provincial curriculum should be:

Minimal – Focusing on fewer topics, but in greater depth.
High-level – Clear on what concepts and skills are required, without prescribing context or pedagogy.
Ordered – Organising concepts in a logical order, based on research into how children learn.

This could also form the basis for an excellent school curriculum, in addition to the context-rich schemes of work that would be necessary at this level. But the advantages of having it as a common national or provincial curriculum is that it establishes a curricular entitlement that is not dependent on the individual school;[237] it ensures consistency, allowing for children moving schools, and it even contributes to the equity of a system.[238]

It needn't mean a lack of autonomy for schools either, for two reasons. The national curriculum is not the same as the curriculum; what a school actually teaches is and ought to be so much broader than that which is prescribed[239] – one reason why governments must resist the urge to keep adding more to the national curriculum to align with new initiatives or the demands of pressure groups, and instead leave the inclusion of most additional material to the school (I've lost count of the number of times people who don't work in education have told me that the education system would be so much better if only they would teach 'insert pet interest here').

Secondly, even within the remit of a national curriculum, schools will have autonomy over how this is taught, so long as the national curriculum has stuck to the remit of being high-level and providing concepts but not contexts. A school might have to teach changes of state (the idea that materials change from solid to liquid to gas and back again as the particles they are made up of, gain or lose energy), but whether they choose to use the example of ice cream melting on a hot day, or teach it as part of a unit on what happens inside the local steel plant, is up to the teachers and their assessment of the children's interests.

Adapting provincial curricula content in a way that is motivating for children is something they are particularly good at in Canada – I went to maths lessons involving pumpkins and science lessons in which they grew their own beansprouts in yogurt pots. When a Canadian teacher friend read over my earlier comments on the importance of subject knowledge, she wrote in red pen in the margin, 'it won't stick unless you make it meaningful to their lives' – this is why it's so important for teachers to know the children they teach as individuals. Finland's national curriculum is adapted at two levels; at the level of the local authority teachers from different schools collaborate to create a local curriculum that is relevant to the area, and then this is further adapted in individual schools to make it relevant to the children in their care.

What closes this autonomy down is attaching too much importance to an external test; if this is the case, the freedom to interpret the national curriculum becomes irrelevant, as teachers will teach based on exam syllabi, or past papers. While Shanghai, Japan, Singapore and Finland share the principle of designing curricula concepts for mastery (Canada has too many provinces to say), the ability of their teachers to design the context for motivation varies due to the importance of external tests in their country and at their level of schooling. I wouldn't have had to hear the story about Bird and Frog as many times as I did if questions about Bird and Frog were not in the end of term exam. All children should be entitled to the same important concepts, but for engagement and enjoyment, these ought to be taught in ways that are motivating to the children in question.

Principle 3: Support Children to Take On Challenges, Rather than Making Concessions

If you are just to remember one principle from this book, let it be this one. It applies to parents, to teachers, to school leaders and to system leaders, and its effects can be seen in homes, classrooms, schools and whole countries.

I've talked quite a lot about intelligence during this book, because what we believe about intelligence is fundamental to how we behave when designing and working in educational contexts. Research suggests that intelligence develops over childhood in all but the most severe cases of intellectual disability, and that the speed and ease of development depends partly on genetic factors, and partly on the environment. What with the diminishing number of low-skill jobs due to improvements in technology, this means that it becomes not only possible but desirable to educate almost everyone to higher levels than we have done historically.

Additionally, children's performance at school is highly correlated with their current level of intelligence, but not defined by it – teaching quality, parental support and student effort make a difference too. So even if the above weren't true – even if your genetics entirely determined your intelligence – believing that effort could make a difference to your intelligence and subsequently working hard would still improve your school grades. Thankfully there is no need for this noble lie – the facts and the helpful beliefs match up.

At a system level, how do these countries support their children to take on challenges, and support the idea that intelligence is malleable? Of the five top-performing systems I went to, four of them had common standards that nearly all children were expected to reach, right up until the age of 15. The teachers and the parents supported less able students to reach these standards through additional teaching and tutoring, and through having high expectations of those children – 'I'll help you get there but you've got to put in the effort' – rather than making concessions, saying 'Don't worry, we can't all be good at maths', and sending them to a different school, putting them in a different class, or giving them a different curriculum. There are, of course, some exceptions to this in the case of children with more severe special needs, where parents agree that their children might benefit from more specialist provision, but these cases are based on psychological diagnoses, rather than doing badly in school tests.

As I discovered in Finland, the research on school selection suggests that separating students into different schools at an early age leads to greater inequity and inequality in a system; a larger spread of results, with these results being more heavily determined by parental background (and immigration status[240]). Delaying selection seems to improve the results of lower performers, without disadvantaging high achievers,[241] and in the case of Poland, a delay of school selection by just one year was estimated by the World Bank to have led to gains in PISA scores of over 120 points, which they describe as 'a dramatic improvement, hardly comparable to effects of any known educational policy'.[242]

Delay selecting children into different schools based on ability until age 15 or 16.

Of course, a delay in school selection by itself is not necessarily enough. You can have all students in the same school, but still put them into different classes based on ability, teach them less challenging things and have lower expectations of them. They didn't do this in Finland, Canada, Shanghai or Japan. They had them all together, in mixed-ability classes, attempting the same challenging curriculum, right up until the end of lower secondary school. This works in combination with Principles 1 and 2. Because formal academic requirements only begin once most of the children have the prerequisite skills to meet them, the spread of ability isn't as wide from the beginning, making it easier to bring everyone along with you in a class. And because there is an emphasis on mastery, fewer topics are covered, meaning that everyone has the opportunity to reach at least a minimum standard in their understanding of each topic, and those who pick it up quickly have the opportunity to explore it in greater depth.

Teach children in mixed-ability classes until 15 or 16.

Even then, unhelpful expectations about children's potential can slip in and adversely affect children's opportunities. Sweden, for example, has a comprehensive system and mixed-ability classes, and yet students within these classes choose individualised grade-related study tracks, depending on what grade they are aiming for.[243] Those who choose the 'pass' track are given work that requires only lower-order thinking. The alternative, practised by Singapore (within classes), Canada, Finland, Shanghai and Japan is to expect all students to work towards the same curriculum, which is pitched at a reasonably high level, but alter the amount of help given. In-class differentiation is in the form of extra attention from the teacher or support by more able peers in class, rather than in the long-term outcome expected.

Mainly though, the support offered is through additional one-to-one or small group attention with a teacher. In Finland and Canada these are additional qualified teachers who take students out of class for short periods of time, or help them at lunch or after school. In East Asia it is the subject teacher who makes use of the breaks between lessons and study periods after school, and communicates with the parents to suggest that children then receive further help from them (parents) or tutors after school if necessary.

Although it doesn't happen much in the countries I visited

(Canada being the exception), I think including gifted children in these small groups to extend them beyond the curriculum is only fair as well. These groups can be flexible, with different children receiving support or extension depending on the specific topic, therefore preventing children from developing a fixed mindset (i.e. 'I'm in the gifted group, so I won't take any intellectual risks in case they decide I'm not gifted after all').

Provide small, flexible group support from qualified professionals before/during/after lessons.[244]

Principle 4: Treat Teachers as Professionals

Let's look at what distinguishes jobs that are considered to be professions – doctors, lawyers and accountants – from jobs that are usually not. Entry into any of these professions requires a period of study of at least a few years, in which the prospective doctor/lawyer/accountant begins to become familiar with the body of knowledge with which her chosen profession works. This course is rigorously assessed, and passing it confers recognition upon the mini-professional as a junior member of the profession, registered with the national professional body. At this stage, our junior professional will begin to practise, but their level of responsibility will be limited, and they will be heavily supervised by more senior members of the profession who will guide them in how to get better in their role. They will gradually get more responsibility as they demonstrate their skill, and upon further study and the passing of another exam, they will move up the career ladder and begin to be responsible for the training of those less experienced than them. They are respected for their certified knowledge, as everyone knows how hard the courses are, and reaching the top of the career ladder can bring a substantial salary. As a result, the profession can take their pick of newly-minted graduates.

All of the top-performing systems I visited take a similar approach to teaching, and do most or all of the following: they are selective about who enters their teacher training programmes; their teacher training programmes are hosted in respected institutions and last at least a year; they only confer teacher certification on those who both successfully pass these programmes and an induction period and they ensure teachers are mentored in their first few years and remain in close collaboration with experienced colleagues beyond that through weekly planning sessions. This means they can then give teachers autonomy to get on with their work (supported by further professional development), which makes the profession attractive, and allows the teacher training programmes to be selective. It is a professionalising cycle, and it means that teachers have the three things – mastery, autonomy and relatedness – which enhance intrinsic motivation.

> *Require prospective teachers to undergo a rigorous teacher training programme of at least a year, which is recognised by a professional body and includes the study of pedagogical content knowledge.*

> *Ensure newly-qualified teachers have a reduced teaching load, and time with a dedicated mentor who also has a reduced teaching load. Encourage teachers to plan and evaluate lessons in small teams, so that all teachers are pedagogically supported and learn from one another.*

The alternative approach is to let in anyone who meets minimum standards; to let any institution run teacher training programmes with minimal oversight; to give certification to anyone who ticks all the boxes (or to not require certification at all) and to have little or no formal mentorship or collaboration. The trouble with this is that it then means you'd have to restrict autonomy in order to ensure minimum standards by controlling how these teachers taught, and because this will impact on intrinsic motivation, you might also try raising their performance using bribes or threats. This would make the profession unattractive, which may lead to a teacher shortage, making it very difficult to be selective and lowering the status of the profession further. Those that remained would be overworked and demotivated. I describe this alternative approach as an illustration of the converse of the above, a 'deprofessionalising cycle' if you like; any resemblance to real systems, living or dead, is purely coincidental.

It's all very well describing what these systems do, but what if your education system is stuck in the latter cycle; where is the opportunity to steer it in a more professional direction? Finland went in at step number 2 – they closed down their teacher training colleges and moved all teacher training to eight highly-respected universities. Singapore made their teacher training programmes more attractive by paying for them (along with a stipend), in exchange for a return of service in teaching. In Canada teaching remains attractive because the unions have fought for good pay and conditions (teacher salary is one of the few things that correlate with PISA scores), though this varies between the provinces. China sought to increase the status of teachers in society by developing rigorous qualification requirements, and introducing a teacher career structure.

There are good reasons for requiring teachers to study in universities and pass rigorous training other than the positive effect it can have on the status of the profession: there are actually things that it is useful for them to learn there. It seems crazy that I have to say it, but like any other profession, there (increasingly) exists a body of knowledge, derived from research, that teachers ought to know: child development, cognitive psychology and subject didactics (also known as pedagogical content knowledge).[245] This isn't always taught in initial teacher training courses,[246] which explains why teacher training doesn't have a unanimously positive impact – but when teachers do have this knowledge, it makes a measurable difference to teacher quality.[247] Interestingly but perhaps not surprisingly, some of the teaching practices observed in top performing countries are also the ones supported by research (see Box 6).

Box 6: Effective pedagogy match-up

It's very difficult to draw firm conclusions about the kinds of teaching going on in any country, as the sample sizes of studies and visits investigating them are usually small, and often not randomly selected. But I will tentatively suggest that some of the practices I observed and read about may have contributed to (although on a couple of occasions detracted from) these systems' high scores in international tests. I don't say this based on personal ideas about what 'good' teaching is, but based on the alignment between many of the practices I saw and have written about in this book, and what research has consistently shown to be effective.[244] I include a list of evidence-based practices that are relevant to the descriptions in this book, along with a few that have been shown to be ineffective (which in the main, the countries explored in this book did not do).

Examples of evidence-based practices used by teachers in top-performing systems:

- **Reviewing previous learning:** Review key elements of course content at the beginning of lessons, and after a delay of several weeks or months.
- **Modelling and examples:** Make content explicit through

carefully-paced explanation, modelling and examples. Alternate problems with their solutions provided, and problems that students must solve.

- **Posing probing questions**: Asking students 'why?', 'how?', 'what if?' and 'how do you know?' requires them to clarify and link their knowledge of key ideas.

- **Motivating students**: Students are more motivated if they believe that intelligence and ability can be improved through hard work. Teachers can encourage these beliefs by praising productive student effort and strategies (and other processes under student control) rather than their ability. Students are also more motivated and successful in academic environments when they believe that they belong and are accepted in those environments.

- **Memorisation:** Each subject area has some set of facts that, if committed to long-term memory, aids problem-solving by freeing working memory resources and illuminating contexts in which existing knowledge and skills can be applied. The size and content of this set varies by subject matter.

- **Low-stakes testing**: Teachers can explain to students that trying to remember something makes memory more long-lasting than other forms of studying. Teachers can use low- or no-stakes quizzes in class to do this, and students can use self-tests.

- **Providing feedback**: If teachers provide regular, clear, purposeful feedback to students, which is compatible with students' prior knowledge, it can help students to understand, or develop their own strategies for understanding or mastering the knowledge or skills being taught.

Examples of ineffective practice:

- Praising children for ability

- Leaving learners to discover key ideas for themselves
- Presenting information to learners in their preferred learning style
- Ensuring learners are always active, rather than listening to the teacher

---

Where these countries differ from one another is where and when they require teachers to acquire that knowledge and master the accompanying skills. Finland front-loads its training, with a five-year master's degree required of primary teachers, but this may not suit every country, especially those at a stage where bright young things might not want to commit such a long time training to join what they see to be an unfashionable profession (if they see it as a profession at all). Japan has all its formal certification at the beginning, but has ongoing informal professional development through mentoring and lesson study, and then formal training again before teachers can move into school principal roles. China and Singapore formalise this further, so that although they have a more limited period of initial teacher training than Finland, teachers are expected to develop both their knowledge and skills as they advance through the profession, receiving further certification and responsibilities for developing new teachers as they go up a career ladder of several steps.

For countries stuck in the 'deprofessionalising cycle', a ladder might be just what is needed to get them out, and up onto a route that requires more professional development, but affords teachers more respect.

Principle 5: Combine School Accountability with School Support (Rather Than Sanctions)

I'd be lying if I said I didn't feel particularly strongly about this one. There were many times during my trip where I felt inspired by the sheer good sense of the approaches to school improvement taken by various governments, while at the same time, wanting to cry a little bit about the alternative approach to school improvement taken in my own country (which is to demand that they improve, and if they don't, to change the school's governance and/or management).

The difference isn't in whether or not schools are held accountable. All of the systems I visited required their schools to submit nationally or provincially comparable data to local government, whether based on moderated teacher assessment (Finland), school-based exams (Japan, Shanghai, Singapore), or provincial examinations (Ontario and British Columbia in Canada). At an international level the existence of standardised external examinations is significantly associated with both PISA outcomes and equity in those outcomes (though is obviously not a necessity for these positive effects, as the case of Finland shows), and Singapore and some provinces in Canada also make these results public at the school level. Schools in all the places I went to also have some form of oversight through school visits, although these differ in their frequency and focus. In order to support schools to improve, you need to know which ones need support, and what kind of support they need.

Monitor school performance at a local or national level using school-level data or irregular national assessments.

That is what this information was used for – to support schools. Accountability in these settings means responsibility and answerability, rather than culpability and liability. Let's look at some examples. We discussed the set-up of schools in most provinces in Canada; they are grouped into 'families' under a school board, which employs school superintendents (usually ex-principals). If a school does badly in their provincial exams, the superintendent will sit with the principal, ask them what they think happened, work out with them what steps to take forward, and may link them up with other schools in the 'family' to learn from. Principals from different schools meet regularly to share strategies.

Singapore takes a similar approach – each cluster of schools is overseen by a cluster superintendent, who develops, guides and supervises the school leadership teams to see that they're effectively run, and encourages collaboration between them. In both places though, schools are unlikely to be poorly run in the first place, because the systems invest in leadership training (cf. Principle 4) and succession planning.

Make use of or create a network of successful former school leaders, to visit schools regularly and provide practising school leaders with advice, support and connections.

In Japan, school inspections are made up of five members of the board of education, who are often ex-teachers and principals. Mr Hashimoto told me that in his prefecture, 'they come to school five times over the course of the year, and watch lessons and talk to teachers, and at the end very of the year they make this,' he reached out to the shelf behind him and took down a bound booklet, 'which is the advice and recommendations for the school.' I told Mr Hashimoto that in England inspectors came for just three days and he raised his eyebrows. 'They can't understand a school in three days!'

Another way that Japan, Singapore and Shanghai support weaker schools is by intentionally sending them strong teachers. In Shanghai, this is part of a bigger scheme called 'commissioned administration'. One of the schools I visited there had been very successful at providing a holistic education along with high results in a relatively deprived area, and so was asked by the government to pair up with a weaker school. They were provided with the funding to enable them to send some of their teachers and one senior leader to work alongside the teachers and leaders in the other school, training up the staff and even taking over the management of the school for a little while, before returning to their original school and leaving those they trained to carry on the good work. This was beneficial for the recipient school, which subsequently improved its results dramatically, and for the teachers who were sent over for a while, who got to lead on teacher development.

Incentivise demonstrably good teachers and middle leaders to work in struggling schools, and provide pedagogical leadership to other staff.

There is an alternative logic of school improvement practised in some countries, which is formally called 'administrative accountability', but more commonly known as 'high-stakes' accountability. In these countries, accountability is based on Motivation 2.0 – the carrot and the stick. Mainly the stick. Schools that perform below a certain threshold are threatened with closure, takeover (permanent) or a financial sanction. School leaders are fearful for their jobs, and even if these are safe, they are fearful for their reputations. These schools are usually those doing the hardest work – working with the most disadvantaged communities, sometimes with the least money.

The logic, I believe, is that teachers and school leaders will be motivated to avoid these sanctions, and so work harder, or work differently. But being stressed doesn't help you come up with innovative new solutions that you hadn't thought of previously – it shuts down your creativity. Highly evaluative contexts decrease creative performance.[249] A McKinsey study of top-performing systems quotes an 'Asian system leader' who gave this as a reason for not publishing school-level data: 'Making results public demotivates staff and results in their paralysis... They stop being open to trying and learning new things.'[250] So if you are working harder (if that is possible), you are just doing more of the same, which if it wasn't working in the first place, isn't going to help much.

Alternatively, as suggested above, you might not do more of the same but change your behaviour for the worse, as the policymaker went on to say: 'Instead, they would focus on protecting themselves and finding ways to make their students look good on tests.' Research on high-stakes accountability in the United States and in England has found that it leads to teachers focusing narrowly on complying with policy demands,[251] giving extra attention to certain 'threshold' students at the expense of others,[252] putting low attaining students into special education programmes to exempt them from the tests,[253] and in some cases – to cheating.[254]

What top-performing systems understand is that when schools are underperforming it is often because the teachers within them lack the knowledge, expertise or capacity to make that change, and so they support them in whatever way is required to make the school better for the children. In the unusual situation that a principal is unwilling or unmotivated to change their behaviour then it may involve moving them on, but this is an extreme case, not a general strategy.

All Together Now

Following just one of these principles may help to raise a system's performance, but can be quite difficult in the absence of the others. For example, supporting children to reach minimum common standards is more challenging if these standards are unachievable for many children right from their first term at school, creating a core of students who are behind before they even begin. Treating teachers as professionals may be your intention, and you may get top graduates attracted by the quality of your new training offer, but if you then threaten to shut down their workplace unless they produce the grades, they will leave.

All the parts of a system need to be consistent with each other: even if you have a fantastic central curriculum, carefully designed for mastery of concepts, few will pay any attention to it if there are high-stakes exams which can be aced by rote learning and teaching to the test. The principles above are mutually reinforcing, and though they were addressed in different ways in the different places I visited, they acted together in these systems to bring about high-quality, equitable education in the subjects of maths, reading and science.[255]

In general, it is better to pursue these principles in a way that suits your context, and to take inspiration from the particular methods that other countries have used, rather than copying them outright. One example of this that has proved successful is the use of a 'Maths Mastery' programme by a group of English primary and secondary schools, which is based on the approach to mathematics teaching in Singapore. What distinguishes this from a normal British maths programme is that fewer topics are covered in greater depth (Principle 2), every child is expected to reach a certain level before the class move on (Principle 3), it is accompanied by a professional development programme for teachers (Principle 4) and the sharing of best practice amongst a network of schools (Principle 5).

Two British researchers carried out a randomised control trial (the gold standard of research methods) evaluating the impact of this programme in 87 primary schools and 50 secondary schools after one year, and found that it had a modest but significantly positive effect, which they estimate would lead to non-trivial economic returns (i.e. its effects would lead to lifetime earnings significantly outweighing the cost of the programme).[256]

But what if you don't care about economic returns? What about everything else? Education is about more than just maths after all. Are these principles at odds with other important things? In the next chapter, we will consider whether these approaches necessitate trade-offs.

Principles underlying high performance and equity

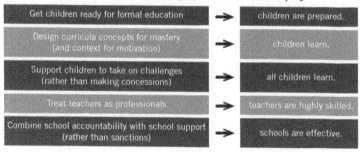

Get children ready for formal education	children are prepared.
Design curricula concepts for mastery (and context for motivation)	children learn.
Support children to take on challenges (rather than making concessions)	all children learn.
Treat teachers as professionals	teachers are highly skilled.
Combine school accountability with school support (rather than sanctions)	schools are effective.

Chapter 18: Trade-Offs?

I don't have children yet. But I've been imagining all the way around the world whether I'd like to send my future children to the schools that I visited, to be educated in these high-achieving systems.

I'd like my children to be excellent readers and solid mathematicians, just like the vast majority of American parents said they did in a recent national survey.[257] I want them to have a good understanding of science too (I'd be embarrassed if they didn't given that I was a science teacher), but I don't know if I want them to be doctors, lawyers or engineers like 38 per cent of parents in a worldwide survey did[258] – I've not even met them yet. So far, all of this is consistent with the five principles underlying the education systems of our five top-performing countries.

I'd also like them to have a broader education. They may not be good at art or dance if talent in those subjects has anything to do with genetics, but I'd like them to throw themselves into the creative arts, and learn to express themselves through these mediums. I'd like them to come home from school covered in mud from a rugby game, or stinking of BO after their basketball match, and I wouldn't mind if they came home a bit late to accomplish that. I'd also like their school to encourage them to think about their community, their society and their role within it, and for them to be held to high standards of moral conduct. None of these things are ruled out by sending them to a school in a system that gets high PISA scores.

Children in Canada, Finland and Japan spend less time per week than the average OECD country does on maths, science and language-of-instruction lessons, leaving ample time for other things. Children in Shanghai and Singapore do spend more time in these subjects than the OECD average, but in Shanghai it's only six minutes weekly more than American students, and 25 minutes more than British students – not enough to significantly narrow the rest of the curriculum. Even at junior high level, when Chinese students are preparing for their high school entrance exams, they have lessons in politics, Chinese, maths, a foreign language, history, geography, physics, chemistry, biology, physical education, music, art and household skills. And I'd be particularly pleased about my children learning that last one.

What are the trade-offs then? Are these systems getting these high results without having to compromise on anything at all? If other systems were to apply the principles outlined in the last chapter, their PISA scores might rise, but at what cost?

Jobs and Vocational Education

You're 14, you struggle at maths, and there's no way you want to stay in school past 15 or 16 to do anything that requires sitting at a desk – which has been the only option 'marketed' to you by your teachers. You're therefore not that fussed about doing your homework, or paying attention in class. If, on the other hand, there was a well-regarded vocational institution not that far away from your auntie's place that taught car mechanics, which is what you've always wanted to do, but that only lets you in with a minimum grade in maths and English and a decent report from your teachers, well, you'll try considerably harder.

Having high-quality vocational training available has obvious advantages beyond giving those who don't want to continue with academia a reason to study. Employability is the one that will no doubt spring first to your mind, but there is a less functional, more fundamental reason why governments ought to invest in this too: education should be for all. It shouldn't be a ladder to university, with those who can't or don't want to get there falling off at different rungs onto the pavement of unemployment; it should be a tree, with a trunk of essential knowledge leading to various, valued branches of specialisms, encompassing the full range of potential vocations.

As previously argued, I don't think that trunk should split off into different branches until children are about 15, for two reasons. In the 21st century, jobs increasingly require employees to be more educated. Whereas a primary-school education might have been enough for the loggers and factory workers of the 20th century, their grandchildren require more cognitive skills to do the jobs that have not been replaced by machines, and deserve to experience the fruits of education just like everyone else. Secondly, splitting into different routes before this increases the impact of parental background on test scores, which is fine if your parents are doctors, but unfairly limits your options if your parents are uneducated, unemployed, or absent all together. Leaving selection into academic and vocational tracks until after lower secondary school is also not at odds with better employment outcomes.[259]

Beyond 15, Finland, Japan, Shanghai and Singapore have separate vocational schools, which specialise in various forms of technical and vocational education. In Finland and Singapore, these can subsequently lead to tertiary-level education, and in both countries, some children who would qualify for academic high schools choose instead to go to the technical institutes – a sign that attitudes towards them are changing. In most provinces in Canada, children can also go to high schools that provide both academic and vocational education, allowing them to combine courses from both before deciding what to specialise in beyond high school. This trip broadened my ambitions for an education system – rather than solely focusing on getting students from poor backgrounds into university, we should ensure we provide excellent educational opportunities for those who choose not to go, whatever background they're from. Thankfully, high-quality academic outcomes in a system are not at odds with the provision of high quality vocational education – if anything they complement one another.

Enjoyment of School and Learning

There is a widely held belief in the West that in East Asia students are high-performing but miserable, all enjoyment of learning drilled out of them by boring teachers and constant testing. I hope I've shown you that it's a bit more complex than that. Students in Singapore, Shanghai and Japan are under a lot of pressure, but they are not all miserable; in fact, many of them actually enjoy school, and are more interested in their school subjects than Brits or Americans. The results of questionnaires that were given to students along with the PISA test help to illustrate this, as they asked them some interesting questions on their feelings about school.

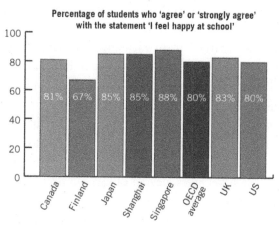

Figure 5: Student-reported happiness[265]

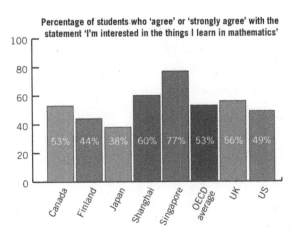

Percentage of students who 'agree' or 'strongly agree' with the statement 'I'm interested in the things I learn in mathematics'

Figure 6: Student-reported interest in mathematics[266]

You can see that students in Shanghai, Singapore and Japan actually report enjoying school more than students in Canada, Finland, the UK and the US (although Korea – another high-performing Asian country, lands right at the bottom of this chart). Having a high-performing education system neither precludes children from enjoying school, but (as the case of Finland indicates) nor does it guarantee it.

It is a similar story with intrinsic motivation; more Shanghainese and Singaporeans said they were interested in the things they learned in mathematics than any of the other countries looked at in this book. You'll remember the two suggested reasons for this as discussed when we were in China: that students there have internalised the importance of education, so are working hard of their own volition, and that mastering a topic or a subject leads to its own intrinsic enjoyment. Our stereotypes about Asian education systems are misinformed; they are not all exam hellholes, devoid of joy and deep learning, and nor are they all the same.

Nevertheless, there is self-evidently a lot of pressure put on children in these countries; parents I met in Singapore and

Shanghai lamented that their children had to study so hard, and saw it as a necessary evil given the education system they were a part of. I wonder whether a high number of children in Shanghai and Singapore find school relatively enjoyable because it is more fun than what they are doing when they're not at school – studying (and conversely perhaps Finnish children rate school as relatively less enjoyable because when they're not there they're playing in the woods). Here is one trade-off between high performance and something else we value. Having an education system with key exams that have high stakes for the pupils (like the *gaokao* in China, or the PLSE in Singapore) was not one of the principles I drew upon to illustrate the key features of high-performing systems, because it was not common to Finland and Canada. However, this pressure no doubt contributes to parents' tendency to seek out extra homework and extra tuition for their children, and subsequently raises both their scores and their stress levels. It is no surprise then that East Asian jurisdictions dominate the top of the PISA tables.

What if the government of a non-Asian country was willing to put the children in their care under this much pressure, in order to 'beat the Chinese'? They can certainly try, but it's unlikely to be worth the hassle. Most of the pressure in East Asian countries comes from the parents' response to these exams; they hold academic education in high regard, they recognise the long-term impact of their children's exam performance, and are typically competitive. Unless you can somehow get the parents in your country to think like this too, and to take leave from their jobs to privately coach their children in big exam years, you won't be catching up any time soon.

I do think that cultures can change, but it might be more productive to focus on changing the culture within schools rather than changing the values and behaviours of all the adults that have chosen to reproduce. This will limit non-Asian nations' ability to reach the top of the PISA charts, but I don't personally think this is a problem. Much better to focus on changing the things you can change, reach the PISA top 15 perhaps, and then focus on growing your nation's talent in the things that the Chinese aren't winning at (yet).

21st-Century Skills

With the exception of expertise in the most recent information technology, '21st-century skills' existed well before the 21st century. Skills often referred to under this label include problem-solving, critical thinking, communication, and creativity; skills that our ancestors have been making use of for centuries. There has been a renewed focus on these skills more recently because a greater proportion of the jobs of the present and the future rely on them – and to a greater degree – than they ever did before.

I'm not going to attempt to go into any detail about how education systems should best address the teaching of these skills – that is not the subject of this book – but I will address the question of whether the approaches to high-performing education systems suggested in the previous chapter are at odds with their development. Is there a trade-off between high-quality academic outcomes and 21st-century skills? Some people have suggested that there is – they see the high performances of the East Asian countries, and the fact that their own governments have been lamenting the lack of creativity and critical thinking amongst their young people, and they assume that the same things that lead to their high performance are the cause of these concerns. There is some truth in this, but I don't believe it's the whole picture.

The same feature of these systems that puts children under great pressure is the one that stifles creativity and critical thinking – the high-stakes exam culture. In such a culture, where a few exams can have such a dramatic effect on your educational opportunities and subsequent job prospects, there isn't much space for alternative answers that are not on the mark scheme. While for mathematics, and to some extent science, this is less of a problem (I have to agree with Rony that while it is good to find different ways of reaching the answer, getting answers wrong in maths is not 'creative'), educating for standardised tests in language, literature, history and politics discourages divergent and critical thinking, and encourages teaching children the mark scheme. Combine this with learning in countries where the governments are wary of criticism (Singapore and China) or where conformity is prized (Japan) and there is even less incentive for teachers to encourage children to think outside the box.

This is not an inevitable consequence of having standardised tests – only of aligning incentives for teachers and students to focus on the tests exclusively, at the expense of deeper, broader or more applied learning. Both Shanghai and Singapore are attempting to move away from this exclusive focus, and have adapted their curricula to encourage more focus within lessons on the children applying what they learn and discussing what they think about it. A common mantra in Shanghai is now 'to every question there should be more than a single answer'. Singapore and Japan both made a decision to cut down on the content in their curricula to make time for this kind of learning. Japan also tried to encourage more 21st-century skills by introducing separate inter-curricular lessons more than a decade ago.

Whether teachers actually follow any of this guidance though, when the high-stakes tests remain, is the crucial question. Several teachers I spoke with in Singapore and Shanghai told me that what they really needed to focus on was preparing students for the test, as that is what the parents know and care most about – something the respective governments are battling to address. In

Japan, research on the 'relaxed education' curriculum suggested that while primary teachers embraced it (possibly enabled by the lack of primary-school exams), teachers at junior high school and high school got away with doing as little of it as they could.

With a complete absence of national exams in primary and junior high school, Finnish teachers have the freedom to teach and assess in a way that they think best meets the demands of the curriculum and the needs of their children. Canadian provinces offer an example of a balanced use of standardised testing – irregular provincial tests at elementary and middle school that have no impact on the children but act as a 'dip stick' to see how schools are doing and where they need intervention and support, and then yearly provincial exams in high school, which make up the credits for about half of each student's school leaving certificate, along with teacher-graded courses. This leaves space for teaching beyond the test, and for more nuanced assessment of skills that can take place over a longer period of time.

An Enhancement, Not a Replacement

Japan put the brakes on its 'relaxed education' when it noticed that its PISA results were going down, re-introduced material that it had formerly cut out of the curriculum and reintroduced Saturday schools. Is there a trade-off between international test scores and 21st-century skills? It appears to me that there might be a quantitative one. In any school year there is a finite amount of time; the number of hours spent on learning and understanding new content is in direct competition with the number of hours spent applying, thinking critically about, and working creatively with that content.

This can all be happening within the same lessons, with one type of learning leading on seamlessly from the other, but both take up time. Writing an extended essay that requires you to make the case for your own interpretation of who was to blame for the Cold War, based on a thorough understanding of the events at the time and a discussion of secondary sources, takes significantly longer than learning those facts by heart, and learning what points to make in an exam essay. Using what you've just learned about heat transfer to design a super-cool lunch box or explain to your classmates how double-glazing works takes longer than learning definitions of different types of conduction. In each of these cases, 21st-century skills are developed by expanding the time on each topic and deepening the learning through creative or critical application.

There are a couple of seemingly clever solutions to this time trade-off. One is to dismiss the need for knowledge all together, and just focus on teaching the skills – after all, if I want to know anything I can look it up on Google. Unfortunately, this wouldn't work, because skills such as problem-solving, critical thinking and creativity rely on domain-specific knowledge to be of any use. If I'm able to think critically about education systems, it's largely because I know a lot about them. I couldn't contribute any intelligent comment however on a debate about whether or not Scotland should become independent from the UK, because I don't know enough about economics, or Scotland. My partner is a doctor and can solve many medical problems, but he won't be the first person I go to when I need help with marketing this book, because he doesn't know much about the book industry, or marketing.

These skills need to be taught through subject content in order for students to actually be able to problem solve or think creatively about anything; attempting to teach thinking skills without a strong base of factual knowledge does not promote transfer to new situations or problem-solving ability.[260] To the extent that features of problem-solving,[261] self-regulation strategies[262] or creativity[263] can be taught as heuristics or strategies

271

to use when working with already available knowledge, they are best taught directly by a teacher with a chance to then practise in a particular domain, rather than by putting students in situations where they are required, and hoping they develop. This does not mean that topics cannot be introduced through presenting an interesting problem to be solved, as they are in many primary schools in Japan, but that students require sufficient knowledge to solve most problems, and will therefore most likely benefit from some teacher instruction in order to solve it.

Another idea to overcome this time trade-off would be to accept that we want our children to both know and understand things, and to be able to be creative, think critically and solve problems in these areas, and so decide that an effective way of doing both would be to teach the content through the use of these skills: to teach maths through problem-solving for example, or to teach history through critical thinking. This would be a qualitative change in the way the academic concepts are taught, rather than just a quantitative change in how much time is spent on teaching each concept or idea, and would be a step change away from how subjects are being taught in Singapore, Shanghai, Japan, Finland and some of Canada. Is this more effective at teaching children concepts or skills?

It might save time compared to teaching the concepts first and then using them, but it is a false economy, because children don't learn the concepts as well this way.[264] Due to limitations in working memory (recall the dog stealing the ingredients from the kitchen counter), children find it difficult to discover concepts for themselves without having a secure understanding of the relevant concepts first. It is essential that they realise things for themselves, and have that light bulb moment, but this is best brought about in a lesson that is heavily structured by the teacher, in which she builds up students' knowledge and understanding through clear explanations, open questioning, and modelling. Only when they've understood a concept can they think critically about it, make use of it to solve problems and be creative with it.

Rather than attempting to teach maths through problem-solving, you can teach problem-solving through maths. Rather than attempting to teach history through critical thinking, you can teach critical thinking through history. The only trade-off between educating for conceptual understanding and educating for 21st-century skills is how many concepts you can cover. Learning concepts deeply doesn't take away from the skills our children need, it enhances them, just as subsequently applying these skills enhances children's understanding of the concepts.

Last Word

When I decided, at age 20, that I wanted to work in education, it was because I couldn't think of anything else that I thought was more important. Ten years later, that ideological belief has both grown and matured into something more tangible, first through my experiences as a teacher, and then through my encounters with children and young people in five different education systems.

Education has the ability to nurture talent, inspire passions, increase social mobility and provide a framework for the adults of tomorrow to develop into knowledgeable, creative, community-minded citizens. Education systems are also just as capable of demotivating students and teachers, limiting the life chances of certain individuals and amplifying pre-existing social inequality. This book was not written as a 'How-To' guide for developing the perfect system, but I hope that by exploring the approaches and policies employed by some of the world's top-performing education systems, I have helped you come to a fuller understanding of what might work in your own. And lest you lament that it's all about the culture, remember this. Finnish teachers haven't always believed that all children can be educated to a higher academic level; the culture of the 'old system' took a while to disappear. Japanese parents haven't always considered education to be important; when compulsory education was first introduced it was a challenge to get children to attend school. And Singaporean graduates haven't always considered teaching to be an attractive profession; back in the 1980s there was a shortage which necessitated the employment of teachers from overseas. To attribute these countries' enviable outcomes to culture and therefore dismiss their value as models would be a grave mistake. Culture can change. And it is schools and school systems that have the power to change it.

Endnotes

1 Charlemagne. Some remedial lessons are needed for European leaders. 2006. Available at: www.economist.com/node/5655172

2 *New York Times*; 6th December 2000; Available at: www.nytimes. com/2000/12/06/us/worldwide-survey-finds-us-students-are-not-keeping-up. html; Date accessed: 27th May 2016.

3 Coughlan S. Pisa tests: UK stagnates as Shanghai tops league table. 2013. Available at: www.bbc.co.uk/news/education-25187997

4 Bita N. PISA report finds Australian teenagers education worse than 10 years ago. 2013. Available at: www.news.com.au/national/pisa-report-finds-australian-teenagers-education-worse-than-10-years-ago/story-fncynjr2-1226774541525

5 Sjøberg S. PISA, politics, problems. Recherches en Education 2012;14(4):1–21.

6 Helsingin Sanomat. As translated in: Chung J. *An Investigation of Reasons for Finland's Success in PISA*. PhD thesis. University of Oxford. Oxford, 2001.

7 Mahoney J. Canadians ace science test. 2007. Available at: www. theglobeandmail.com/news/national/canadians-ace-science-test/ article18150672

8 The eighth grade sample is defined as: 'All students enrolled in the grade that represents eight years of schooling counting from the first year of ISCED Level 1 (beginning of formal education), providing the mean age at the time of testing is at least 13.5 years.'

9 Bergesen OH. *Kampen om Kunnskapsskolen*. Oslo: Universitetsforlaget, 2006. As translated in Sjøberg (2012).

10 Thrupp M. When PISA meets politics – a lesson from New Zealand. 2014. Available at: theconversation.com/when-pisa-meets-politics-a-lesson-from-new-zealand-26539

11 In case you worry that this is what I've done, please be reassured that I changed this whole section just one week before my final draft was due in, in response to coming across some convincing evidence that did not support what I'd previously said. I've taken the same approach across the book.

12 Barber, M., Donnelly, K., & Rizvi, S. (2012). Oceans of innovation: the Atlantic, the Pacific, global leadership and the future of education. Institute of Public Policy Research.

Barber, M., & Mourshed, M. (2007). How the world's best-performing schools systems come out on top. McKinsey & Company.

Mourshed, M., Chijioke, C., & Barber, M. (2010). How the world's most improved school systems keep getting better. McKinsey.

Organisation for Economic Co-operation and Development (OECD). (2013). Strong performers and successful reformers in education: lessons from PISA 2012 for the United States. OECD, Paris, France.

Stewart, V. (2012). A world-class education: Learning from international models of excellence and innovation. ASCD.

Tucker, M. S. (2011). Surpassing Shanghai: An agenda for American education built on the world's leading systems. Cambridge, MA: Harvard Education

Press.

13 An exception to this is Amada Ripley's engaging book on the experiences of American exchange students in schools in Finland, Korea and Poland:Ripley, A. (2013). The smartest kids in the world: And how they got that way. Simon and Schuster.

14 For more information on my methodology, go to my website: www.lucycrehan.com.

15 OECD. *Learning Beyond Fifteen: Ten Years After PISA*. Paris: Organization for Economic Co-operation and Development (OECD), 2014.

16 Whitebread D. *The Importance of Play*. London: University of Cambridge, 2012.

17 Kupiainen S, Hautamäki J, Karjalainen T. *The Finnish Education System and PISA*. Helsinki: Ministry of Education Publications, Helsinki University Print, 2012.

18 Antigua and Barbuda, The Bahamas, Barbados, Bermuda, Cayman Islands, Dominica, Grenada, Malta, Mauritius, Samoa, St Kitts and Nevis, St Lucia, St Vincent and the Grenadines, Tonga, Trinidad and Tobago.

19 Suggate S. School entry age and reading achievement in the 2006 Programme for International Student Assessment (PISA). *International Journal of Educational Research* 2009;48:151–61.

20 McGuinness C, Sproule L, Bojke C, Trew K and Walsh G. Impact of a play-based curriculum in the first two years of primary school: literacy and numeracy outcomes over seven years. *British Educational Research Journal* 2014;40(5):772–95.
Schmerkotte H. Ergebnisse eines Vergleichs von Modellkindergarten und Vorklassen in Nordrhein-Westfalen. Results from a comparison of typical kindergartens and preschools in North Rhine-Westphalia. *Bildung und Erziehung* 1978;31:401–11.
Marcon R. Moving up the grades; relationship between pre-school model and later school success. *Early Childhood Research and Practice* 2002;4(1):517–30.

21 Prais SJ. School-readiness, whole-class teaching and pupils' mathematical attainments. *Discussion Paper No.111*. London: National Institute of Economic and Social Research, 1997.
Kavkler M, Tancig S, Magajna L, Aubrey C. Getting it right from the start? The influence of early school entry on later achievements in mathematics. *European Early Childhood Education Research Journal* 2000;8(1):75–93.

22 Suggate S, Schaughency E, Reese E. Children learning to read later catch up to children reading earlier. *Early Childhood Research Quarterly* 2013;28:33–48.

23 My scepticism never leaves me completely – it's dangerous to be too convinced of anything in a field this complex.

24 Dee, TS, Sievertsen, HH. *The Gift of Time? School Starting Age and Mental Health*. 2015. Available at: www.nber.org/papers/w21610

25 Black S, Devereux P, Salvanes K. Too young to leave the nest? The effects of school starting age. *The Review of Economics and Statistics* 2011;93(2):455–67.

26 DfES/Institute of Education. The effective provision of pre-school education (EPPE). *Project: Technical Paper 12 – The final report: effective pre-school education*. London: University of London, 2004.

27 OECD. PISA 2012: *Key Results in Focus*. France: OECD Publishing, 2012.

28 Save the Children. *Early Language Development and Children's Primary School Attainment in English and Maths.* Save the Children, 2016.

29 National Audit Office. *A Literature Review of the Impact of Early Years Provision on Young Children, with Emphasis Given to Children from Disadvantaged Backgrounds.* London: National Audit Office, 2004.

30 Sylva, et al. (2004).

31 Melhuish (2004). Melhuish does not define what is meant by 'developmentally appropriate', but recent research has shown that the key factor in determining whether a child is ready for a particular activity is not their age (as children develop at different rates) but whether or not they have mastered the prerequisites for that activity.

32 Suggate S. The parable of the slower and the long-term effects of early reading. *European Early Childhood Education Research Journal* 2015;23(4):524–44.

33 Goswami U, Bryant P. *Children's Cognitive Development and Learning.* Cambridge: University of Cambridge Faculty of Education, 2007. Available at: http://cprtrust.org.uk/wp-content/uploads/2014/06/research-survey-2-1a.pdf

34 Sylva, K, Nabuco, ME. Research on quality in the curriculum. International Journal of Early Childhood 1996;28(2):1–6.
Elkind D, Whitehurst G. Young Einsteins. Much too early: much too late. *Education Matters* 2001;1(2):8–21.
See also Spinath and Spinath (2005) and Jacobs, et al. (2002) who show that children's perceived self-competence affects their learning motivation.
Spinath B, Spinath FM. Longitudinal analysis of the link between learning motivation and competence beliefs among elementary school children. *Learning and Instruction* 2005;15(2):87–102.
Jacobs JE, Lanza S, Osgood DW, et al. Changes in children's self-competence and values: Gender and domain differences across grades one through twelve. *Child Development* 2002;73:509–27.

35 *All Work and No Play?* Presented at: Hay Festival, Hay-on-Wye, 27 May 2016.

36 Kiiveri K, Määttä K. Children's opinions about learning to read. *Early Child Development and Care* 2012;182(6):755–69.

37 Leppanen U, Niemi P, Aunola K, Nurmi JE. Development of reading skills among preschool and primary school pupils. *Reading Research Quarterly* 2004;39:72–93.

38 *Ibid.*

39 Suggate (2009)

40 Chung J. *An Investigation of Reasons for Finland's Success in PISA.* PhD thesis. University of Oxford. Oxford, 2001.

41 Ministry of Justice. Greater focus on education in youth estate. 2013. Available at: www.gov.uk/government/news/greater-focus-on-education-in-youth-estate

42 Begin to Read. Literacy statistics. Available at: www.begintoread.com/research/literacystatistics.html

43 Hanushek E, Woßmann L. Does educational tracking affect performance and inequality differences in evidence across countries. *Economic Journal* 2006;116:63–76.

44 Woessmann L. International evidence on school tracking: a review. CESifo DICE report in: *Journal for Institutional Comparisons* 2009;7(1):26–34. The UK is not included as it did not enter both of these tests

45 Woessmann L, Luedemann E, Schuetz G, West, M. *School Accountability, Autonomy and Choice around the World*. Cheltenham: Edward Elgar, 2009.

46 Horn D. *Age of Selection Counts: A Cross-Country Comparison of Educational Institutions*. Mannheim: Unniversität Mannheim, 2008. Available at: www.mzes.uni-mannheim.de/publications/wp/wp-107.pdf
Duru-Bellat M, Suchaut B. Organisation and context, efficiency and equity of educational systems: What PISA tells us. *European Educational Research Journal* 2005;4(3):181–94.

47 Solsten E, Meditz S. *Finland: A Country Study*. Washington: Government Publishing Office for the Library of Congress, 1988.

48 Schuetz G, Ursprung H, Woessmann L. Education Policy and Equality of Opportunity. *Kyklos* 2008;61(2):279–308.

49 OECD. *Reviews of National Policies for Education*: Lithuania. Paris: OECD Publishing, 2002
OECD. *The Impact of the 1999 Education Reform in Poland*. Paris: OECD Publishing, 2011.

50 Kerr S, Pekkarinen T, Uusitalo R. School tracking and development of cognitive skills. *Journal of Labour Economics* 2013;31:577–602.

51 Both John Hattie and the Education Endowment Foundation provide summaries of this research. Hattie J. *Visible Learning: A Synthesis of over 800 Meta-analyses Relating to Achievement*. New York: Routledge, 2008.
Higgins S, Katsipataki M, Kokotsaki D, Coleman R, Major LE, Coe R. *The Sutton Trust-Education Endowment Foundation Teaching and Learning Toolkit*. London: Education Endowment Foundation, 2013.

52 Aho E, Pitkänen K, Sahlberg P. *Policy Development and Reform Principles of Basic and Secondary Education in Finland since 1968*. Washington: World Bank, 2006..

53 Pink DH. *Drive: The Surprising Truth About What Motivates Us*. New York: Riverhead Books, 2009.

54 Deci EL, Ryan RM. The 'what' and 'why' of goal pursuits: Human needs and the self-determination of behaviour. *Psychological Inquiry* 2000;11:319–38.
Deci EL, Ryan RM. Facilitating optimal motivation and psychological well-being across life's domains. *Canadian Psychology* 2008;49:14–23.

55 Grant AM. Relational job design and the motivation to make a prosocial difference. *Academy of Management Review* 2007;32:393–417.

56 Strictly speaking, this addition is not something that contributes to intrinsic motivation, but does contribute to internal (as opposed to external) motivation. These distinctions will be addressed in the Singapore section.

57 Menzies L, Parameshwaran M. Why Teach? Available at: www.lkmco.org/why-teach; 2015.

58 Varkey GEMS Foundation (2013). *Global Teacher Status Index*. London: Varkey Foundation, 2013. Available at: www.varkeyfoundation.org/sites/default/files/documents/2013GlobalTeacherStatusIndex.pdf

59 According to some data which is somewhat contested (Altinok. *An international perspective on trends in the quality of learning achievement*. Paris: UNESCO, 1965–2007.), Finland's international test results began improving in the mid-1960s. This is a decade before teacher training in Finland was moved from colleges to the universities as a master's-level profession in the mid-1970s. However, they did then continue to improve for 30 years,

leaving open the possibility that the newly trained graduates contributed to this continuing improvement.

60 Izadi R. *The impact of school closures on student achievement – evidence from rural Finland.* Helsinki: VATT Institute for Economic Research, 2015.

61 Autti O. *The Role of Small Primary Schools in Rural Communities.* European Conference on Educational Research, 2011.

62 Leanna CR. The missing link in school reform. *Stanford Social Innovation Review.* Stanford: Stanford University, 2011. Available at: www2.ed.gov/programs/slcp/2011progdirmtg/mislinkinrfm.pdf

63 Sahlberg P. The most wanted: Teachers and teacher education in Finland. In Lieberman A, Darling-Hammond L (eds.), *Teacher Education Around the World: Changing Policies and Practices.* New York: Routledge, 2012;1–21.

64 Norris N, Asplund R, MacDonald B, Schostak J, Zamorski B. *An Independent Evaluation of Comprehensive Curriculum Reform in Finland.* Helsinki: National Board of Education, 1996; p29.

65 Savola L. Comparison of the classroom practices of Finnish and Icelandic mathematics teachers. *Journal of Mathematics Education at Teachers College* 2010;7–13.

66 Sahlberg P. *Finnish Lessons 2.0: What Can the World Learn From Educational Change in Finland.* New York: Teachers College Press, 2015.

67 OECD. *TALIS 2013 Results: An International Perspective on Teaching and Learning.* Paris: TALIS, OECD publishing, 2014.

68 Sahlberg P (2015).

69 Statistics Finland (2011). Population Structure. In Sahlberg P. (2015).

70 Harju-Luukkainen H, Nissinen K, Sulkunen S, et al. *Selvitys maahanmuuttajataustaisten nuorten osaamisesta ja siihen liittyvistä taustatekijöistä* PISA 2012 – tutkimuksessa. As reported by the University of Jyväskylä, 2014. Available at: www.jyu.fi/en/news/archive/2014/08/tiedote-2014-08-15-14-56-41-604088

71 Reischauer EO. *Japan: The Story of a Nation.* Tokyo: Tuttle, 1981;127.

72 Benjamin GR. *Japanese Lessons: A Year in a Japanese School Through the Eyes of an American Anthropologist and Her Children.* New York: NYU Press, 1998.

73 Quoted in: Tanikawa M. Free to be. 2003. Available at: www.nytimes.com/2003/01/12/education/free-to-be.html?pagewanted=all; 1998.

74 Morita Y, Taki M, Hata M. *Nihon no ijime Bullying in Japan.* Toky Kaneko shobo. Available at: http://apjjf.org/-Shoko-YONEYAMA/3001/article.html; 1999.

75 Yoneyama S, Naito A. Problems with the Paradigm: The School as a Factor in Understanding (Bullying (with special reference to Japan). *British Journal of Sociology of Education* 2003;24:3:315–30.

76 Yoneyama S. *The Japanese High School: Silence and Resistance.* New York: Routledge, 2012.

77 Preamble to the Fundamental Code of Education, 1872 Government Document, in *Children and Youth in History,* Item 129. Available at: http://chnm.gmu.edu/cyh/primary-sources/129

78 Ministry of Education, Culture, Sports, Science and Technology. *The Establishment of Elementary Schools and Attendance.* Available at: www.

mext.go.jp/b_menu/hakusho/html/others/detail/1317264.htm

79 Ellington L. *Japan*. California: ABC-CLIO, 2009.

80 Rosenthal R, Jacobson L. Pygmalion in the classroom. *The Urban Review* 1968;3(1):16–20.

81 It has recently been brought to my attention that this study has come under some criticism for its design. A more recent review of research in this area suggests that self-fulfilling prophesies in the classroom do exist, but their effects are smaller than those seen in the famous Rosenathal study: Jussim L, Harber KD. Teacher expectations and self-fulfilling prophecies: Knowns and unknowns, resolved and unresolved controversies. *Personality and Social Psychology Review* 2005;9(2):131–55.

82 Babad EY. Pygmalion in reverse. *Journal of Special Education* 1977;11:81–90.

83 Benjamin GR (1997).

84 Yamamoto Y. Social class and Japanese mothers' support for young children's education: A qualitative study. *Journal of Early Childhood Research* 2015;13(2):165–80.

85 Kariya T. *Education Reform and Social Class in Japan: The Emerging Incentive Divide*. New York: Routledge, 2012.

86 Dang, L. Almost 50% of Japanese women are told they're 'causing trouble' for being pregnant. 2015. Available at: http://nextshark.com/japan-women-pregnant-harassment

87 Benjamin GR. (1997).

88 Stigler JW, Hiebert J. *The Teaching Gap: Best Ideas From the World's Teachers for Improving Education in the Classroom*. New York, NY: Free Press, 1999.

89 Stevenson HW, Stigler JW. *The Learning Gap: Why Our Schools Are Failing and What We Can Learn From Japanese and Chinese Education*. New York: Summit Books, 1992.

90 A similar point is made by the National Mathematics Advisory Panel. National Mathematics Advisory Panel in: *Foundations for Success: The Final Report of the National Mathematics Advisory Panel*. Washington, DC, US. Department of Education, 2008. Available at: www2.ed.gov/about/bdscomm/list/mathpanel/report/final-report.pdf

91 Two asides for those following this from the perspective of the 'progressive' vs 'traditional' debate who have been led to believe that Japanese classrooms follow 'progressive' pedagogy:

   1. I spoke with a Japanese secondary-school teacher who was at school in the 90s, and was telling me that in her experience, both secondary and elementary teachers just taught the content and then got students to practise it. When I told her that some people in England and America thought that Japan did so well in international tests because the teachers gave children space to create and solve their own problems, and that this was based on their visits to schools, she leaned back in her chair in surprise, and her eyebrows shot up. 'Really?! Which school did they go to? That's really strange. Wow.'

   2. The percentage of Japanese elementary school teachers reporting that they frequently used the three often-related teaching practices of small group work, Information and Communications Technology (ICT) and projects lasting longer than a week, was the lowest of the countries that took part in TALIS. (TALIS, 2012. Fig 6.3).

   As I've implied in the text, based on my interviews, observations and reading,

I believe that they use reasoning and problem-solving tasks to good effect in a very structured way, alongside more 'traditional' practices like whole class teaching and memorisation.

92 This analysis is from the blog of Tom Loveless at the Brookings Institution. Available at: www.brookings.edu/research/papers/2014/08/07-new-york-times-math-loveless

93 Stevenson & Stigler (1992).

94 OECD. TALIS 2013 *Results: An International Perspective on Teaching and Learning*. Paris: OECD Publishing, 2014.

95 Only Mexico, Columbia and Chile have worse student-teacher ratios of all of the OECD and non-OECD countries surveyed. OECD (2015). *Education at a Glance 2015*: OECD Indicators. OECD Publishing, Paris.

96 Whitman NC. Learning from Japanese Middle School Math Teachers. *Phi Delta Kappa Fastbacks* 2003;505:7–46.

97 Catherine Lewis and Ineko Tsuchida. Planned educational change in Japan: the case of elementary science instruction. *Journal of Education Policy* 1997;12(5):313–31.

98 Japanese education system – school year and juku. Available at: http://members.tripod.com/h_javora/jed3.htm

99 Weisman, SR. How do Japan's students do it? They cram. 1992. Available at: www.nytimes.com/1992/04/27/world/how-do-japan-s-students-do-it-they-cram.html?pagewanted=all&src=pm

100 Bjork C. Local implementation of Japan's Integrated Studies reform: a preliminary analysis of efforts to decentralise the curriculum. *Comparative Education* 2009;45(1):23–44.

101 Kariya T, Rappleye J. The twisted, unintended impacts of globalization on Japanese education. In Hannum E, Park H, Goto Butler Y (eds.) *Globalization, Changing Demographics, and Educational Challenges in East Asia, Research in the Sociology of Education*. Bingley: Emerald Group Publishing; 2010;Vol 17:17–63.

102 Bjork C. Local implementation of Japan's Integrated Studies reform: a preliminary analysis of efforts to decentralise the curriculum. *Comparative Education* 2009;45(1):23–44.

103 Fish, R. Japan: Recent trends in education reform. 2016. Available at: http://asiasociety.org/global-cities-education-network/japan-recent-trends-education-reform

104 Primary school education only became compulsory in Singapore in 2003. Secondary education is still not compulsory – children only need attend school until they have completed P6, although the vast majority do progress to secondary education and beyond.

105 Unless you took a gamble and applied for the direct admissions scheme, where schools can accept students based on other talents such as music or languages, prior to PLSE results being released.

106 These change slightly every year. As they are approximations only, they don't add up to 100%.

107 Hoh, WK. How David Hoe fought his way to university. 2014. Available at: www.straitstimes.com/singapore/how-david-hoe-fought-his-way-to-university

108 Said to stand for 'Single, Desperate and Ugly' by those who looked down on

this programme.

109 I have drawn on the work of Scott Kaufmann for information on the history of intelligence testing. For a fuller account of this history, see his book *Ungifted – Intelligence redefined*. (Basic Books, 2013).

110 This word literally means 'less advanced in mental, physical, or social development than is usual for one's age'. The more common understanding of it being a permanent trait developed from the history we are about to explore.

111 Binet A. Modern ideas about children. Trans. Heisler S. In: Kaufman, SB. *Ungifted: Intelligence Redefined*. New York: Basic Books, 2013.

112 Asbury K, Plomin R. *G is for Genes – The Impact of Genetics on Education and Achievement*. Chichester: Wiley, 2013.

113 It is actually way more complicated than this – genes and environment interact for a start, but my account is accurate, if simplified. For a proper explanation of all this, read K Asbury and R Plomin's book *G is for Genes – The Impact of Genetics on Education and Achievement*, (Chichester, Wiley, 2013).

114 Asbury and Plomin (2013), *op. cit.*, 92

115 Singapore is not alone in this, England does it to a lesser extent in areas where grammar schools still exist.

116 MPs call for rethink of streaming, specialist schools, emphasis on exams. 2016. Available at: www.channelnewsasia.com/news/singapore/mps-call-for-rethink-of/2462490.html; Accessed date: 27th May 2016

117 *Survey on Attitudes & Lifestyle among Primary 4–6 Pupils*. Singapore Press Holdings November, 2000. Available at: http://app.msf.gov.sg/portals/0/Summary/publication/SF4-Children.pdf

118 Singapore Window. Minister's plea not to belt children. 2000. Available at: www.singapore-window.org/sw00/001127a1.htm

119 Education Minister Heng Swee Keat is reported as saying, 'We have to be very thoughtful and we have to think long term, and not just focus on one bit or another bit. This is not how we develop an education policy. You must have the big picture and then you must have all the pieces in place, not just one little piece.' Mr Heng added that the Education Ministry's plans are comprehensive and well thought through and have gone through many rounds of analytical and consultation work with students, teachers, parents and employers. Available at: www.channelnewsasia.com/news/singapore/education-policy-has-to/2086914.html

120 Singapore 'still world's most expensive city'. 2016. Available at: www.bbc.co.uk/news/business-35765378

121 Economist Intelligence Unit, 'Starting well: Benchmarking early education across the world'. Singapore's preschool system includes some good preschools based on sound curricula principles, but the government is struggling to find enough well-qualified staff to fill the number of positions needed for universal access. This is a recognised problem, and therefore an area of focus for the Singaporean government.

122 D A Bell. *The China Model: Political Meritocracy and the Limits of Democracy*. Princeton: Princeton University Press, 2015: 126.

123 Saad, I. MP proposes pilot schools without streaming nor PSLE. 2014. Available at: www.channelnewsasia.com/news/specialreports/parliament/news/mp-proposes-pilot-schools-without-stream/962284.html

124 Lee Yock Suan, Minister for Education, reported in *Straits Times*; issue: 14th June 1994.

125 Youth unemployment in Singapore: an overview. 2013. Available at: www.elmmagazine.eu/articles/youth-unemployment-in-singapore-an-overview

126 Bol T, Van de Werfhorst HG. Educational systems and the trade-off between labor market allocation and equality of educational opportunity. *Comparative Education Review* 2013;57(2):285–308.

127 OECD Singapore. Available at: www.oecd.org/education/school/programmeforinternationalstudentassessmentpisa/49765882.pdf

128 Deci EL, Ryan RM. *Intrinsic Motivation and Self-determination in Human Behaviour.* New York: Plenum, 1985.

129 Deci EL, Koestner R, Ryan RM. A Meta-analytic Review of Experiments Examining the Effects of Extrinsic Rewards on Intrinsic Motivation. *Psychological Bulletin* 1999;125(6):627–68.

130 Deci EL, et al. (1985).

131 Ryan RM, Deci EL. Intrinsic and Extrinsic Motivations: Classic Definitions and New Directions. *Contemporary Educational Psychology* 2000;25(1):54–67.

132 Ryan RM, Deci EL. (2000)

133 Choi K, Ross M. (Cultural differences in process and person focus: Congratulations on your hard work versus celebrating your exceptional brain. *Journal of Experimental Social Psychology* 2011;47(2):343–9.

134 Chen C, Stevenson HW. Motivation and mathematics achievement: a comparative study of Asian-American, Caucasian-American, and East Asian high school students. *Child Development* 1995;66:1215–34.

135 Wang Q, Pomerantz EM. The motivational landscape of early adolescence in the United States and China: a longitudinal investigation. *Child Development* 2009;80(4):1272–7.

136 Stevenson HW, Stigler JW. *The Learning Gap: Why our Schools Are Failing and What We Can Learn from Japanese and Chinese Education.* New York: Summit Books, 1992: P105

137 Wang, et al. (2009)

138 Heine SJ, Kitayama S, Lehman DR, et al. Divergent consequences of success and failure in Japan and North America: an investigation of self-improving motivations and malleable selves. *Journal of Personality and Social Psychology* 2001;81(4):599.

139 *Ibid.*

140 Ng FF, Pomerantz EM, Lam S. European American and Chinese parents' responses to children's success and failure: Implications for children's responses. *Developmental Psychology* 2007;43:1239–55.

141 Li J. *Cultural Foundations of Learning: East and West.* Cambridge: Cambridge University Press, 2012:p7.

142 Stipek DJ. Motivation to Learn: Integrating Theory and Practice (4th ed). Boston: Allyn & Baker, 2002.

143 Tobin J, Wu D, Davidson D. *Preschool in Three Cultures: Japan, China, and the United States.* New Haven, CT: Yale University Press, 1989.

144 Hess RD, Chang C-M, McDevitt TM. Cultural variations in family beliefs about children's performance in mathematics: Comparisons among People's Republic of China, Chinese-American, and Caucasian-American families. *Journal of Educational Psychology* 1987;79:179–88.

145 Heine SJ, etal.

146 Dweck C. *Mindset: How You Can Fulfil Your Potential.* London: Hachette UK, 2012.

147 Pualengco RP, Chiu CY, Kim YH. (2009). Cultural variations in pre_emptive effort downplaying. *Asian Journal of Social Psychology* 2009;12(1):12–9.

148 Dweck CS. *Mindsets and Math/Science Achievement.* New York: Carnegie Corp. of New York –Institute for Advanced Study Commission on Mathematics and Science Education, 2008.

149 Li J. (2012);14.

150 *ibid.*

151 Li J. (2012); 13.

152 Dweck CS. (2008).

153 Ng, F. F. Y., Pomerantz, E. M., & Lam, S. F. (2007). European American and Chinese parents' responses to children's success and failure: implications for children's responses. *Developmental Psychology*, 43(5), 1239.

154 Greenberger E, Chen C, Tally SR, Dong Q. Family, peer, and individual correlates of depressive symptomatology among US and Chinese adolescents. *Journal of Consulting and Clinical Psychology* 2000;68(2):209.

155 Chao R, Tseng V. Parenting of Asians. *Handbook of Parenting* 2002;4:59–93.

156 East China Normal University (2015) Gaokao to be reformed: A better Channel for social mobility?; Available at: http://english.ecnu.edu.cn/df/cf/c1706a57295/page.htm

157 Qian H, Walker A. In: Tony Townsend and John MacBeath (eds.), *International Handbook of Leadership for Learning.* Germany: Springer, 2011: 209-25.

158 Researchers have independently found private migrant schools to be of worse educational quality than public schools. See Chen, Y., & Feng, S. (2013). Access to public schools and the education of migrant children in China. China Economic Review, 26, 75-88.

159 Strauss V. So how overblown were No. 1 Shanghai's PISA results? 2014. Available at: www.washingtonpost.com/news/answer-sheet/wp/2014/03/20/so-how-overblown-were-no-1-shanghais-pisa-results

160 OECD. *PISA 2012 Results in Focus. What 15-year-olds Know and hat they can do with what they know.* Paris: OECD, 2013. Available at: https://www.oecd.org/pisa/keyfindings/pisa-2012-results-overview.pdf

161 An SH. Capturing the Chinese way of teaching: the learning-questioning and learning-reviewing instructional model. In: *How Chinese Learn Mathematics: Perspectives From Insiders.* Fan LH, Fan NY, Wong, Cai JF, Li SQ (eds). Singapore: World Scientific, 2014:462–482.

162 Fan L, Miao Z, Mok I. How Chinese teachers teach mathematics and pursue professional development: perspectives from contemporary international research. In: *How Chinese Teach Mathematics: Perspectives from Insiders.* Singapore: World Scientific, 2014:43–70.

163 Schleppenbach M, Flevares LM, Sims LM, Perry M. Teachers' responses to student mistakes in Chinese and US mathematics classrooms. *The Elementary School Journal* 2007;108(2):131–47.

164 Qiong LI, Yujing NI. Dialogue in the elementary school mathematics classroom: a comparative study between expert and novice teachers. *Frontiers of Education in China* 2009;4(4):526–40.

165 Fang Y. The cultural pedagogy of errors: teacher Wang's homework practice in teaching geometric proofs. *Journal of Curriculum Studies* 2010;42(5):597–

619.

166 Biggs JB. The Paradox of the Chinese Learner. *Asian Contributions to Cross-Cultural Psychology* 1996:180–199.

167 Watkins DA, Biggs JB. *The Chinese Learner: Cultural, Psychological, and Contextual Influences.* Hong Kong/Melbourne: CERC & ACER, 1996.

168 Li J. US and Chinese cultural beliefs about learning. *Journal of Educational Psychology* 2003;95(2):258.

169 Rao ZH. Understanding Chinese students' use of language learning strategies from cultural and educational perspectives. *Journal of Multilingual and Multicultural Development* 2006;27:491–508.

170 Deci E, Ryan R. *Handbook of Self-determination Research.* Rochester, NY: University of Rochester Press, 2002.

171 Wang Q, Pomerantz EM. The motivational landscape of early adolescence in the US and China: a longitudinal investigation. *Child Development* 2009;80:1280–96.

172 Stevenson HW, Lee SY, Chen C, et al. Contexts of achievement: a study of American, Chinese, and Japanese children. Chicago: University of Chicago Press, 1990.

173 OECD. *Ready to Learn: Students' Engagement, Drive and Self-beliefs – Volume III.* Paris: OECD, 2013.

174 Zhou N, Lam SF, Chan KC. The Chinese classroom paradox: a cross-cultural comparison of teacher controlling behaviors. *Journal of Educational Psychology* 2012;104:1162–74.

175 Chua A. *Battle Hymn of the Tiger Mother.* London: Bloomsbury Publishing, 2011:29.

176 Pratt D, Kelly M, Wong S. Chinese conceptions of "Effective Teaching" in Hong Kong: towards a culturally sensitive evaluation of teaching. *International Journal of Lifelong Education* 1999;18(4): 241–58.

177 Reuters. Wen says rote learning must go in Chinese schools. Available in: www.reuters.com/article/us-china-education-idUSTRE67U18Y20100831; 2010.

178 Tan C. *Learning from Shanghai: Lessons on Achieving Educational Success.* Germany: Springer, 2013.

179 BBC News: China universities 'must shun Western values'. Available at: www.bbc.co.uk/news/world-asia-china-31052682

180 Adams GL, Engelmann S. *Research on Direct Instruction: 25 Years beyond DISTAR.* Seattle: Educational Achievement Systems, 1996.
Hattie J. *Visible Learning: A Synthesis of Over 800 Meta-analyses Relating to Achievement.* New York: Routledge, 2008.

181 Glaser R, Chi MT. Overview. In: *The Nature of Expertise* . Hillsdale: Erlbaum, 1988: xv-xxvii.

182 New to BC. Diverse British Columbia: Immigration in Western Canada. Available at: http://newtobc.ca/2015/05/diverse-british-columbia-immigration-in-western-canada

183 OECD. Ontario, Canada: reform to support high achievement in a diverse context. In: *Strong Performers and Successful Reformers in Education: Lessons from PISA for the United States.* Paris: OECD, 2011.

184 Statistics Canada. *Immigration and Ethnocultural Diversity in Canada.* Available at: www12.statcan.gc.ca/nhs-enm/2011/as-sa/99-010-x/99-010-x2011001-eng.cfm

185 If you were to be irritated by the inconsistency between China entering different regions separately and Canada entering its different provincial systems as one country, you could say Canada came sixth in 2009 and ninth in 2012 out of all the countries (were we to lump China's scores together as one entry).

186 Entorf H, Minoiu N. What a difference immigration law makes: PISA results, migration background and social mobility in Europe and traditional countries of immigration. In: ZEW-Centre for European Economic Research Discussion Paper, (04-017), 2004.

187 National Centre for Education Statistics International Data Explorer.

188 The three territories opted not to participate in PISA, partly due to inaccessibility (there are no roads connecting communities in Nunavut, you'd have to get a plane), which excluded 1.1 per cent of Canada's student population from the tests.

189 Despite their similarities, provinces have quite different scores, much of which can be explained by differences in student background. This explains more of the score difference between provinces than it does between countries, which makes sense given the similarities in policy. If all the countries in the world had identical education systems, they still wouldn't all have the same results, but most of the variation would be due to student background. So it is with Canadian provinces – their similar approaches to education mean that less of the variation in their scores can be explained by their systems, and so more is explained by the children's home lives.

190 Neil Guppy, Professor of Sociology and author of textbook on education in Canada, interviewed by the OECD for 'Ontario, Canada: Reform to Support High Achievement in a Diverse Context', Lessons from PISA for the United States, (OECD, 2011).

191 Cappon P. Think Nationally, Act Locally: A pan-Canadian strategy for education and training. (2014).

192 An evaluation of Quebec's early years programme found negative effects on five-year-olds, with the authors suggesting that this was due to the children going in too young, for too long, and to poor quality settings without sufficient qualified staff.
Lefebvre P, Merrigan P, Verstraete M. Impact of Early Childhood Care and Education on Children's Preschool Cognitive Development: Canadian Results from a Large Scale Quasi-Experiment. In: CIPEE. Working Paper 06–36, 2006. Available at: www.cirpee.org/fileadmin/documents/Cahiers_2006/CIRPEE06-36.pdf

193 The significant growth in the proportion of five-year-olds attending kindergarten (from about a third to almost all) happened during the 1960s.

194 Cornelius-White J. Learner-centered teacher-student relationships are effective: a meta-analysis. Review of Educational Research 2007;77(1):113–43.

195 Jennifer Walner. Learning to School: Federalism and Public Schooling in Canada. Toronto: Toronto University Press, 2014:54.

196 OECD (2014). Are grouping and selecting students for different schools related to students' motivation to learn? PISA in Focus 39. Paris: OECD.

197 Pashler, H., McDaniel, M., Rohrer, D., & Bjork, R. (2008). Learning styles concepts and evidence. Psychological Science in the Public Interest, 9(3), 105-119. p105.

198 In Ontario they have grade-level rubrics too, but they cannot include any 'negative language' like you see in BC's 'not yet within expectations' box. Instead they focus on what the child did achieve.

199 For a much better explanation of this idea, see Daisy Christodoulou's blog 'The Wing to Heaven' in which she writes about comparative judgement.

200 In a sense, even criterion-referenced exams are based on what is normal for a particular age-group, because it is human beings deciding on the criteria, and their decision is likely to be based on what children have been able to achieve in previous years. If the scenario above actually happened, and all Grade 4 Canadian children met or exceeded the grade-level expectations, there would no doubt be criticism, or at least self-reflection, about whether the expectations were high enough. Nevertheless, there is still a clear distinction between an assessment in which children are judged against standards, and an assessment in which they are judged against each other.

201 British Columbia Ministry of Education. Gifted Education – A Resource Guide for Teachers. Available in: www.bced.gov.bc.ca/specialed/gifted/giftedlearners.htm; accessed dates: 2nd June 2016

202 Hattie J. *Visible Learning: A Synthesis of Over 800 Meta-analyses Relating to Achievement*. Abingdon: Routledge, 2008.

203 Kanevsky LS. A survey of educational acceleration practices in Canada. *Canadian Journal of Education* 2011;34(3):153–80.

204 King LA, Burton CM. The hazards of goal pursuit. In: Chang EC, Lawrence J (eds). *Virtue, Vice, and Personality: The Complexity of Behavior*. Washington, DC: American Psychological Association, xxvi, 2003:53–69.

205 Dunae P. The School Inspectorate 1856 – 1973. Available in: www2.viu.ca/homeroom/content/Topics/Programs/inspect.htm

206 Hough LM, Oswald FL. Personnel selection: Looking toward the future—remembering the past. *Annual Review of Psychology* 2000;51:631–64.

207 Döbert H, Klieme E, Sroka W. *Conditions of School Performance in Seven Countries*. Waxmann Verlag, 2004.

208 Stokke A. What to do about Canada's declining math scores. Commentary 427, CD. Howe Institute, Toronto, 2015. Available at: www.cdhowe.org/sites/default/files/attachments/research_papers/mixed/commentary_427.pdf

209 Here problem-based learning is defined after Gijbels (2005), who outlined six core characteristics: learning is student-centred; learning occurs in small groups; a tutor is present as a facilitator or guide, authentic problems are presented at the beginning of a learning sequence; the problems encountered are used as tools to achieve the required knowledge and the problem-solving skills necessary to eventually solve the problem; and new information is acquired through self-directed learning. Often the terms 'problem based learning' and 'discovery learning' are used interchangeably, although Hmelo-Silver et al. suggest that there are clear distinctions between them; that discovery based learning involves less teacher guidance and is therefore less effective. As the research quoted refers to problem-based learning, the overall lack of evidence of its effectiveness on supporting knowledge and understanding in school-aged children should therefore worry us even more.

Gijbels D, Dochy F, Van den Bossche P, Segers M. Effects of problem-based learning: a meta-analysis from the angle of assessment. *Review of*

Educational Research 2005;75(1):27–61.

Hmelo-Silver CE, Duncan RG, Chinn CA. Scaffolding and achievement in problem-based and inquiry learning: a response to Kirschner, Sweller, and Clark (2006). *Educational Psychologist* 2007;42(2):99–107.

210 Kirschner PA, Sweller J, Clark RE. Why minimal guidance during instruction does not work. *Educational Psychologist* 2006;41(2):75–86.

211 Hattie J. Visible learning: a synthesis of over 800 meta-analyses relating to achievement. Abingdon: Routledge, 2008.

212 Echazarra A, Salinas D, Méndez I, et al. *How Teachers Teach and Students Learn*. Paris: OECD, 2016.

213 This is the argument that due to working memory limitations, children are limited in the extent to which they can solve problems without relevant prior knowledge – as expressed in Kirschner et al. (2006).

214 Haeck C, Lefebvre P, Merrigan P. *All students left behind: an ambitious provincial school reform in canada, but poor math achievements from grade 2 to 10.* Available at: SSRN 1966937; 2011.

215 Coe R, Aloisi C, Higgins S, Elliot Major L. *What makes great teaching? Review of the underpinning research.* Centre for Evaluation and Monitoring/ The Sutton Trust, Durham, 2014.

216 Didactique has a lot in common with PCK, but it's not quite the same thing. Within the continental European tradition (which is the Quebecois use of diadctique comes from) it also includes issues of curriculum design, such as the relative strength and weakness of various metaphors for teaching mathematics. Examples are whether you introduce negative numbers as bank balances, temperatures, heights below sea-level, and so on. Many thanks to Dylan Wiliam for pointing out this distinction.

217 Hattie (2008): 211

218 Not every country I visited adheres to all five principles, but each principle is followed by at least four of the five top-performing systems.

219 Formby S. *Children's early literacy practices at home and in early years settings: Second annual survey of parents and practitioners.* National Literacy Trust, 2014.

220 Aunio P, Aubrey C, Godfrey R, et al. Children's early numeracy in England, Finland and People's Republic of China. *International Journal of Early Years in Education* 2008;16(3):203–21.

221 Alexander R. *The Education of Six Year Olds in England, Denmark and Finland: An International Comparative Study.* London: Ofsted, 2003.

222 Nah KO. A comparative study of mathematics education practices in English and Korean preschools focusing on implementation of curriculum content. *KEDI Journal of Educational Policy* 2011;8(1):

223 Whitburn J. Contrasting approaches to the acquisition of mathematical skills: Japan and England. *Oxford Review of Education* 1996;22(4):415–34. Although this research was conducted in 1996, the findings are still true – Japanese preschool is still entirely play-based.

224 Bassok D, Latham S, Rorem A. Is Kindergarten the new first grade? *Working Paper Series, No. 20.* Available at: http://curry.virginia.edu/uploads/ resourceLibrary/20_Bassok_Is_Kindergarten_The_New_First_Grade.pdf; 2015.

225 Sylva K, Nabuco M. Research on quality in the curriculum. *International*

Journal of Early Childhood 1996;28(2):1–6.

Elkind D, Whitehurst G. Young Einsteins. Much too early: much too late. *Education Matters* 2001;1(2):8–21.

Dee T, Sievertsen H. The gift of time? School starting age and mental health. *NBER Working Paper No. 21610*, 2015. Available at: http://www.literacytrust.org.uk/assets/0002/4082/EY_Final_report_2014.pdf

Black S, Devereux P, Salvanes K. Too young to leave the nest? The effects of school starting age. *The Review of Economics and Statistics* 2011;93(2):455–67.

226 Kavkler M, Tancig S, Magajna L, Aubrey C. Getting it right from the start? The influence of early school entry on later achievements in mathematics. *European Early Childhood Education Research Journal* 2000;8(1):75–93.

McGuinness C, Sproule L, Bojke C, Trew K, Walsh G. Impact of a play-based curriculum in the first two years of primary school: literacy and numeracy outcomes over seven years. *British Educational Research Journal* 2014;40(5):772–95.

Schmerkotte H. Ergebnisse eines Vergleichs von Modellkindergarten und Vorklassen in Nordrhein-Westfalen Results from a comparison of typical kindergartens and preschools in North Rhine-Westphalia. *Bildung und Erziehung* 1978;31:401–11.

227 Marcon R. Moving up the grades; relationship between pre-school model and later school success. *Early childhood Research and Practice* 2002;4(1):517–30.

Suggate S, Schaughency E, Reese E. Children learning to read later catch up to children reading earlier. *Early Childhood Research Quarterly* 2013;28:33–48.

228 Aunio P, Aubrey C, Godfrey R, Pan Y, Liu Y. Children's early numeracy in England, Finland and People's Republic of China. *International Journal of Early Years Education* 2008;16(3):203–21.

229 Heckman JJ. Schools, skills, and synapses. *Economic Inquiry* 2008;46(3):289–324.

230 *ibid.*

231 Aunio, et al. (2008).

232 Ee J, Wong K, Aunio P. Numeracy of Young Children in Singapore, Beijing Helsinki. *Early Childhood Education Journal* 2006;33(5).

233 Nurturing Early Learners: A curriculum for kindergartens in Singapore. Numeracy. Available from: www.moe.gov.sg/docs/defaultsource/document/education/preschool/files/nel-edu-guide-numeracy.pdf

234 OECD (2015). Helping Immigrants Succeed at School – and Beyond. Available from: https://www.oecd.org/education/Helping-immigrant-students-to-succeed-at-school-and-beyond.pdf

235 Bransford JD, Brown AL, Cocking RR. *How People Learn: Brain, Mind, Experience, and School.* Washington DC: National Academy Press, 1999.

236 I have drawn heavily on the work of Tim Oates (2010) and Schmidt and Prawat (2006) for this section, and recommend their work for further reading.

Oates T. *Could Do Better.* Cambridge: Cambridge Assessment, 2010.

Schmidt WH, Prawat RS. Curriculum coherence and national control of education: issue or non_issue? *Journal of Curriculum Studies* 2006;38(6):641–58.

237 NB. Having a national curriculum needn't mean it is designed by the

government – it could be a national non-governmental body. The important thing is that it is credible to teachers.

238 Van de Werfhorst HG, Mijs JJ. Achievement inequality and the institutional structure of educational systems: a comparative perspective. *Annual Review of Sociology* 2010;36:407–28.

239 Thanks to Tim Oates for pointing out this distinction.

240 PISA finds that, after accounting for socio-economic status and performance in reading and mathematics, immigrant students are 44 per cent more likely than non-immigrant students to be enrolled in vocational programmes. The systematic tracking of disadvantaged immigrants into vocational tracks and less-demanding courses not only limits the academic skills they may acquire, but also creates an additional barrier into high-status professional occupations later on.

241 Hanushek E, Woßmann L. Does educational tracking affect performance and inequality? Differences-In-Differences Evidence Across Countries. *Economic Journal* 2006;116:63–76.
Woessmann L. International Evidence on School Tracking: A Review. CESifo DICE Report – *Journal for Institutional Comparisons* 2009;7(1):26–34.
Horn, D. Age of selection counts: A cross-country comparison of educational institutions. *Arbeitspapiere – Mannheimer Zentrum für Europäische Sozialforschung*; 107. Available from: http://www.mzes.uni-mannheim.de/publications/wp/wp-107.pdf; 2008.
Duru-Bellat M, Suchaut B. Organisation and context, efficiency and equity of educational systems: what PISA tells us. *European Educational Research Journal* 2005;4(3):181–94.

242 Jakubowski M, Patrinos HA, Porta EE, Wisniewski J. The Impact of the 1999 Education Reform in Poland. *Policy Research Working Paper 5263*. Human Development Network Education, 2010.

243 Carlgren I. The Swedish comprehensive school—lost in transition? *Zeitschrift für Erziehungswissenschaft* 2009;12(4):633–49.

244 Although it was a qualified teacher fulfilling this role in all of the countries I went to, there is some evidence that academic and non-academic gains can be made using well-educated, committed tutors who do not necessarily have formal teacher training. E.g. Cook et al (2014), The (Surprising) Efficacy of Academic and Behavioral Intervention with Disadvantaged Youth: Results from a Randomized Experiment in Chicago, *NBER Working Paper No. 19862*.

245 Hill HC, Rowan B, Ball DL. Effects of Teachers' Mathematical Knowledge for Teaching on Student Achievement. *American Educational Research Journal* 2005;42(2):371-406.
Sadler PM, Sonnert G, Coyle HP, Cook-Smith N, Miller JL. The influence of teachers' knowledge on student learning in middle school physical science classrooms. *American Educational Research Journal* 2013;50(5):1020–49.
Deans for Impact (2015). *The Science of Learning*, Austin, TX: Deans for Impact, available at: www.deansforimpact.org/pdfs/The_Science_of_Learning.pdf

246 Pomerance L, Greenberg J, Walsh K. Learning about learning: *What Every New Teacher Needs to Know*. Washington, DC: The National Council of Teacher Quality, 2016.

247 Coe R, Aloisi C, Higgins S, Elliot Major L. *What Makes Great Teaching? Review of the Underpinning Research*. Durham: Centre for Evaluation and

Monitoring/The Sutton Trust, 2014.

248 I have drawn on five reviews of what makes effective/great teaching and learning –

Ko J, Sammons P. *Effective Teaching: A Review of Research and Evidence.* Reading: CfBT Education Trust, 2013.

Coe R, Aloisi C, Higgins S, Elliot Major L. *What Makes Great Teaching? Review of the Underpinning Research.* Durham:Centre for Evaluation and Monitoring/The Sutton Trust, 2014.

Deans for Impact (2015). The Science of Learning, Austin, TX: Deans for Impact. Available at: www.deansforimpact.org/pdfs/The_Science_of_Learning.pdf

Pashler H, Bain PM, Bottge BA, et al. Organizing Instruction and Study to Improve Student Learning. *IES Practice Guide NCER 2007-2004.* Washington, DC: National Center for Education Research, 2007.

Hattie J. (2008).

249 Byron K, Khazanchi S, Nazarian D. The relationship between stressors and creativity: a meta-analysis examining competing theoretical models. *Journal of Applied Psychology* 2010;95(1):201.

250 Mourshed M, Chijioke C, Barber M. *How the World's Most Improved Systems Keep Getting Better.* New York: McKinsey & Co, 2010:70.

251 Diamond J, Spillane J. High-stakes accountability in urban elementary schools: challenging or reproducing inequality? *The Teachers College Record* 2004;106(6):1145–76.

252 Neal D, Schanzenback DW. Left behind by design: proficiency counts and test-based accountability. *The Review of Economics and Statistics* 2010;92(2):263–83.

253 Jacob B. Accountability, incentives and behavior: the impact of high-stakes testing in Chicago public schools. *Journal of Public Economics* 2005;89(5–6):761–96.

Jennings J. Below the bubble: educational triage and the Texas accountability system. *American Educational Research Journal* 2005;42(2):231–68.

254 Jacob BA, Levitt SD. *Rotten Apples: An Investigation of the Prevalence and Predictors of Teacher Cheating* (No. w9413). Cambridge, MA: National Bureau of Economic Research, 2003.

255 Shanghai and Singapore have not yet delayed the selection of different children into different schools (although Shanghai is trying) so these systems are high-performing but not yet equitable.

256 Jerrim J, Vignoles A. *The Causal Effect of East Asian 'Mastery' Teaching Methods on English Children's Mathematics Skills* (No. 15-05). Department of Quantitative Social Science-UCL Institute of Education. London: University College London, 2015.

257 Zeehandelaar D, Northern AM. *What Parents Want: Education Preferences and Trade-offs: A National Survey of K-12 Parents.* Washington DC: Thomas B. Fordham Institute, 2013.

258 HSBC. The Value of Education: Learning for Life. Available at: www.google.com/search?client=safari&rls=en&q=The+Value+of+Education:+Learning+for+Life%E2%80%99&ie=UTF-8&oe=UTF-8&gfe_rd=cr&ei=u65aV6X1E-Hc8geTho3wCA; 2015; accessed at: 6th June 2016.

259 Bol T, Van de Werfhorst HG. Educational systems and the trade-off

between labor market allocation and equality of educational opportunity. *Comparative Education Review* 2013;57(2):285–308.

260 Bransford JD, Brown AL, Cocking RR. *How People Learn: Brain, Mind, Experience, and School.* Washington, DC: National Academy Press, 2000.

261 Pellegrino JW, Hilton ML. *Education for Life and Work: Developing Transferable Knowledge and Skills in the 21st Century.* Washington, DC: National Academies Press, 2012.

262 Dignath C, Buettner G, Langfeldt HP. How can primary school students learn self-regulated learning strategies most effectively? A meta-analysis on self-regulation training programmes. *Educational Research Review* 2008;3(2):101–29.

263 Scott G, Leritz LE, Mumford MD. The effectiveness of creativity training: A quantitative review. *Creativity Research Journal* 2004;16(4):361–88.

264 Kirschner PA, Sweller J, Clark RE. Why minimal guidance during instruction does not work: An analysis of the failure of constructivist, discovery, problem-based, experiential, and inquiry-based teaching. *Educational Psychologist* 2006;41(2):75–86.

Glossary

Autonomous motivation When a person fully endorses a behaviour and experiences volition and choice.

Differentiation A change in teacher behaviour to cater for students with different needs.

Equality In this context, this means the spread of student/school results being narrow.

Equity/equitable In this context, this refers to the extent to which students' results depend on their parental background. Equitable would mean there was no relationship.

External (controlled) motivation When a person feels coerced or seduced into behaving, with the experience of pressure and obligation.

Extrinsic motivation Motivation that comes from external sources, such as the pursuit of a reward or the avoidance of punishment.

Fixed mindset The belief that you only have a certain amount of ability/intelligence/skill, and that there is nothing you can do to change this.

Gaman Japanese term meaning 'enduring the seemingly unbearable with patience and dignity'.

Growth mindset The belief that you can improve your abilities or level of intelligence through hard work and training.

Guanxi Chinese term meaning 'connection' which refers to a network of mutually-beneficial relationships that can help you in your personal life or in business.

Han A Japanese term meaning 'group', used to refer to the small groups students are put into at school.

Hukou A record of household registration in China. This affects which public services one is entitled to in other parts of the country.

Intrinsic motivation Acting because the action is inherently interesting or enjoyable.

Juku In Japan, a private school or college attended in addition to an ordinary educational institution.

Lesson study A professional development practice in which teachers plan a lesson together, observe how effectively the children learn in the lesson, and discuss possible changes on the basis of this.

Pedagogy (pedagogical) The method and practice of teaching (relating to teaching).

Problem solving (As defined by the OECD) Engaging in cognitive processing to understand and resolve problem situations in which a method of solution is not immediately obvious.

Relatedness The extent of one's positive relationships with others.

'Resilient' students (As defined by the OECD) Resilient students come from the bottom quarter of the distribution of socio-economic background in their country and score in the top quarter among students from all countries with similar socioeconomic background.

Setting   Separating students into different classes for different subjects on the basis of exam scores or perceived ability.

Social capital   The strengths of the relationships a person has with others, and the value arising from those relationships.

Socio-economic background   A family's economic and social position in relation to others, based on income, education, and occupation. References to measurements of this are based on the PISA index of social, cultural and economic status.

Working memory   The cognitive structure in which processing occurs (where you process things that you are consciously thinking about). Limited in capacity.

yutori kyōiku   Japanese term meaning 'relaxed education'. This was the name of an approach taken by the government to make schooling more relaxed in response to fears that children were too stressed.

Acknowledgements

I would not have had the confidence to travel around the world staying with strangers, nor to write this book, were it not for the love and support of my parents, Jill and Dominic Crehan. To them, and the rest of my wonderful family, I owe a huge debt of gratitude that I will never be able to repay.

The teachers I stayed with quickly became my friends, and it is these open-minded educators that really made this trip, and this book, possible. One in particular took a chance on me right at the start, and welcomed me to her home, her school, and her Zumba classes on the basis of a single Skype conversation; Reeta, you made this happen.

Other notable teachers and students who generously leant me their time and their hospitality (and on two occasions even took me to hospital) include Sini, Maarit, Heli, Emma, Ilpo, Marilyn, Loree, Eric, Deirdre, Nadine, Trevor, Jacob, Shaun, Heidi, Anne, Berinder, Bulpreet, Monica, David, Alan, Marcus, Glynis, Isao, Anna, Aya, Ellie, Sayaka, Ricky, Sunny, Wendy, Michelle, Jenny, Angela, Rony, Raye, and Nancy. You are all welcome to come and stay with us in Bath whenever you like!

Once I'd had the idea that I might write a book, the stars aligned to help me make that happen. Their names are Georgia Odd, Jimmy Leach, Mathew Clayton, Isobel Kieran, DeAndra Lupu, Craig Adams, Lauren Fulbright and Amy Winchester – the team at Unbound. I had no idea how much hard work and creative genius goes into making a book that has little to do with the author herself. I'd like to thank them in particular for their guidance and their patience with me as a first-timer. I also quite literally could not have done this without the wonderful patrons who paid for my book before it even existed – thank you.

The ideas in this book went through several iterations, and reached their final form with the help of the friends and family who looked through it: Mark O'Brien, Tessa Roberts, Dom Weinberg, Kiran Gill, Harry Fletcher-Wood, Andrew Sabisky and Mum and Dad. I was also honoured to have the renowned Sir Michael Barber, Professor Dylan Wiliam and Sir Clive Woodward look through the book and offer their generous endorsements.

One person stands out for the time and thought they have dedicated to helping me develop my ideas. Tim Oates has become my unofficial mentor during the past year, and has offered me invaluable critique and public support. His organisation, Cambridge Assessment, also kindly sponsored my flights to Shanghai. Tim gave me confidence that my ideas could be taken seriously.

Finally, I would like to thank my fiancé Mark for his unswerving emotional support during the ups and downs of the writing process. My happiness at reaching this point is doubled by my sharing it with him.

Supporters

Unbound is a new kind of publishing house. Our books are funded directly by readers. This was a very popular idea during the late eighteenth and nineteenth centuries. Now we have revived it for the internet age. It allows authors to write the books they really want to write and readers to support the writing they would most like to see published.

The names listed below are of readers who have pledged their support and made this book happen. If you'd like to join them, visit: www.unbound.com.

Stephen Adcock

Seliat Agboola

Valeria Agostini

Imad Ahmed

Beth Allard

Ian Armitage

Ed Arthur

Stephen & Regina Ash

Josie Azoff

Maya Bahoshy

Sarah Bailey

Karen Baines

Peter Batty

Jen Baxter

Wendy Baxter

Oliver Beach

Jeffrey Beard

Simon Belk

Emma Bell

Ian Bergson

Fiona Bibby

William Blad

Roy Blatchford

Mike Blyth

Rachael Boddy

Anne Bohbot

Caroline Booth

Kristopher Boulton

Jaime Martinez Bowness

Neil Brading

Kelly Bristow

Beckie Brown

David Bryan

Aaron Buff

Steve Bullock

Paul Burgess

Joseph Burne

David Buxton

Thomas Byrne

Tom Campion

Linda Campling

Jill Cansell

Xander Cansell

Selina Carmody

Geraldine Carter

Ian Casswell

Matthew Chisambi

Daisy Christodoulou

Anne Clark

Matthew Clark

Bridget Clay

Alice Coates

Victoria Cockram

Michael Coleman

Stevyn Colgan

Jane Considine

Sophie Cooper

Simon Coopey

Dominic Crehan

Emily Crehan

Oscar Crehan

Mike Crowhurst

Jesse Crozier

Charlie Crutchley

Adam D'Souza

Jonathan Dando

Simon Darling

Geoffrey Darnton

Sophia Darwin

Neil Davies

Tomos Davies

Stacey Davies-Boyle

Alice Davis

Michelle Day

James de Winter

Vincent Della Puppa

Michael Denhart

Joanna Dennis

Margaret Desmond

Annette Deutschendorf

David Didau

Sarah Dilnot

Annette Dobson

Robert Dole

Richard Donnelly

Lisa Donoghue

Chimé Metok Dorjee

Jenny Doughty

Kimberly Douglas

Catherine Dufour

Gabrielle Dumont

Lydia Dyckhoff

Gillian Eastwood

Joshua Eisenthal

Ruth Elborn

Peter Ellis

T Ellis

Katharine Elwis

Gemma Escott

Daniel Ethier

David Evans

Joan and Kingston Evans

Lauren Evetts
Phillip Evitt
Nathan Ewin
Lee Faith
Simon Faulkner
Alex Fiennes
Sally Fincher
Nicola Fleming
Nik Fleming
Harry Fletcher-Wood
Alex Fontanelli
Rowan Fookes
Mandy Forbes
Clare Forrester
Lucinda Foulkes-Arnold
Sarah Freck
Hilary Gallo
Ben Gibbs
Daniele Gibney
Tom Gibson
Laura Gilbert
Simmi Gill
Tarjinder Gill
Jamie Godd
Ada Gokay
Ashley Gordon
Jonathan Gower
Clarissa Grandi
Helen Gregory
Victoria Greybrook
Virginia Lynn Grimaldi
Flora Grimston
Liz Gunstone
Sinead Harold

John Hart
Ellie Haworth
Gemma Hay
Crista Hazell
Mark Healy
Emily Higgs
Eileen Hinds
Philip Holdaway
Guy Holloway
Tom Holroyd
Matthew Hood
Verity Howorth
Robin Humphreys
Ray Hunter
Aliyah Hussein
Edison Huynh
Rebecca Isaacs
Bodil Isaksen
Daniel Jackson
Ceri James
Josh James
C Jenkinson
Rhodri Jervis
Christine Jolliffe
Russell Jones
Jasmeen Kanwal
Julia Karmo
Augusta Kaufmann
Jan Keeling
Alex Kelly
Hilary Kemp
Hugo Kerr
Kate Kettle
Laura Kettle

Naureen Khalid

Dan Kieran

Darren King

Georgina Klein

Doron Klemer

Christine Knight

Doreen Knight

Simon Knight

Mark Knightley

Arend Koeditz

Amina Ado Kurawa

Jonathan Lafferty

Clare Lee

Andy Lewis

Craig Lewis

Pancho Lewis

Richard Lewis

The LKMco team

Gill Lloyd

Stuart Lock

Dr Robert Loe

David Longman

Andre Louis

Helen Lundebye

Rob MacAndrew

Charlie Mackenzie

Donald Mackintosh

Julien Manhood

Jennifer Martin

Sarah Mary

Abbie Mason

Gazz Matthews

George Matthews

David Maxwell-Lyte

Benedict McAleenan

Justine McDonald

Sonia McDonnell

Laura McInerney

Lorenzo McLellan

Dotty McLeod

Phillip McShane

Hannah McVey

Carrie-Ellen Mitchell

Shelly Mitcheson

John Mitchinson

Neha Modha

Henry Moore

Sasha Morgan

Mark Morley

Liane Mount

Hannah Mowat

Megan Murray-Pepper

Karen Murtfeldt

Helen Nash

National Education Trust

Carlo Navato

Lizzy Nesbitt

Ruth Newbury

Kathryn Nutbeem

Beryl O'Brien

Mark O'Brien

Mark O'Neill

Georgia Odd

Par Olsson

Lara Osmotherly

Shaun Palmer

Adrian Park

Natalie Parker

Sophia Parkinson

Himesh Patel

Rahul Patel

Sejal Patel

Simal Patel

Michelle Paterson

Helle Patterson

Katrina Patterson

Bryan Penfound

Allan Pengelly

Luisa Plaja

Diana Ples

Philip Podmore

Justin Pollard

Mike Pope

Natasha Porter

Daniel Potter

Joshua Press

Matthew Prestshaw

Paula Purkiss

Siobhan Quinn

Jodie Rabin

Anthony Radice

Neil Record

Bruno Reddy

Claire Redmond

Wynn Rees

Fiona Reid

Simon Rennie

Susan Rennie

Lyn Revie

Alex Reynolds

Chris Richards

Benjamin Riley

Jennifer Riley

Jon-Carlos Rivera

Naveen Rizvi

John Roberts

Ros Roberts

Tessa Roberts

Mark Robinson

Nicole Rodden

Annah Ross

Penny Russell

Maricel Salazar

Kate Salisbury

Dominic Salles

Tzen Sam & Daniel Crehan

Seb Sander

Billy Saxton

Annabel Scott

Oliver Seeley

Rebecca Sickinger

Jonathan Simons

Melanie Sinclair

Michael Slavinsky

Marleen Slingenbergh

Andy Smart

Catherine Smith

Georgina Smith

Karen Smith

Marc Smith

Natalie Smith

Fiona Snailham

Lisa Southam

Heather Speight

Teresa Stark

Lottie Stenntopht

Matthew Stevenson

Elizabeth Style

Ian Sudbery

Katie Sutcliffe

Susan Sutherland

Andy Szebeni

Shohei Takaya

Justin Tan

Ezra Tassone

Angelo Tata

Jo Taylor

Jonathan Taylor

Michael J Taylor

Nayan Thapa

Katy Theobald

David Thomas

Heather Thomas

Jane Thomas

Jack Thomlinson

Richard Thousand

Amanda Towers

James Townsend

Julia Tratt

David Trembath

Laura Turner

Sophia Ufton

Tamsin V-Robinson

Stephen Vahrman

Zach Van Stanley

Ellen Vanderhoven

Mark Vent

Robin Verschoren

Richard Visick

Nick von Behr

Sarah Waite

Rob Walden

Nick Walpole

Ben Ward

Charlotte Warner

Roisin Watson

Alex Weatherall

Dom Weinberg

David Weston

Helen Wheeler

Louise Whitbread

Angela Wiggan

Charlie Wild

Edward Wild

Suzie Wilde

Sarah Williams

Charlie Wilson

Kathryn Wilson

Rosanna Wilson

Sora Wondra

Alistair Wood

Alison Woodrow

Steve Woodward

Carolanne Wright

Glen Wright

Ke Wu

Emma Zymanczyk